C000224761

# SEND IT BY SEMAPHORE

## *The Old Telegraphs During the Wars With France*

HOWARD MALLINSON

THE CROWOOD PRESS

First published in 2005 by
The Crowood Press Ltd
Ramsbury, Marlborough
Wiltshire SN8 2HR

**www.crowood.com**



**British Library Cataloguing-in-Publication Data**
A catalogue record for this book is available from the British Library.

ISBN 1 86126 734 7

Typeset by Textype, Cambridge

Printed and bound in Great Britain by Cromwell Press, Trowbridge, Wilts

# Contents

# Maps and Diagrams

# Acknowledgements

I have been helped in many ways in researching the semaphore story, but the encouragement that I received from friends, both those who, like me, live near a preserved semaphore station and others not otherwise familiar with the first long-distance communication medium and who expressed their interest as enlightenment unfolded was an important driver to my completing my research. I should mention the Royal Signals Museum in Blandford: their archive material was very helpful, particularly the unpublished work by Geoffrey Wilson (a notable author on the subject) who had deposited the results of some of his research into the work of the Revd John Gamble.

I have developed a high regard for archivists and librarians who are notably helpful in their work: it makes the researching of historical records possible, of course, but enjoyable too. The staff at the British Library and of the public libraries in Norwich, Plymouth, Redruth, Richmond and Camden deserve my thanks and particularly those in Portsmouth, where I had the *eureka* moment of discovering that the news of Waterloo arrived there by telegraph – a fact not previously recorded in the literature. The library of the National Maritime Museum in Falmouth, Cornwall must also be mentioned along with the cathedral library in Canterbury. In Paris, the archives of the Musée des Arts et Metier were opened for me, and help was also given there by the Musée de la Poste and the Musée National de la Marine, and by the Musée de la Poste in Caen as well as by the Waterloo Museum near Brussels.

Christine Ward gave me thoughtful help with the translation of many documents in French, while Tony Allen was an enthusiastic companion on a research trip to France, performing not only the same function, but helping to unravel some of the mysteries of the subject and, through his linguistic skill and charm, enabled us to gain access to a private residence and site of a former semaphore station outside Paris. I am grateful to them both and to Candida Gill who helped by proof reading an earlier text and making thoughtful suggestions. David Evans cheerfully upgraded my computing capacity when the demands of the book put strain on the old, while my son Dudley kept me from despairing at being outflanked by a computer, both the new and the old, whose personalities often seemed perverse. He achieved this often from a range of 11,000 miles, which illustrates how far we have travelled since our forbears used to *Send It by Semaphore.*

My final thanks are to all those householders, many in England as well as the one in France, who live in converted signal stations and who have, without exception, graciously allowed me into their homes. As well as enabling me to absorb the atmosphere of their former use, being able to marvel at the views from their upper levels towards the sites of their corresponding signal stations, was a rare privilege; I am deeply grateful. Only my respect for their privacy stops me from thanking them by name: they know who they are.

*Howard Mallinson*
*Claygate*
*July 2004*

# Preface

The historical context of this book is the French Revolutionary and the Napoleonic Wars; it is a book for readers who like their history and who are intrigued, as I am, by its turning points. The book is about the development of the telegraph during this astonishing period, a period of transition from communication at the speed of the horse or sailing ship, to speeds of hundreds of miles an hour; it is about England's deliverance from the threat of invasion; of the gradual military ascendancy of Britain in the period 1793 to 1815 over one of the greatest military leaders and military forces the world has ever known, sometimes with allies, often alone; it is about how Napoleon exploited the telegraph as an instrument of his centralized power over much of the Continent; and it is about the sublime primacy of the Royal Navy, which had a central place in the national psyche, and it is about how the Admiralty used the new telegraphic technologies.

The first historical research into the old visual telegraphs was conducted as long ago as 1911 by Capt R. Hudleston, RN and was written up in 'The Coast Signal Stations and the Semaphore Telegraph' in the journal of the Society for Nautical Research, *The Mariner's Mirror* (vol.1, no.7, July 1911). This was the first occasion on which material from the Public Record Office on the subject of telegraphs had been analysed and made available generally, albeit to a specialized audience: it is interesting that Hudleston felt the need to use the word 'semaphore' as an adjective qualifying telegraph, seemingly as a tautology; I shall come back to this point.

It seems likely that Hudleston's work was the inspiration for Instructor Capt O. Tuck, RN, who, some thirteen years later, in September 1924, published an article in *The Fighting Forces* entitled 'The Old Telegraph'. Tuck's writing was an important contribution to knowledge of the visual telegraphs: in giving the first account of the establishment of the earliest telegraph lines he introduced his British audience to the fact that the telegraph was a French invention by Claude Chappe – how it was first developed in France and how a different version of it was invented and made operational in England. But if Hudleston was the first modern historian of the telegraph and Tuck the one who substantially advanced our knowledge of the subject, it was Cdr H.P. Mead, RN who, in the 1930s, completed some definitive research on the subject and wrote substantively on telegraphs and the technologies of semaphore signalling. It is no accident that all these pioneering historians were senior officers in the Royal Navy: the history of the development and application of the visual telegraphs in England, across both land and the seas, is dominated by one issue alone – British sea power. By the mid-eighteenth century the Navy had become a major force by its combination of skilled seamanship, fighting spirit, oceanic reach and the stratified cultural endowment of an island race which was supported in Westminster by a cross-party convention: in essence, this was the achievement of naval supremacy in support of English merchants (who, in 1800, conducted nearly 30 per cent of world trade), the maintenance of supremacy in the late eighteenth and the early nineteenth century being politically non-partisan. The telegraph may have been invented in France, and, indeed, far better exploited there as an instrument of central government, but in England it was to be the Admiralty, although not always gloriously, which was to be in control of the application of the new technology.

Mead wrote extensively in *The Mariner's Mirror* through the 1930s:

'The Story of the Semaphore I' (vol.19, no.3, July 1933)
'The Story of the Semaphore II – Manual Signalling' (vol.20, no.1, Jan. 1934)
'The Story of the Semaphore III – Semaphore Machines' (vol.20, no.2, Apr. 1934)
'The Story of the Semaphore IV – Popham and Pasley' (vol.20, no.3, July 1934)
'The Story of the Semaphore V – Development in the Royal Navy and Other Services (vol.21, no.1, Jan. 1935)
'The Admiralty Telegraphs and Semaphores' (vol.24, no.2, Apr. 1938)
'The Portsmouth Semaphore' (vol.25, no.3, July 1939).

Collectively, the writings of Hudleston, Tuck and Mead represented the substantive knowledge about the old telegraphs; but even in their own day, and certainly now, their work is available only in specialist libraries, usually those with a naval character. Moreover, the highly informative, well researched article 'Telegraphs and Telegrams in Revolutionary France', by Duane Koenig scarcely crossed the Atlantic: it was published in the USA in *The Scientific Monthly* (vol.59, Dec. 1944); if it had been produced in a more expansive version, this book would scarcely have been necessary. The wider public was well served, therefore, by much more recent publications: building on the work of the earlier writers (but not Koenig) and covering new ground themselves, two authors have written valuable extensions to our knowledge: in 1976 Geoffrey Wilson gave us *The Old Telegraphs*, to be followed in 1983 with T.W. Holmes's *The Semaphore*. Wilson's book was for twenty years considered to be the definitive work on the visual telegraphs worldwide. Holmes's work, although much less ambitious, had the enormous benefit of having been written with the emotion which can only be brought to the subject by a former signaller, a successor to the first telegraphers, who served in the Royal Navy in both world wars; few could know better the truth of the observation that nothing has ever been achieved by the Navy in the pursuit of sea power without a signaller being close at hand. He it was who knew how with later technology, itself now obsolete, a warship could challenge the identity of a vessel as it appeared over the horizon by means of a 20in signal lamp and the now almost obsolete Morse code; only such a man who had practised signalling with flags could accurately describe how the crews of a semaphore line from the Admiralty could get the 1pm time signal down to Portsmouth and the acknowledgement back in 45 seconds. Both books are recommended for their technical content, and, in Holmes's case, his coverage of the lives of the signallers.

This was the situation until 1995 when the result of a massive amount of research, a joint US/Swedish recognition of the 1993 bicentenary celebrations in France of the first telegraph, was published in the USA; the diligently referenced book, with the apparently Delphic but, in fact, profound title of *The Early History of Data Networks* is a mine of technical description of the early telegraphs and an important contribution to historiography. It was written by Dr Gerard J. Holzmann, a computer scientist with Bell Laboratories (a name with more than passing relevance to the subject) and Dr Björn Pehrson, who at the time was chairman of the Royal Institute of Technology in Stockholm.

Why is there a need for a new book on the subject and where does this one fit in the literature reviewed above? The book by Holzmann and Pehrson, enduring scholarly work that it is, is not readily available in the United Kingdom. The inaccessibility of that important contribution apart, my focus is in any event quite different, it is the application of telegraphy, as first practised in England and France, in one of the most dangerous but exciting periods in European history. Consider: a man who was twenty-five years old at the time of Waterloo would have grown up in England knowing a succession of important news stories – the Glorious First of June; the Nile; invasion scares; Trafalgar; Napoleon's great victory at Austerlitz, and the great gloom that followed it; the blockade and the failed harvests; the Peninsular War with its carefully executed victories; the retreat from Moscow; the Battle of the Nations at Leipzig and the fall of Paris, twice; and the eclipse of Napoleon. All these events took place after the telegraph had been invented; if such a young man had lived his normal span, he would have seen the rise of the railways and of the electric telegraph and its use to convey orders from London to our armies in the Crimean War; and then the connection of continents by submarine cables, all of it an astonishing period of history. In my book, resisting the temptation to give much in the way of technical explanation of the old telegraphs, the ground of which is already well covered, I wanted to explain how the new technology, the precursor of the electric telegraph, the telephone and the internet, changed (or did not change) how the holders of power operated in its early days. My story is intertwined with the histories of France and England as enemies, for the history of the first telegraphs starts shortly after the French Revolution began in 1789, and ends after Waterloo, which, as well as marking the starting point for the history of the nineteenth century also marked a large punctuation in the history of the telegraphs in England.

As we shall see, the Waterloo news came to Portsmouth by the shutter telegraph: as Victor Hugo was to remark 'On that day the course of mankind was altered. Waterloo was the hinge of the nineteenth century.' But it was also a hinge in the history of telegraphy in England. Waterloo marked the end of the use of the shutter telegraphs and, for a period, the Admiralty became blind: if there were any urgent intelligence to be sent to London, it would make its way on the Portsmouth Road by mail coach. But there were to be new experiments with semaphore, with a trial line to Deal, followed by the operational connection of Portsmouth to the Admiralty – a semaphore line using a twenty-year-old idea from France – which started life in 1822 and which lasted until the electrical telegraph replaced it in 1847. By the time Charles Dickens died in 1870, a middle-aged man of fifty-eight, his life had encompassed the second phase of the history of telegraphy: the transition from shutter technology, through semaphore and then to electrical telegraphs, and well before his death, to the intercontinental submarine cable. Dickens, being a newspaperman, would have been among the first to absorb the nature of the revolution that was wrought by the electric telegraph, and the juxtaposition of his own lifespan (he was born three years before Waterloo) to the spread of fast communication at a distance. Apart from the early days of the shutter telegraphs, Dickens saw it all: having moved around with his father's jobs with the Navy, in Portsmouth, Chatham and then London, the young nascent writer on social conditions would have been aware of the semaphore telegraph in all these locations. When he started work in London in 1824 at Hungerford Stairs he would have seen the semaphore at work on the Admiralty roof; he would retain his infant memory of the Waterloo news, and, later in his life, he would have been able to telegraph in an instant to first Paris, then the USA, India and Australia.

In a period of about sixty years, the horse had given way to the great communications revolution. In the researching of the book it became plain that the second phase of the history of the telegraphs – the beginning of the communication age seen by Dickens – is a story which needs to be divorced from the first phase, one which is inextricably bound up with the wars between England and France: the book had to become the story of the old telegraphs during the wars with France.

In writing about the old telegraphs an author soon encounters semantic problems, and it would be as well to clear up this difficulty here, in the preface, to avoid distractions later. What is the difference between a semaphore and a telegraph? Specialists could spend an evening discussing such a question, and arrive at a long answer – an answer that is of no interest to my audience, the general reader. In at least two of his novels, *David Copperfield* and *A Tale of Two Cities*, Dickens uses the word 'telegraph' as a more convenient word (for his purposes) than 'semaphore': he used the word telegraph allegorically as a verb (it being possible to say 'telegraph it', but inelegant to say 'semaphore it') to describe the capacity of body language to convey the mind's true feeling and, as a result, to 'send it by semaphore'. Dickens deliberately substituted the word semaphore by telegraph. Over the years this substitution has been done more and more carelessly: the words telegraph and semaphore have been used as if they meant the same thing. Even if Capt Hudleston were not the first to use the two words either together, as a tautology, or interchangeably as synonyms, he was certainly the first thoughtful writer on the subject to propagate the semantic inaccuracy; and, so far as the title of this book is concerned, *Send It by Semaphore*, I have followed his lead. The title correctly suggests the transmission of a dispatch, that is what the book is about, but, in the period covered by it, the Admiralty was not using semaphore but an earlier type of telegraph using shutters. If my book had been called, with more semantic exactness, *Send It by Telegraph*, the reader would not be able to determine immediately that this was one about the visual telegraphs: it might have been about the electric variety, and there would certainly be connotations of a popular newspaper. It seems probable that the wrong use of the words as if they were synonyms arose in the mid-nineteenth century, after the telegraph was electrified, for typically all references to the telegraph from then were, unless qualified, references to the electric telegraph. After that time, where a writer, other than Dickens, wanted to refer to visual telegraphs, that is, the by then obsolete technology, the use of the single word semaphore was a convenient way of making the distinction. But it was sometimes wrong to do so, for, although all semaphores were telegraphs, not by a long way were all telegraphs also semaphores, both of which words entered English from the French, via ancient Greek.

Before the telegraph was invented, the words in general currency for messages were signal or dispatch; when the telegraph was invented, a new word was required to describe a new process, the transmission of infinitely variable text over long distances. A French classicist coined the word *télégram*, from *télégraphe*, that word coming from the Greek 'to write at a distance'. Although created to describe the new visual distance-writing invention, the word was retained all over the world to refer to the electric telegraph that superseded it. Once this was established, it needed no adjectival qualification, and we still have telegraph poles, even though we do not have telegraphs any more. In due course, the word telegraph became synonymous with everything which was fast and up-to-date: stage-coach services and many journals used the word in their titles to make a point, the most obvious current example being the *Daily Telegraph* newspaper, founded in 1855, by which time, the global expansion of the electric telegraph was taking place. In this book 'telegraph', where no qualification is given, means a general reference to the visual telegraphs, of whatever type. Just as many journals adopted the word telegraph in their title, both before and after electricity was introduced; a similar thing had had happened earlier, when some journals adopted the word semaphore (to make a sign) to suggest alertness or speed.

Why is all this semantic discussion necessary? I have already confessed to following the lead of Capt Hudleston in using the terms semaphore and telegraph synonymously in the book's title, but a book about a technical subject, even if it is not about the technicalities, ought to be precise about language. I shall cite one more author who overcame the same difficulty in the same, technically inaccurate way: Sir Arthur Bryant in his book *The Great Duke*, writing about Wellington's victorious soldiers in the Peninsular War, observed that, had they only been able to see it, a part of the means of their success was due to 'the semaphore watchers on the Admiralty roof gazing across the river to the wooded Surrey heights'. There was no semaphore on this roof during the wars with France; in the period being referred to it was the shutter telegraph that transmitted their orders. But that was not the point that the author was about, he was referring to something which at the time was novel, a new, fast way of sending messages over long distances, and he did not want to clutter his text with explanations of the fact that he was not talking about the electric telegraph. So it is with me: 'SEND IT BY SEMAPHORE' was not an instruction that would have been heard in the Admiralty for an operational command before 1822; in France, on the other hand, 'L'ENVOYEZ PAR SÉMAPHORE' would undoubtedly have been heard from about 1801 when a coastal semaphore system was introduced in France. The sub-title of the book, 'The Old Telegraphs during the Wars with France', faithfully describes the period covered here. The Battle of Waterloo and the eclipse of Bonapartism changed the whole strategic aspect of telegraphy in England, as well as much else, and it was only in the second, post-Waterloo phase of the visual telegraphs that the Admiralty copied the French semaphore. This was retained until 1847, when the electric telegraph took over. If it were not exactly a wholly twilight period of the visual telegraphs, it was certainly one of unbroken peace for Britain, whereas this story is about Britain at war.

When France declared war on Britain in 1793 only ten years had elapsed since the end of the previous round of hostilities, when France, keen to damage her old enemy, had sided with the USA in her revolutionary war against Britain. Through the eighteenth century war had been a commonplace state: at the start of the French Revolutionary conflict, Britain had been at war for twenty-four out of the previous sixty years and stood on the threshold of new wars that would last until 1815. But the French Revolutionary and Napoleonic Wars were different from any that had preceded them because not since the Normans had there been any significant attempt to invade England; 250 years had passed since Drake had defeated the Spanish Armada. Seven centuries had seen Norman England, then Great Britain, become a great European power, so, unlike nearly all the other countries of Europe, the islanders knew nothing of foreign dominion, it was too long ago for anything to have been handed down through the generations and they were fiercely independent as a result; these islanders, growing rich by trade, were special people, the peasants as well as the privileged, for they had only one resounding call from their genes when invasion threatened, a call that needed no pause for rationalization: the survival of their own Christian way of life. Whatever deficiencies and injustices there were in the kingdom, and there were many, the centuries-old gene pool caused the whole population to stand and face the tyrants' might. When London learned of the French king's execution the news was greeted with indignation: the revolutionaries should have heeded this instinctive loathing of despotism. Confronted by revolutionary France, it was to be a war not just of territory and trade but of causes. Initially uncontrolled and uncontrollable, the French Revolution mutated into a dictatorship, led by a genius who was probably the most brilliant soldier that had ever lived but who certainly controlled the greatest military power the world had ever seen, and who was the first tyrant in the world to understand the power of the telegraph to give immediate effect to his orders over great distances, to manipulate news and to turn it quickly into propaganda.

Edmund Burke (1729–97), considered to be one of the most brilliant and original thinkers of his time and perhaps of any who had sat in the House of Commons, denounced the Revolution in his famous *Reflections on the Revolution in France* (1790), dwelling on the benefits of continuity, a concept so conservative and appealing to the English and yet not just alien to the Revolution so much as diametrically in conflict with its *raison d'être.* He was one of the first to perceive that it was portentous; the Revolution was certainly a volte-face so that when sufficient time had passed for its residual impact to be assessed, it was considered by a French cleric that, 'In two thousand years of recorded world history so sharp a revolution in customs, ideas, and beliefs has perhaps never occurred before.' As Burke said:

> We are in a war of a peculiar nature. It is not with an ordinary community . . . We are at war with a system which by its essence is inimical to all other governments; and which makes peace or war as peace and war may best contribute to their subversion. It is with an armed doctrine that we are at war.

Armed doctrine! Burke lived long enough to see the worst doctrinal outrages, but, even before this, he spotted that there was a central flaw in the new French thinking; according to him, their passion for logical abstractions recognized the existence of neither religion nor morality. Unwittingly the revolutionary philosophers were opening the way for tyranny: 'If the present project of a republic should fail,' Burke predicted, 'all security to a moderate freedom must fail with it.' It was to be mob-rule; in May 1790 the new rulers of France, professing peace, sent troops to Avignon, an enclave of Papal territory since the Middle Ages, to take it back, not by the ballot box, but by force in response to a riot that reflected an anti-Christian aspect of the Revolution. Burke predicted the excesses and the killing and was quickly proved right; the revolutionary fervour was, of itself, to make the wars unprecedented. None of the many wars that had been waged in the past was anything like that which broke upon Europe in 1793. The liberal tide that had begun to flow in England since the American Revolution suddenly turned, electoral reform and the abolition of the slave trade were shelved, it was no time for innovation, but rather one in which to cling to old certainties. The new wars with France were to be different for another reason: technical innovation was rife. A different tide was flowing and its force could not be ignored: rather than liberalism or revolution, which was for the most part rejected in England, it was to be a new technology, embraced with zeal in France, which provided the other new aspect of the wars.

These wars were to be the first where the visual telegraphs allowed news, intelligence and commands to be transmitted at hundreds of miles an hour along the hilltop telegraph lines. The dominion of the horse was to be challenged for the first time in the ascent of man; this in itself was a revolution, one which would see its zenith not in the days of the electric telegraph, of which the new visual telegraphs were themselves portentous, nor radio but in the late twentieth century with communication satellites and the Internet. This challenge to the horse was to evolve quite differently in Revolutionary France from its course in a slowly adapting England. In England the Admiralty virtually monopolized the development and operation of the telegraphs, which were never an instrument of government as they were in France. Moreover, in France the centralizing use of the telegraph was so institutionalized that there was continuity in the telegraph service that survived the defeat of Napoleon twice and also the two restorations of the monarchy, with scarcely a pause. In England the telegraphs were only considered to be a facility to be available for the duration of the wars.

Routinely from 1794, dialogue at a distance was possible for the first time in history. It was bound to alter the world; it was no coincidence that this astonishing change came shortly after the French Revolution (Chapter 3), in a period in which Britain was at war with France (Chapters 7 and 10); it was no coincidence either that the period saw the telegraph dancing to Napoleon's tune as he carried all before him. Stumbling at the hands of the Royal Navy (Chapters 6 and 8), now equipped with a telegraph system of its own (Chapter 5), then after a stunning series of Continental triumphs by his armies, Napoleon failed, finally, to achieve his goal of a United States of Europe, after defeats in Russia, at Leipzig, in the Iberian peninsula, and ultimately, after his escape from Elba, his defeat at Waterloo (Chapters 11, 12 and 13). All this took place during the first chapter of human enterprise which I call 'the first telegraph age'.

In a definitive history of the period, *The New Cambridge Modern History:* Vol.XI, *War and Peace in an Age of Upheaval 1793–1830*, the index contains only two references to semaphore and none to telegraph, and barely a few lines of text to the subject. All the books on the period, whether great or indifferent, give scant coverage of the growth of the nascent telegraphs. There is the great trilogy by Bryant, *The Years of Endurance 1793–1802*, *Years of Victory 1802–1812* and *The Age of Elegance 1812–1822*, written during and shortly after the Second World War, when the threat of invasion had again been made and parried, in which the period of the wars with France is dealt with at length, sensitively and with a passion informed by the contemporary writings which enrich his text. But even in these most readable accounts, if all references to semaphore and telegraph were expunged, only a handful of paragraphs would be affected. It was as if Claude Chappe, the central figure behind the French telegraph system so warmly embraced by revolutionary and Napoleonic France, had invented something unimportant or insignificant, even if the innovation were not in itself war-winning.

So, readers have been given the choice, so far, of either reading a text about the wars with France in which, however well the subject is covered, there is no enlightenment on the role of semaphore, or good books about the semaphore with no great insight into how its application was woven into the astonishing events happening as it was being developed and applied to meet the new urgencies of the age. My book is an attempt to bridge the two extremes. For the would-be student of the wars with France it will be found no more than an appetizer; for those interested in the old telegraphs and wanting to know how they worked and other technical matters or stories of their operatives, the texts already mentioned are admirable. It is for the readers who revel in Britain's past greatness, who wish they knew more about the Revolutionary and Napoleonic Wars, who marvel at the turning points in science and history and how the telegraphs fitted in with their course, that I have written. There is nothing new here about the wars, but there is much that is new about the telegraphs and the historical context of their application. None of the previous writers on the subject has explained the state of cartography while the first telegraph lines were being developed; marvelling at the speed at which some of the lines were surveyed, planned and built, these authors told us nothing about how the process could have been achieved. By a stroke of fortune, the triangulation of the south of England had been completed just before the Revolution; I explain how this came about (Chapter 2) and how it facilitated the planning, initially from the surveyor's desk, of the telegraph lines. The book is designed to be attractive to the curious. It is written from an English point of view but with an admiration for France and things French that lies just beneath the surface.

I came to be intrigued by the old telegraphs, like many before me, because I grew up in their presence. In Hinchley Wood, near Esher in Surrey there remains, admirably restored to a comfortable family home, one of the signal stations on the old semaphore line from the Admiralty to Portsmouth. In writing a local history (*Hinchley Wood: the Origins of a 1930s Settlement*) and touching on the semaphore line, I found that I wanted to know more. I had romantic notions of that old hilltop semaphore station sending brilliant news like that of Trafalgar or Waterloo down Bryant's Surrey heights from the Admiralty to Portsmouth, but it was not like that at all. That semaphore line, which replaced the previous shutter line, which was closed down after Waterloo, did not open until 1822 and there was no war in which Britain was engaged which took place before the line closed in 1847. Moreover, the telegraph was not used by the Admiralty as a news service: the imperative of the time was the operational effectiveness of the Navy and it was used by the Admiralty only for prosaic communication in prosecuting that business. Having discovered that the London to Portsmouth semaphore line was in phase two of the story of the old telegraphs in England, from 1822 to 1847, this left the story of the earlier phase, which came to an end after the Battle of Waterloo, inextricably bound up with the French Revolution and its wars and with Napoleon and his wars. What started as a story of the whole visual telegraph age – 1793–1847 – was found to be two stories: this first one is confined to the war-time application of the telegraphs.

Howard Mallinson

# 1
# When Speed Was Measured by the Horse and the Sailing Ship

*A thousand shall flee at the threat of one . . . until you are left like a beacon on top of a mountain, like a signal on top of a hill.*
Isaiah xxx: 17

*But mostly he watched with eager search*
*The belfry tower of the Old North Church . . .*
*And lo! as he looks, on the belfry's height*
*A glimmer, and then a gleam of light!*
*Longfellow: 'The Midnight Ride of Paul Revere'*
*O, for a horse with wings.*
Shakespeare[1]

## Signalling in Ancient Times

There is a Darwinian desire to communicate urgently which is common among the species; whether this is by audible, visual or other means may vary, but the distress call of the blackbird and the 'follow me' white rump of a deer are examples of perfectly adapted warning signs of danger from the animal kingdom. Ingenious man discovered that an audible signal could be carried a greater distance by cupping the hands round the mouth and from this the megaphone was developed, and the method continues to be favoured today for voice communication over a short stretch of water. Visual signalling over distances beyond hearing has been practised since before recorded history. Fire and smoke had been in use in the old world for millennia without achieving, except in the most highly developed ancient civilizations, the means of sending anything other than signals of which the meanings were pre-arranged. In the New World, as recently as the late nineteenth century and no one knows since when, for it seems unlikely that the extent of their signalling ability was ever properly researched, the primitive native Americans made smoke signals as a method of communication.

Such signals, even if not in dialogue, allowed them to send messages with variable meanings and, by means of primitive relay stations, they succeeded in making transmissions over great distances. They achieved variations not just by altering the number of puffs but by changing the colour of the smoke with different agents. Equally vague is what the ancient Chinese achieved in the field of signalling, but we may safely assume that their cleverness was aimed at the problem of distance communication.

On the battlefield, if no horse were available, runners would be used for sending messages, a method, which remains the final fallback for the soldier if all else fails. Carrier pigeons have, evidently, been used from the early Christian period,[2] their use having been brought back from the east to Europe by Dutch navigators. Julius Reuter (1816–99) used them in the 1850s to distribute news reports, and they were used in twentieth-century warfare.* In the early days of man's successful communication at a distance, no method prevailed more than the use of fire at night: examples have been handed down in the Old Testament. For example in *Isaiah*, thought to have been written not long before Christ, 'Then the Lord will create over the whole site of Mount Zion and over its places of assembly a cloud by day and smoke and the shining of a flaming fire by night' (iv, 5). But audible signalling, as well as visual, also has biblical reference: in *Jeremiah* vi, 1: ' Flee for safety . . . Blow the trumpet . . . for evil looms out of the north, and great destruction.'

In our own history, when invasion loomed in 1940, it was the low-tech church bells which would toll to give their singular, but not unexpected message, 'The invaders are coming'. According to the Athenian historian, Thucydides (*c.* 460–400BC), the Greeks arranged torch signals to have two meanings: to give notice of the approach of an enemy, in which case, 'the torches were shaken by those who held them' or to foretell the arrival of friends, when the torches 'were kept steady'. The Greek philosopher, logician and scientist Aristotle (384–322BC) tells us that through all the territories of Persia, fire signals were so disposed on towers, that in twenty-four hours he could receive advice of trouble in distant parts of the country.[3] Although the heliograph was not developed by the British Army for use in India until the late nineteenth century, its precursor, the flashing of light reflected from burnished shields, was in use in ancient times.

The movements of Roman armies were directed by flags or by the sound of trumpets or drums; wherever they formed a camp, an elevated spot was chosen for a signal station for communication with distant detachments. The Roman army is thought to have had an advanced form of signals by

*Experiments with carrier pigeons by submariners were abandoned when, after surfacing and being released, the birds had the wisdom not to leave the vessel.

which it could direct troop movements in the rear areas. Their method was based on two sets of torches: the alphabet was divided into groups of five letters, and the first torch indicated to which group the second torch was to be applied to fix a letter of the alphabet, enabling a message to be spelt out letter by letter.[4] The Romans had a chain of coastal signal stations along the Yorkshire coast; archaeological evidence has shown that they were occupied in the years around AD370–395. They were part of the defensive works against invaders from across the North Sea, and it is supposed that, operating in conjunction with a fleet based on the Humber, they could send signals inland to York.[5] Although scholars are certain of the existence of these signal stations there and in other areas too, we are not told whether messages were actually spelled out, although it seems likely that they were. We can be certain that, if an alphabetic method were used, the Romans took the method with them when they left, because there was no signalling inheritance for those whom they left behind.

If the spelling out of messages was not in general application throughout the Roman empire, we can be certain that the Romans introduced beacons wherever they held dominion; they were certainly in early use in Britain: the derivation of the word is from the Saxon, meaning 'a signal' and gives to our language the verb to beckon. In the early Middle Ages, English beacons were simply stacks of faggots set up on hills and fired when enemies were coming. Later, the process was refined so that fabricated fire beacons were erected, with bowls containing pitch, to provide an alarm system which was funded by local taxation. For the giving of alarm in daylight hours during periods of crisis guns might be fired and horses and riders would have been retained on standby. This would have been the state of signals technology at the time of the Armada in 1588. This marked the limit of signals evolution, or, more accurately, the limit of what had been retained from the ancient civilizations, until some new war need coincided with and was allied to an advance in technology. The news of an invasion could be spread rapidly, but the speed that was achieved was possible only by sending a pre-arranged message: no dialogue was possible. Until the new technology became available, a message continued to travel at the speed of the horse and a reply would take the same time to be received.

There is a legendary story from New England which serves to demonstrate the limits which the science of signalling had reached just shortly before the great leap forward was made in France. At the start of the colonial revolt in Boston, Massachusetts the folk hero Paul Revere, informed by a light-signal from across the Charles River, made his famous midnight ride to inform the rebels along the road to Lexington that 'the regulars', meaning the British Redcoats, 'were out'. Henry Wadsworth Longfellow told the story in his poem 'The Midnight Ride of Paul Revere':

Hang a lantern aloft in the belfry-arch
Of the North Church tower as a signal light –
One if by land, and two if by sea;
And I on the opposite shore will be,
Ready to ride and spread the alarm.

The year was 1775 and the church was the Old North Church in the North End of Boston, which remains to this day as the oldest surviving one in the city;* the hero was Paul Revere, the son of a French immigrant. That there was a French ingredient in the signal which led to the successful skirmish against the British was ironic: the French, in testament to the eternal truth 'my enemy's enemy is my friend', would later side with the USA, after the Declaration of Independence, in her revolutionary war against Britain. The French Revolution would follow only six years after the end of this war, and the first telegraph age would begin only four years after that. Revere's story marks the military end of the whole signalling story before the invention of the telegraph. The light in the belfry of Old North Church meant that the Redcoats were coming: one lantern meant that they were coming by land and two by sea. The signal was seen by Revere across the river. By prior arrangement its meaning was plain: now king horse would play his part, for the message had to be conveyed 16 miles: all this was as it had been since time began. Revere's story demonstrates the limit of man's signalling capacity as the eighteenth century drew to its close. All this was about to change.

## Communication by Sea

If the horse controlled the pace of news transmission on land, at sea it was even slower. In the early days of Britain's involvement with India a message sent there by ship, round the Cape of Good Hope, would not get a reply inside a year. It is only to be expected of an island race, leaving aside issues of jealously guarded sovereignty, that their communications by sea should be developed faster than those of her continental competitors. In the eighteenth century, British merchants followed the Empire and extended greatly their overseas reach. The rapid expansion of Britain's trade created the need for an independent and reliable diplomatic, postal and communications service. This was formalized in 1689 when the Post Office appointed an agent in Falmouth, in Cornwall, to set up a regular service to Spain. By 1702, so-called packet-boats were sailing regularly to Lisbon and to Barbados and Jamaica. New York was added in 1755 and, by 1764,

*The church was built in 1723 in the Georgian style, based on a design by Wren similar to that of St. Andrew's-by-the-Wardrobe, Blackfriars, London.

packets were serving Gibraltar and several ports in the American colonies. Routes were opened up to South America and into the Mediterranean at the beginning of the nineteenth century. These packets operated more than just a mail service; merchants entrusted their money to them, and often the ships carried official dispatches and bullion to pay British troops. The first news of disasters, wars, victories and revolutions reached Britain in the packets and was taken to London by horse.

British shipping was severely disrupted by hostilities with the Americans and their allies during their War of Independence and then again during the wars with France. Packets often had to run the gauntlet of enemy warships and of privateers licensed to take them as prizes; few escaped unscathed. As many as sixty-eight packets were captured between 1793 and 1815.[6] In wartime the risks from enemy action, as well as from the elements, were great, and the long tradition of high security over the mail started then. The instructions to the captains of the packets were plain: 'You must run where you can. You must fight when you can no longer run and when you can run no more you must sink the mails before you strike [capitulate].'

Commercial mail traffic would go by the network of packet routes, but the Royal Navy looked after its own needs: when speed was essential, a frigate or some other small, fast ship would be sent with dispatches; in wartime such ships would be scuttling across the seas at a giddy rate, but not without risk, as this dispatch from Nelson to the Admiralty made clear:

> . . . your . . . letter of April 10th which, notwithstanding it has been afloat in the Mediterranean 6 days, conveys to me very late news. I wish our Government in their important communications with me would direct their dispatches to . . . Madrid, [for forwarding] . . . by confidential person to Barcelona where almost every week I send a frigate for information, then such a distressing circumstance as has happened to the Swift cutter* could not take place. Bonaparte read all the public dispatches on April 16th. I wish they had choked him . . .[7]

## The Telegraph is Invented

We have traced the extent to which fast communication on both land and sea had developed towards the close of the eighteenth century. It is curious that it took so long for the great leap forward in the speed of it to be made: Holzmann and Pehrson referred to it as 'the 2,000 year gap',[8] knowledge, had it seems, regressed from the time of the clever ancients. That the great

---

*The *Swift* was a hired cutter; it had been captured by a French privateer on 5 April and her commander killed, not only dispatches were lost, but a portrait of Lady Hamilton, with whom Nelson was by this time besotted.

leap forward towards the world of communications that we have today was made in France shortly after the Revolution shows how some ideas, if they are to flourish beyond research to development and practical exploitation, need the fertile ground of political imagination and power in which to grow. Revolutionary France gave the world the visual telegraph. The invention by Claude Chappe (1763–1805) of the '*télégraphe*' in 1793 marks the beginning of the remarkably short ascendancy of fast communication by the new mechanical telegraphs; 1793 drew a line under the old communication technologies.

It is no coincidence that this breathtaking new capacity to send a short message at 300 to 400mph (480–640km/hr) was invented and developed in time of war. As we shall see, it is no coincidence either that France was in Revolution and that most of Europe was to be torn apart and temporarily put back together again by Napoleon. Neither was it any coincidence that the introduction of the visual telegraph in Britain marked a point of mortal danger for her. Sir Walter Scott witnessed the state of Britain during the invasion scares at the end of the eighteenth and the beginning of the nineteenth century. He observed that almost every individual was enrolled in either a military or civil capacity for the purposes of resisting any invasion. 'Beacons were erected along the coast,' he tells us, 'and all through the country, to give the signal for everyone to go to his post.' The Navy guarded the Western Approaches: and soon, the Admiralty began to build telegraph stations.

## An Age of Inventions

This was an age of new inventions: oxygen had already been isolated; in the 1790s William Smith, the uneducated blacksmith's son and a precursor of Darwin, made his stratigraphical observations in Somerset coalmines and canal works, portents of his 'map that changed the world' of 1801 and the new science of geology and eventually its upending of Christian orthodoxy; in 1799 the Royal Institution was founded in London, albeit as an elite body, for the dissemination of scientific knowledge; the first crossing of the English Channel by balloon took place in 1785, followed by the first aerial observation of artillery fire at the Battle of Fleurus in 1794; the first patent on a mechanical reaper was granted in 1799; the first harnessing of steam power for navigation was achieved in France on the River Saône in 1783, followed in 1801 by steam tugs being employed on the Clyde. In the same year, the world's first full-size road locomotive, designed by Richard Trevithick (1770–1833), took to the road in Cornwall. In 1804, in south Wales, the world's first steam railway locomotive, also designed by Trevithick, pulled a train for a distance of nearly 10 miles (16km) – ten years before George Stephenson's first locomotive and twenty-five before the famous 'Rocket'. The British at the time were the most ingenious people on earth. A society that venerated freedom of thought and action was a seed-plot for invention. Man in England was a tool-making animal.[9]

The application of steam power to ships did not have any impact on naval warfare in the period we are concerned with, neither did the demonstration to the French navy by an American of a three-man, metal submarine, which proved to be an idea of ultimate awesome application but ahead of its time and not yet capable of exploitation. But not so the telescope or the railways, for they were inventions for which the world was waiting. We should perhaps say the development of the telescope rather than its invention. Although Galileo (1564–1642) constructed a telescope in 1609 and Isaac Newton (1642–1727) developed the instrument further in the seventeenth century, it was John Dolland (1706–61) who made the development breakthrough. He was known in scientific circles in London for his wide optical knowledge and gave his name to an optician's business which still exists today. In 1757 he perfected his achromatic lenses (which transmitted light without separating it into its constituent colours) and had provided the ideal instrument for seeing at a distance. Dolland patented his lens, but even after the patent expired in 1772, Dolland's son Peter (described as 'the father of practical optics') dominated the market. The business created and fostered the public demand for portable telescopes and in 1780 introduced an 'army telescope'. The firm became suppliers of telescopes to both the Army and the Admiralty; as evidence of their quality, a French astronomer observed, 'this telescope is particularly fine'.[10] This was probably Jean-Baptiste Chappe d'Auteroche (1722–69), an important French astronomer and uncle of Claude Chappe) who, in 1769, went to California in order to observe for France the big astronomical event, the transit of Venus; he took with him 'two Dolland achromatic refracting telescopes'.[11]

It was an age of invention in France too: unlike the British Royal Society, which appealed to those of brilliant mind *and* status, the egalitarian École Polytechnique opened in 1794, appealing to any of brilliant mind to join the nursery of engineering science; here, for the first time, students went through a systematic scientific and mathematical curriculum under the foremost scientific minds of the day.

A year later, in 1795, was founded the Institut National de France, endowing state patronage of science, the arts and letters, which with the École Polytechnique, together reconstituted as the children of the Revolution to advance excellence and replace, enduringly and tellingly, the orphans of the *Ancien Régime*'s educational system so recently put to death. It was the beginning of the French intelligentsia. The scientific community, so recently compromised by elimination of the *Ancien Régime*, was put on a pedestal in the Revolutionary atmosphere of the time, for:

> In the military emergency of 1793 [the seminal year in our story], the regime had looked to scientists [not for the prosecution of science but] for leadership in war production. It had not looked in vain. For the first time, a scientific community was mobilised to serve the nation in arms. Supply, ordnance, communications, gunpowder – France became a national workshop serving her armies.[12]

The reference to communication is central to this story: the development of the telegraph in France by Claude Chappe was to be part of this, even if he was not part of the École Polytechnique mould. But it was the ground-breaking work on optics by Dolland which was key to Chappe's progress: if Dolland's refinements to the telescope had not preceded Chappe, the story of the development of telegraphy may have been different. In a monument to the quality of the Dolland instruments, when the debate took place in England from 1816 about whether and how to proceed with visual telegraphy, the relative merits of two different systems were compared in bad atmospheric conditions; whatever criticism there was of a particular telegraph apparatus, there was never a word about any lack of quality of the telescopes. So it was then, when Chappe invented his telegraph, telescopes were available which allowed observations of signals that sometimes were as much as 11 miles (18km) apart. For the Admiralty, the telescope had been a godsend in advancing the development of sea power. When the telegraph was introduced in Britain, from 1796, the Admiralty monopolized its development for fast communication with ports; it was to be thirty years before any commercial exploitation of the technology was possible. The Admiralty telegraph lines were built with only two aims in mind: to give the Navy the best strategic and tactical advantage it could have in its key role in war, including the supply of our armies overseas; and in defence against invasion. Until the telegraphs came, the Admiralty, like everyone else, had to rely on the post and horse for the inland delivery of dispatches.

## Postal Communication at the Time of the New Telegraph

Even before the shutter telegraphs came to England in 1796, there was a highly developed postal service, which had been set up in Tudor times for the delivery of news of battles and in calling for reinforcements and other needs of the army; this was the 'Royal Mail'. Charles I created the Post Office and, in a 1635 Act of Parliament, opened the royal post to the public; opened, that is, at least to the richer elements of it. By now mail was being sent routinely to Europe and the volume grew with increasing trade following the Industrial Revolution from the mid-eighteenth century. Once the improvement in the quality of the roads had been achieved, brought about by the turnpike trusts of the same century, journey times quickened, and the days of the highwaymen were in decline. Mail would be delivered, albeit at high cost, to all cities in Britain, and even to the most distant within a few days; certainly Admiralty dispatches would only be a day's journey away from Portsmouth and Deal by mail coach. The first specially designed mail coach was put into service between London and Bristol in 1784; although they could carry passengers, they were built for speed. Two Scots, Thomas Telford (1757–1834) and John Macadam (1756–1836), civil engineering geniuses of their day, provided the country, during the first quarter of the nineteenth century, with smooth-metalled highways which allowed the speed of post-chaises to rise from 4 or 5mph (6–8km/hr) to 10 and even 12mph (16–19km/hr). Teams of four horses would be changed every hour or so, as they strove to keep a strict timetable. By 1799, the south-west was served by mail coach as far as Falmouth, connecting with the packets that took the mail overseas. The mail coaches were privately owned, with the Royal Mail providing the armed guard.

The first telegraphs to Deal and Portsmouth were able to improve by about five hours on the slower speeds of the mails during the early stages of the wars, an urgent dispatch taking the greater part of a day, and more than two days for Plymouth and Yarmouth. Mail was timetabled to take forty-three hours from the General Post Office in London, to the drop in Exeter, with a further twelve hours to Falmouth;[13] but road improvements allowed this to be reduced in the early nineteenth century. In 1815, when the telegraph to Plymouth had been reinstated, the mail was only two days from London. That the mail was expensive at this time was not an issue for the Admiralty; the mail of the government and the king was carried free (Queen Victoria being the first monarch to pay for her own). The subsidizing of official mail by private mail was sufficient for the Post Office to be a contributor to the national finances. Thus, when the telegraph came, it was able to do for the Admiralty in minutes, although at great cost, what otherwise would have taken a day or more, at no cost.* This curious

*The great Post Office reforms of Rowland Hill in 1840 are not relevant here, although they were significant for the civil population, first, by reversing the previous practice of the receiver of the letter paying its postage, which was calculated by reference to the distance it had travelled, and, secondly, by introducing the penny post, which for the first time, by promoting a simple, single tariff, encouraged greater usage. These reforms not only stimulated a vastly increased volume, which was economically self-sustaining, but also made the service accessible to ordinary people; a great increase in wealth creation followed, as well as imitation all over the world. There had already been a penny post in London set up by William Dockwra in 1660, but the significance of Rowland Hill was that the one-penny tariff applied irrespective of distance. The counter-intuitive aspect of the economics of this move was inspired.

juxtaposition of economics was to be important when the wars with France were over.

The Admiralty's gain in transmission time achieved through the shutter telegraph was measurable as the greater part of a day to a few days, but it was achieved at great cost: in the money of the day, the first shutter telegraph line cost about £40 per mile to build and about the same amount per annum per mile to operate. In war, the cost was secondary to the ultimate imperative of stopping the French. It is almost certain that it was because the telegraph lines were expensive to operate that the Admiralty was so keen to close down the shutter telegraphs, prematurely as it turned out, in 1814. The highly developed Royal Mail, which by 1814 was not unduly vulnerable to robbery, was a costless alternative for the Admiralty's dispatches. In France, where the superior telegraph system did not close until the electric telegraph came, the mail was not so well developed. But this is not to say that its importance was not recognized; the very next day after the storming of the Bastille on 14 July 1789 the Revolution declared that the post was under the control of a permanent committee on behalf of the people and that it would be free from interference from prying eyes. Why did the French take so readily to the new technology? It was the centralized government machinery, the product of the Revolution, and the greater distances which must have influenced them to embrace the telegraph; the distance from Paris to Toulon, their Mediterranean fleet base, was over 500 miles (800km), about the distance of Aberdeen from London, one which, before the railways came, was to say the least, formidable. When they did come, the railways speeded up the mail even before the electric telegraph could send a message in no longer than it took to transcribe it. The railways, and the emerging scientific understanding of electricity, were to have a decisive impact on the later history of telegraphy.

## Electricity Was Nearly Understood

We must make a temporary departure from chronology in order to clear out of the way the history of the evolution of the understanding of electricity and its place in the development of the visual telegraphs: it is a story of what might have been. We must cover the ground now because, in part, the story of the electric telegraph, even though it did not emerge until the railways came, predates the Chappe visual telegraph and the later phases of the visual telegraph story. There could be endless speculation about how Europe would have evolved if Napoleon had won the Battle of Waterloo. One aspect would have been, I assert, the introduction of the electric telegraph much earlier than it was: we must examine the case. The first imperative for the visual telegraphs had been the waging of war. Revolutionary France, with its power base in Paris, needed to exploit fast communication as its one major strategic advantage over its enemies, who were able to communicate with each other only at the speed of the horse; Britain's imperative was the need to defend herself from invasion and keep trade routes open, hence the Admiralty's interest in telegraphs. The size of Britain's merchant fleet was prodigious: in spite of war losses, it grew during the war years by over 50 per cent to over 24,000 ships Were it not for these powerful drivers, the visual telegraphs, which were very expensive, may not have been introduced by the Admiralty at all before the railways started using the electric telegraph. But the situation in France in 1793 was that she had a communications demand that was clamouring for solution: the visual telegraph was developed to meet it. After the Revolution began and the urgencies of the moment, there was no time to experiment, but after Waterloo there was plenty, and if Napoleon had been master he would have found the electric telegraph as manna from heaven, like the British empire did when the submarine cables were laid.

That there was something about electricity and its power to be used for sending a message had emerged somewhat mysteriously at an astonishingly early date. On 17 February 1753, a letter signed by a certain 'C M', never identified, was published in the *Scots Magazine.* In it the author set out a plausible if rudimentary method of sending a signal using one wire for each letter of the alphabet. At the time, electricity was not taken seriously. Further experiments took place in Spain forty years later but these did not proceed beyond the development stage either.[14] As we shall see in Chapter 3, even Claude Chappe experimented with electrical telegraphs before the imperatives of revolutionary France caused him to put on one side what was not deliverable as a working system to concentrate on the low-tech and low risk, but deliverable visual method.

After Chappe had abandoned his experiments with electricity, there was no recorded attempt to use it for sending a signal for over twenty years. In his *Descriptions of an Electrical Telegraph and some other Electrical Apparatus,* published in 1823, the inspirational physicist Sir Francis Ronalds (1788–1873), pays his tribute to 'Dr Watson and his friends who in 1748 proved that electrical shocks might be conducted through long circuits [of two miles] with immeasurable velocity'[15] and to Volta and Cavallo, who suggested 'a method of conveying intelligence, by passing given numbers of sparks through an insulated wire in given spaces of time'. Ronalds wrote:

> In the summer of 1816 I amused myself . . . in trying to prove by experiments . . . [the practical employment of an electrical telegraph]. Electricity . . . may be compelled to travel many hundreds of miles . . . Why has no serious trial yet been made of the qualifications of so diligent a courier? Why should not our Kings hold councils at Brighton with their ministers in London? Why should not our government govern in Portsmouth almost as

> promptly as in Downing Street? Why should our defaulters escape by default of our foggy climate? . . . Let us have electrical conversazione offices, communicating with each other all over the kingdom, if we can.

Ronalds's clear vision and Chappe's own ideas on electricity were to be realized, but not yet. The fact that most impressed Ronalds, as he experimented in his Hammersmith garden, was the instantaneous transmission, through 8 miles (13km) of wire, of an electrical discharge. The reader must pause; we are speaking of an era when electricity was not been properly understood; Ronalds had observed, what was later to be established, that electricity travelled at the speed of light. He was convinced, with monumental prescience in 1816, that his experiments afforded 'no grounds for abandoning the project of an electric telegraph'; he added, 'By the use of a telegraphic dictionary, a word or even a whole sentence could be conveyed . . .'.[16] He was on to something, his invention of a dial telegraph that worked was quite brilliant; that it was not exploited for twenty more years can be explained more easily than it can be justified. There is no doubt that the means to develop an electric telegraph existed shortly after Waterloo. If the railways had already been invented (they were only a few years away), the idea may have been given a trial, but in their absence as a convenient and cheap place to lay a grid of cabling, the only alternative for the Admiralty – alternative to the semaphore line that they actually built to Portsmouth in 1822 – would have been to install 70 miles (113km) of telegraph poles down the Portsmouth Road; the Admiralty was not in that business. They were by that time operating in peace-time conditions and in the business of running a navy, a task they had recently performed with such skill and dash; they saved the nation. The Navy was peerless, but impecunious: after victory in 1815, the wars had to be paid for.

Ronalds, a scientist not an entrepreneur, was never motivated to take out a patent on his telegraph (as neither was Alexander Fleming after he had identified penicillin over a century later); instead he offered his invention to the Admiralty, who had the monopoly on the telegraph, and to the world. In France there was no Ronalds; if there had been, the centralized French state apparatus, in which the telegraph was a key component, may have taken more interest in some proving trials. With no Ronalds in France, Europe at peace at last and a desultory attitude in the Admiralty towards innovation, the electric telegraph's moment was not yet at hand. Here is the story of how the Admiralty rejected it.

Ronalds wrote to the First Lord of the Admiralty, Lord Melville (1742–1811) (the former Sir Henry Dundas) on 11 July 1816:

> Mr Ronalds presents his respectful compliments to Lord Melville, and takes the liberty of soliciting his Lordship's attention to a mode of conveying telegraphic intelligence with great rapidity, accuracy and certainty, in all states of the atmosphere, either at night or at day, and at small expense, which has occurred to him while pursuing some electrical experiments.

This seems all very fair and reasonable, if not immediately eye-catching. He continued:

> Having been at some pains to ascertain the practicability of the scheme, it appears to Mr Ronalds and to a few gentlemen by whom it has been examined, to possess several important advantages over any species of telegraph hitherto invented, and he would be much gratified by an opportunity of demonstrating those advantages to Lord Melville by an experiment which he has no doubt would be deemed decisive, if it should be perfectly agreeable and consistent with his Lordship's engagements to honour Mr Ronalds with a call; or he would be very happy to explain more particularly the nature of the contrivance if Lord Melville could conveniently oblige him by appointing an interview.

No interview took place, and after further correspondence, the Secretary to the Admiralty wrote on 5 August, 'Mr Barrow presents his compliments to Mr Ronalds, and acquaints him with reference to his note of the 3rd inst., that telegraphs of any kind are now wholly unnecessary; and no other than the one in use will be adopted.'

Following the Battle of Waterloo, the Admiralty's telegraph lines were closed down in the interests of economy, and the finest army England had ever had was dismissed arbitrarily and without regret or gratitude, and according to Bryant, without compassion:

> In 1815 a naval officer in charge of a Sussex . . . [coastal telegraph station] received sudden orders to discharge his men in the dead of winter, though they were on a hilltop miles from anywhere. The men who had fought their way from . . . [Portugal to Waterloo] were given neither pension nor medal.[17]

In this parsimonious atmosphere, Ronalds's timing had been unfortunate: the Admiralty's dismissive attitude disguised the received wisdom that, with the need for economy or not, to have no telegraphic contact with the coast was unacceptable and new methods were under consideration at the very time that the electric telegraph was suggested. In the same month that

Ronalds wrote to Melville, the Admiralty had just appointed the signalmen for a new experimental telegraph line to Sheerness, which by the end of the month was operational. It was a new line, using a new method – the semaphore, invented by Rear-Adm Sir Home* Riggs Popham (1762–1820), a man who will reappear in our story as a telegraphic pioneer at sea as well as on land. The semaphore method had been found to be materially better in operation than the original shutter telegraphs; the Admiralty knew it worked because it had been trialled and Ronalds's advocacy of an electric telegraph in 1816 was still-born. The rejection letter has been retained in the archives of the Institution of Electrical Engineers to be cherished as an example of bureaucratic dumbness and bad grace. Ronalds was an equable man, an entrepreneurial pigmy inside a giant of electrical science: he bore no resentment towards the Admiralty.

Thus was an opportunity lost. But what if Napoleon had won the Battle of Waterloo in the previous year? What if he, presiding over his newly restored empire in Paris, which now included Britain, or if on a visit to London, had had Ronalds's letter? Seized as Napoleon was with the benefits of fast communication and the ambition he had had for telegraph communication with London, as well as his restored United States of Europe, the whole history of the development of telegraphy would have taken a different turn. But it was not to be: the semaphore telegraph line between London and Portsmouth was developed, and, because it would have taken a visionary such as Napoleon to understand the extraordinary scope of electricity, its exploitation as a telegraph was delayed for twenty years, even though the proof of its capability lay with Ronalds. Two examples of Napoleon's championing of the sciences may be cited in support. In 1801, the Italian physicist Alessandro Volta was 'called to France' in the language of the Institut de France, to present a paper on his invention of batteries: Napoleon, himself a member since 1797, attended the three-day presentation by Volta at the end of which he was awarded a gold medal by Napoleon and made a Count. Even more remarkable was the honouring by Napoleon of Sir Humphry Davy, a lecturer at the Royal Institution at the time (and of the miner's lamp fame) for his discovery of electrolysis. This was all the more remarkable for he received a safe conduct to cross to Paris for his day of glory in front of the Institut, even though England was at war at the time (1813) with France.[18] These examples of Napoleon's auspicious approach to science and the impact of state-sponsored intellectual elitism, which survived Napoleon's downfall, serve to establish how much faster the electric telegraph would have been developed if Ronalds had worked in Paris instead of London.

But it was not just Ronalds who was to be held back because there was no

---

*To rhyme with 'fume'.

equivalent of the Institut de France to approach with inventions; we shall be hearing the names of Edgeworth and Gamble, both of whom had brilliant ideas on telegraphs twenty years and more before Ronalds. In France *la méritocratie* was practiced well before in Britain: from this we may note a deviation in the way the development of pure science occurred in England compared with the state-sponsored advancement of it which occurred in France after 1794–95. The Royal Society was to become a snobbish club, with social-climbing aspirants to the Fellowship outnumbering genuine contributors to science. The public schools taught no science, 'no more did Oxford, and scarcely more did Cambridge'.[19] The Scottish universities were better attuned but small and poor. There was as yet no such thing as a scientific career in England, and the success which was achieved was in spite of any centralized sponsorship. It is not to say that things did not work here, it was that they worked differently. 'In England the French Revolution came late to science as to politics',[20] but, having explored what might have been, we must return to what actually happened.

# 2
# The Ordnance Survey

*Every Prince should have should have a map of his country, to see how the ground lies within it; which highest; which lowest, and what respect they have to each other and to the sea; how the rivers flow; where are the heaths and bogs. Such a map would be useful in both War and Peace, to order the improvement of a country.*
Thomas Burnet (1684)[1]

*Know . . .*
*On the summit whither thou art bound*
*A geographic labourer pitched his tent*
*With books supplied and instruments of art*
*To measure heights and distances; lonely task*
*Week after week pursued!*
William Wordsworth (1813)

Soon after the French had experimented with their visual telegraphs and then brought them into service, the idea was borrowed in England; we shall discover how it happened, in a quite different way, in the two countries in succeeding chapters. But there is something to be explained, however, before the detail of this development is covered: how was it possible in the England of 1796 to plan, survey, construct, test and commission a chain of twelve telegraph stations covering the 70 miles (113km) from London to Deal in just four months? How could the hilltops needed to allow a continuous line of sight be identified with such giant strides, when the surveyor had only his horse for transport and a cart for his tools? Certainly that was the only method of movement which was available to test the appropriateness of a site; but the key to the speed of commissioning the telegraph route at such speed was the quality of the topographical maps which had emerged just a few years earlier and, in the context of a bitter war with France which brought forth the risk of invasion, with such serendipity. We must consider the problems faced by the surveyors and how they managed their timely work.

## Developments in Cartography in the Late Eighteenth Century

The second half of that century and beyond into the great railway-building age was a golden period for the surveying profession; its status became elevated in a society which marvelled at their achievements, which were at the very heart of the commercial, scientific and engineering innovations which were achieved in just a few decades, and which thrust Britain forward as a leading nation. By 1795, when the surveying of the Admiralty shutter telegraph lines began, the rudimentary maps with no topographical information, which the early canal builders had had to use, had been replaced, at least in the southern part of England with accurate, triangulated maps. The benefits which these maps gave to the later canal builders, the military, the railway builders and the telegraph surveyors, are remarkable; and from the point of view of national defence the progress in mapping was chronologically fortuitous.

As the Industrial Revolution took hold in Britain, shown by the sharp upward movement in industrial production in 1780–90,[2] it was made yet more vital by the demands of the wars with France. As the French historian Jules Michelet was to observe in his retrospective analysis of the Europe of the times, the wars saw the masses of Napoleon's France streaming towards the barracks while in England they headed for the factories.[3] By the end of the wars more than 3,000 miles (4,800km) of canals had been surveyed, engineered and dug: the consumption of coal doubled to one ton per caput in the nineteenth century, and other heavy goods such as iron, timber and pottery had to be carried, much of it to the arsenals that built the ships and guns. Not all of the advantages enjoyed by Britain were unique to her, but in the aggregate, freedom of thought and enterprise; political stability; a widespread advance of scientific knowledge, freely dispersed; national political unity and a large single market following the union with Scotland; a political and social climate which was conducive to innovation, industry and commerce; coal and iron in abundance; geographical advantages which allowed for short hauls; in the aggregate these advantages were immense.

The new and substantial reach of the country's cartographers rose to match these other achievements, but with cartography here having previously lagged behind that in other countries, it was natural that the early canal builders and others should have already voiced dissatisfaction with the relatively poor quality of county maps in the early part of the Industrial Revolution. The Society for the Encouragement of Arts, Commerce and Manufactures, to give it its original title, had taken an interest in the 1750s by offering prizes for new county surveys and by applying pressure for a national survey. In fact, the period from the 1750s to 1800 was to be one of remarkable progress for private mapping, for in that period much of Britain had been surveyed and mapped at 1 mile to the inch, to a tolerable level of accuracy, albeit, until the 1790s, with limited detail.[4]

The surveyors of canals and telegraphs needed to deal with the topographical characteristics of large distances between points on a map. By the last decade of the eighteenth century, the maps that the surveying profession had produced reached a new high standard of both accuracy and topographical presentation. Although no contour maps were available until after 1847, from the 1790s maps drawn from triangulated surveys of land over which telegraph stations were to be built began to be published. The surveyors produced these maps just in time for the war with France for the defence of the south coast and for the telegraphs which came with the war. An appreciation of the evolution of cartography in the latter part of the century gives a better understanding of the process by which it was possible for the first shutter telegraph lines to be surveyed at such speed.

One way or another, the whole country had been mapped by the 1760s, but the deficiencies in terms of the accuracy and the absence of detail in the existing, privately published county maps were being exposed. The surveyors of canals, telegraphs and railways needed to be informed of topography. At the official level, mapping in Britain had actually fallen behind that of other European countries, especially of France, and, somewhat paradoxically, behind many of her colonies including eastern North America. Shortly before the war with France broke out, it was complained that England lacked a general map as well executed and as accurate as those in India. This is not to say that no progress had been made here by then: map makers had hitherto been focused on county maps, but this was changing to meet the needs of canal builders and of national defence, but the improvements were taking place piecemeal. Haphazardly, the provision of maps grew by a blend of private initiative and military demands when invasion scares arose. Topographical maps did not emerge until the 1790s and were not widely available until the new century. It was therefore in an atmosphere of a drift towards better maps that the new Ordnance Survey's influence was brought to bear.

## The Board of Ordnance

The Ordnance Survey Office started as a minor part of the Board of Ordnance, which was an organ of government with its roots in the Middle Ages when the Royal Arsenal at the Tower of London was established. The primary and historic role of the Board was to act as custodian of all lands required for depots and forts which were required to provide for the defence of the country, at home and overseas, and to be the supplier of munitions and equipment to the Army and the Navy. It was, as can easily be imagined, a major organization; although it was a civil body, it maintained its own military force, the Ordnance Corps. It was this Corps from which sprang the artillery and the engineers (out of which emerged, in 1920, the Royal Corps of Signals) that were to provide the officers for the Ordnance Survey. The historical responsibilities of the Board including, as they did, fortifications, ensured a knowledge of military engineering and cartographical expertise. This latter had resulted in the extensive mapping of coastal areas and ports in southern England; indeed, with both the ports of Portsmouth and Plymouth developing into major Ordnance depots, there grew there a nucleus of significant mapping capability, while at the Tower of London, a map-engraving capacity evolved.

Even in 1683, to give some idea of how old was the knowledge, the cartographic qualifications required of the chief engineer of the Board of Ordnance were in the mathematics of volumes and heights and of geodetics (the surveying of the earth not as a plane, but as a sphere so that by making allowance for its curvature an accurate framework for smaller-scale work was provided). By the measurement of distances, heights and depths it became possible to draw maps of any place in its due position and perspective in relation to another. On these foundations the Board of Ordnance was able to build a scientific corps whose training needs were to be satisfied by the founding of the Royal Military Academy at Woolwich. A nucleus of officers of scientific mind were trained there who were sufficiently versed in the specialized mathematics required to begin the Trigonometrical Survey: the first accurate fixing, in absolute terms, of the whole country by triangulation. Two officers, both as closely linked with the scientific life of the country through the Royal Society as they were with the military and both destined to play a major role in the early development of the Ordnance Survey, were the Duke of Richmond (1735–1806) the Master-General of the Ordnance Board at the time of the triangulation, and Maj Gen William Roy (1726–90), a cartographer and soldier from Edinburgh.

## The Early Work of William Roy

Before the Ordnance Survey Office moved to Southampton* in 1841, its headquarters were located in the Tower of London, along with its so-called 'Drawing Room', where its maps and plans were produced. A particular function of the Tower was to train surveyors and draughtsmen; the young recruits would produce military topographical maps and plans of

*During the Second World War, after the bombing of Southampton which caused considerable damage to the Ordnance Survey facility, it was moved to Hinchley Wood, near Esher. By coincidence, this was near the site of one of the semaphore stations on the Portsmouth line which opened in 1822. After the war, the Ordnance Survey moved back to Southampton.

fortifications. From the mid-eighteenth century, the growth in technical and scientific competence achieved by the Board of Ordnance provided the means to conduct a major military mapping exercise, which proved to be what was perhaps the founding episode in the history of the Ordnance Survey – the national survey of Scotland conducted between 1747 and 1755. This was the most extensive of its kind to be made in eighteenth-century Britain. Its origins were the military needs imposed by the 1745 Jacobite rebellion; it was not initiated as some far-seeing public initiative, even though this is what it became, but by the engineer officer on the spot in the Northern Britain Command of the Army. The survey was conducted by William Roy, a Scotsman employed in the drawing room of the engineer establishment in Edinburgh. His superb organization of the project marked him out as a future leader in cartographic projects. His finished maps represented a British variant of the best contemporary European mapping practice; hill features, of particular interest for our telegraph surveyors, were delineated by brush strokes in a hatching laid in the direction of the slope; gradient was differentiated by the steeper slopes having a darker tone and the strokes being laid more closely.

His Scottish survey completed, Roy was appointed in 1765 to survey and make reports on coastal areas around the country and its islands. As part of this process, Roy produced a 'General Map of the Southeast Part of England'[5] – a regional map drawn at 6 miles to 1in, it showed London in relation to the coast of southern England as well as the major hill features, including, of course, the North and the South Downs, just the sort of small-scale map a surveyor would like to have had on his desk thirty years later when planning the possible routes for a chain of telegraph stations from London. Conscious as he was of the need for more accurate and better topographical surveys, but mindful of the great cost of a national survey, he put forward a scheme in 1766 which took advantage of the privately prepared county surveys, many of them at 1 mile to 1in, which were being produced at the time. Roy noted that:

> There are already good surveys . . . of Middlesex, Hertfordshire, Berkshire, Hampshire, Dorset, Devon, Hereford and Shropshire; there is also a tolerable map of Sussex and Cornwall; that of Surrey is almost finished; Kent, Bedfordshire, Buckinghamshire, Oxfordshire, Northamptonshire, Huntingdonshire, Worcestershire, Cumberland and . . . Durham are carrying on in the same manner.[6]

But in a comment relevant for surveyors of canals at the time and for telegraphs later, Roy was to say that, although the contemporary county maps were generally sufficiently exact for common purposes: 'They are extremely defective with regard to topographical representation of the ground, giving scarcely any idea, or at least but a very imperfect one . . . of the lie of the land.'[7] Roy had exposed the general weakness of the two-dimensional nature of the maps of the time, in that high (and low) ground could not be discerned, but equally he exposed the absence of overall geodetic control because of the haphazard derivation of the maps.

## Triangulation

Since the time of Euclid in 300BC, trigonometry, or the mathematics of triangles, had been well understood from the fact that the internal angles of a triangle add up to 180°. This branch of mathematics had evolved simple ways of computing the value of a missing variable, whether an angle or the length of a side, if the values of the other variables were known. The practice of applied trigonometry for the cartographer was directed to the minimization of measurement: if instruments could be developed which could measure angles accurately, as they were to be in the late eighteenth century, then the lengths of the sides of all adjoining triangles could be calculated if the length of one side was measured. Roy proposed (anticipating later work actually done by the Ordnance Survey) that a proper scientific triangulation of the whole country should be conducted, having been protracted from the first measurement of a 'great base of the first triangle' which would be 'six or eight miles [9.7 or 13km] in length, measured with the utmost exactness. . .'. By applying Euclid, Roy asserted that from this baseline by measuring only the angles of every triangle projected from the base to some other landmarks, whether natural or placed for the purpose, the whole country could be mapped with the greatest accuracy.

In fact, Roy's proposals, sound and far-seeing as they were, were not taken up at the time, for in the 1770s trouble in America was preoccupying the government. But in the intervening time considerable advances were made in the development of optical instruments; this delay thus served to allow a major leap forward in cartography to be made. In 1763 Roy made his home in London (at 10 Argyll Street, near Oxford Circus), and in 1767 was elected to the Royal Society. By the latter part of the eighteenth century, London was to become the leading European centre for the design, development and manufacture of scientific instruments,* including the theodolite.

---

*John Harrison, the much abused inventor and developer of accurate sea-going chronometers for the measurement of longitude, produced his prize-winning instrument in 1762.

## An Initiative from France

Between them, the Board of Ordnance, the Society of Arts and the Royal Society brought together brilliant minds which, combined with the impulses of the age, created the capability for Britain to make a huge leap forward in cartography. The catalyst, which fused all the ingredients together, came from France; the irony of this is doubled when considering the history of telegraphy, itself a French invention. In cartography France was more highly developed at the time than Britain. In 1783, following the end of the American Wars of Independence, a short window of peaceful relations started between Britain and France, one which was first partially closed by the Revolution in 1789 and then slammed shut when war broke out again in 1793. But it was open long enough to allow, through a chance of timing, a chain of events which would see the whole country covered by triangulation, and the infilling of it by topographical surveys to give the forerunners of the Ordnance Survey maps we know today. The first of these emerging maps, that of Kent at 1 mile to 1in was published by the Survey in 1801, but private-sector maps based on the official triangulation had started to be produced in the previous decade, just in time for the Admiralty's shutter telegraph to be surveyed. It happened like this.

A continuing difference of opinion had existed, which astronomical measurements were unable to resolve, about the relative positions on the globe of the Royal Observatories in Greenwich and Paris (a fact which illustrated the contacts, unrestrained by politics, of the two scientific communities). To settle the argument, a proposal was made by Cassini de Thury (1714–84), a third-generation member of a famous French astronomical family. This was to lead to not only '. . . the origins of accurate mapping in the British Isles'[8] and the foundation of the Ordnance Survey, but also to ensure that, when war came again between England and France only ten years later, all the coastal counties south of London and Surrey had been triangulated, allowing the shutter telegraph lines to Deal and Portsmouth to be surveyed and quickly built. Cassini wrote, in October 1783 to George III: '*Il est interessant pour le progress de l'astronomie que l'on connaisse exactement la différence de longitude et de latitude entre les deux plus fameux observatories de l'Europe.*'

He went on to suggest that, by triangulation between Greenwich and Dover and then by cross-Channel observations, a connection could be made with the French triangulation which had already linked Calais to Paris, a fact which serves to illustrate the lead which France then had. The Royal Society was consulted and thereby Roy, the master surveyor of Scotland, then working in London. In considering Cassini's proposal, there were several motives at work: political, scientific and practical, but in accepting the challenge all were pulling in the same direction.[9] Thus was the working link made between the highest scientific authority, the Royal Society, and the organization, the Board of Ordnance, with the resources and specialist skill, to be led by Roy, for carrying out the project. He grasped the opportunity and, having an eye for the big picture, saw in it the means of achieving his dream: the extension of the local survey to connect London and Dover by triangulation (and on to Paris) into a national survey: the next year, 1784, the work on what was to become the Ordnance Survey was begun.

## The Triangulation Project is Started

In 1785, the Duke of Richmond, Master-General of the Ordnance Board, issued Roy's *General Instructions for the Officers of Engineers employed in Surveying.*[10] The military driving force for the survey which was to be done and its utility when the invasion threat loomed again ten years later can be gauged by the following extract where, in relation to the coast, the surveyors were to report:

> . . . what parts of it are accessible, and what are not; at what distance from the shore, ships of war may come to an anchor to cover a debarkation from boats; and what sort of communications there are leading from the coast to the interior country, in case an enemy had made his landing good: also the nature of the soil . . . Whether there is plenty of timber and of what sort and size . . .

As to the triangulation:

> Every base should be measured twice . . . for this purpose, one chain should be kept as a standard, with which those in common use will be compared at least at the beginning and end of an operation, that a true mean may be taken . . . and with a view to still greater accuracy it will be proper to observe . . . [the readings of] a thermometer at stated intervals. . . . The principal triangles, connected with the base or bases, will be such as are nearly equilateral, formed by church steeples, windmills, single trees or other conspicuous objects [the sorts upon which signal stations would be placed] and in each of these triangles all the three angles should as often as possible actually observed with the large . . . [theodolite] that the reduction to 180° may be properly made.
>
> With regard to . . . elevation, the relative heights of the angles of the great triangles . . . should be first determined: because these being once settled, the relative heights of all other commanding points of any general range . . . will be subsequently ascertained with respect to the first . . .

The method of measurement was initially with deal rods, later replaced by glass rods because they were more accurately controlled for temperature deviation. However, the great innovation was the 100ft (30m) steel chain, which was to be used by surveyors as a standard method of measurement into the last century. It was developed by Jesse Ramsden, of whom we are to hear more below; the chain came complete with a complex set of apparatus that was required to maintain its accuracy. The baseline Roy chose from which to protract the observations that were to occupy much of the rest of his six more years of life was to be at Hounslow Heath, where the operations excited much interest and took on a carnival character in the summer of 1784. Seldom had a baseline been measured with such care or to such a tolerance of accuracy.[11] The land over which the 5-mile (8km) base was to be measured was flat land in the Thames flood plain. It was not particularly convenient for the triangulation from Greenwich to Dover, but Roy had other things in mind when he chose the site. Reflecting his vision of the survey of the whole country, this was a convenient location, being further to the west, to extend the exercise into something much bigger than the Observatories project; perhaps he could rationalize his choice on the grounds that it was the longest stretch of flat land near London; whatever, the protraction to the whole country from this base is exactly what happened. At the time of the measurement wide wooden pipes marked the terminals, but these rotted and the barrels of surplus cannons, placed vertically, with the centre marking the terminal point, later replaced them. The south-east terminal is at grid reference TQ 137709, in a road named appropriately Roy Grove, in Hampton, Middlesex. The inscription on the tablet placed nearby is shown in the accompanying box.

This tablet was affixed in 1926 to commemorate the 200th anniversary of the birth of Major-General William Roy, FRS, born 4th May, 1726 – died 1st July, 1790.

He conceived the idea of carrying out the triangulation of this country and of constructing a complete and accurate map, and thereby laid the foundation of the *Ordnance Survey.*

This gun marks the S.E. terminal of the base which was measured in 1784 under the supervision of General Roy as part of the operations for determining the relative positions of the Greenwich and Paris Observatories. This measurement was rendered possible by the munificence of HM King George III who inspected the work on 21 August 1784.

The base was measured again in 1791 by Captain Mudge, as the commencement of the principal triangulation of Great Britain.

Length of base

As measured by Roy ——————— 27,404.01 feet
As measured by Mudge ——————-27,404.24 feet

The Great Base ran across what is now Heathrow Airport to the north-east terminal at grid reference TQ077767. In 1944 the cannon which marked the spot was removed to make way for works and placed outside the temporary headquarters of the Ordnance Survey in Chessington, Surrey. It stayed there until 1972 when it was returned to Heathrow.

Contemporary developments in scientific instrument-making allied to the development of optical instruments already discussed led to new theodolite of remarkable accuracy: the 3ft theodolite of Jesse Ramsden (1735–1800), 'the father of accurate theodolites'.[12] Ramsden, born in Halifax, was apprenticed to a mathematical instrument maker in London in 1758, set up in business in 1762 and acquired a rare facility in the accurate working with metal to tolerances the fineness of which were better than anything previously known. In 1777 the Commissioners of Longitude awarded him a prize for his *Description of an Engine for Dividing Mathematical Instruments,* which was followed two years later by his *Description of an Engine for Dividing Straight Lines on Mathematical Instruments.* He was elected a Fellow of the Royal Society in 1786.[13] He reached the pinnacle of his profession with the construction for Roy of the 3ft theodolite. Building on his earlier work, Ramsden produced an awesome, precision-built instrument that could measure both horizontal and vertical angles in units of tenths of a second.[14] The practical benefit was assured by combining such precision with a fine telescope of John Dolland's son Peter. His sister married Ramsden, who received, as part of the marriage settlement, a share in the patent for Dolland's achromatic lenses. It was a rare combination of families: Ramsden gave the surveying profession its theodolites, while the Dollands gave astronomers, sailors and telegraphists their telescopes. Brilliant though Ramsden's theodolite was, he sorely tried Roy's patience in making him wait for it. Ramsden was notorious for his disregard of time and he allowed full rein to the maxim of the perfect being the enemy of the good. Famously, he produced a telescope for a new observatory at Palermo on the very day for which he had promised it . . . but in the wrong year.[15] But at length, the theodolite was delivered to Roy at Hounslow Heath in 1787. This was an instrument which, although delivered late, was just what was wanted, and, its being then at the very limits of contemporary instrumentation, remained in use until 1853. The instrument was retained by the Survey at its headquarters in Southampton, where, unhappily, it was destroyed by enemy action, along with other valuable holdings. The instrument weighed over 200lb (91kg) and was transported in a sprung van; it was capable of measuring angles at up to 70 miles (113km) distant,[16] with an accuracy which was as astonishing at the time as it is remarkable now to reflect how long ago it happened.

In September the French longitude party arrived (including the fourth Cassini) and, in October 1787, the cross-Channel triangulation was completed, thus establishing forever the relationship of England to the Continent. The connections of the triangulation, back from Dover towards London and Hounslow Heath required a total of nineteen hilltop structures or other key features, such as the Royal Observatory at Greenwich, which was, of course, the ostensible object of the whole exercise in the first place. Roy died in 1790, just as the proofs of his paper to the Royal Society giving a full account of the job were nearly ready. He was seventy-four years old, he had seen the start of the French Revolution and he bequeathed, not only the military maps of the south of England which were soon to become most serviceable as the French threatened invasion, but also he gave us, either direct or through others who filled in the map details, the triangulated maps of the whole country. More particularly for this story he gave us the height of every hill (by interpolation where necessary) from London to the coast; only five years after his death these data allowed the telegraph stations to be surveyed at great speed. Roy's work was highly praised by his successor William Mudge, the first effective director of the Ordnance Survey, who wrote[17]:

> It was the first accurate triangulation carried out in this country and it set a remarkably high standard; it amply fulfilled its original scientific purpose; it provided for the first time, a thoroughly reliable framework for map-making; and it led directly to the formal founding of the Ordnance Survey.

The accuracy of Roy's measurement and of Ramsden's theodolite can be appreciated by later empirical evidence: Roy's Great Base was remeasured by Mudge in 1791 and found to be less than 3in (7.6cm) different in over 27,000ft (8,200m). In 1787 another base was laid out on Romney Marsh in order to test the accuracy of the triangulation which had been protracted from the Great Base on Hounslow Heath. This was to be the greatest test of Roy's measurement: by the measurement of the angles in the countless triangulations needed to cover the 70-odd miles (about 113km) distance, the length of the Romney Marsh base was deduced from Roy's at Hounslow to be 28,553.3ft (8,708.8m) – the measurement of the ground showed the calculation to be less than 1ft (30cm) in error.[18]

Even before this triumph, Roy's work had been recognized by the Royal Society, which, in presenting him with their Copley Medal, noted 'the accurate and satisfactory manner in which he has measured a base, for operations of trigonometry, upon Hounslow Heath'. He had done more than this: it was enough to make the case, first postulated by him thirty years earlier, for a national survey to be undertaken. The extension of Roy's work, ultimately to cover the whole country as he had wished, was begun in 1791; that the whole of the south of England had been surveyed before the French threatened and in time for the telegraph stations to be sited and commissioned at great speed can be counted as providential. Roy's legacy of maps with heights was like radar in 1940: it was just in time, for grave danger loomed.

## The Military Imperative

At first, the directional progress of the triangulation was determined by military considerations, not commercial. Essex was a priority, so that, with Kent already fixed by the Paris observatory project, both banks of the Thames estuary were accurately mapped and the high ground known. As war with France loomed (the Revolution started less than two years after the connection by triangulation of the Paris and Greenwich observatories), the priority for the primary triangulation was to fix points along the whole of the south coast and points near to it. In 1793, after France had declared war, the urgent requirement was for military maps of Kent, Sussex, Surrey and Hampshire, any northward movement of the primary triangulation being shelved because of the war. By 1796 the whole area from the Thames estuary to Land's End had been covered; this was sufficient to allow military maps of any area relevant to the war to be drawn up quickly. In addition to being of great help to the early Admiralty surveyors, the triangulation was of equal value when the coastal signal stations were ordered. Their utility to the military planners on whom was to fall the burden of defence in the event of invasion scarcely needs to be mentioned. We can be certain that, thanks to the French initiative in suggesting the connection by triangulation of London and Paris, the height of every major hill in the south of England had been measured in the primary triangulation.

## The Ordnance Survey

The trigonometrical survey started by Roy in 1784, formed the framework for the general map of England by the Ordnance Survey, which was started formally in 1791, as war became likely. It was this primary survey that enabled a rationalization to be made between all the privately surveyed and produced maps, county by county, putting them in proper relation to each other. The primary triangulation through Surrey, West Sussex, parts of Hampshire and the Isle of Wight had been completed by 1792.[19] While the heights of the points used in the primary triangulation were now known, much detail still needed to be filled in by lesser triangulation, within the primary one. This lower order triangulation, known as the topographical survey, took considerably more resources for a given area, locating as it did the geographical features of the landscape – rivers, roads, settlements and hills – and had to follow, necessarily, behind the primary triangulation which was now being driven by military imperatives. But these secondary and tertiary observations allowed maps of publishable quality to be produced, and, where land was graded, it was shaded on the map to illustrate the direction of slope and its steepness. The publication of these maps by the Survey began with the map of Kent at 1 mile to 1in in 1801, that of Essex followed in 1805; by the end of 1809 the primary and secondary triangulation of the whole country had been completed (except Lincolnshire, Norfolk and Suffolk).[20]

These maps were, naturally, of crucial strategic importance. In 1802, when the Peace of Amiens gave a temporary truce and under the pretence of establishing consuls for the protection of commerce, the French sent spies to England. Their orders were to make exact plans of all the harbours and coasts of the United Kingdom, but their activities were observed and they were sent by back to France. According to Lockhart,[21] this treacherous measure was openly denounced 'as a violation of every rule of international law, and a plain symptom of warlike preparation'. This was true, but in the dirty business of espionage the first rule is not to be caught: the English had no scruples in 1803 about drawing plans of the military defences of Boulogne, a sally port which was shortly to be the place of great attention and drama, and bringing them home for military analysis.

# 3
# The First Telegraphs and the French Revolution

*Of all the names that the first telegraph age yielded up: Edgeworth, Gamble, Murray, Depillion; Popham and Pasley; it is the name of Claude Chappe that is pre-eminent.*

*Since things in motion sooner catch the eye*
*Than what not stirs.*
Shakespeare[1]

## Edgeworth's Early Experiments

Although it is reasonable to attribute to Claude Chappe the invention of the telegraph, on a point of accuracy, his telegraphic experiments were not the first: Chappe was the first to develop an operational telegraph, one which was unique, durable and most serviceable, but the concept of telegraphy was not his. The extent of Chappe's knowledge of the earlier exploratory work done with telegraphs is not known, but he is unlikely to have been ignorant of it, neither of the pioneering work on electricity already discussed. Richard Lovell Edgeworth (1744–1817), inventor, landowner, educationalist, was on to the idea well before Chappe, but he did not pursue it through to development before Chappe did. There is an interesting story[2] that dates Edgeworth's work on telegraphy nearly thirty years before Chappe's. In 1767 Edgeworth asserted that he could name the winner of a race in Newmarket by 5pm on the same day in London, something that at the time would be, ostensibly, impossible (and devastating to the bookmakers). A bet was made, but it was called off when it became clear that Edgeworth intended to use one of his 'machines' on reciprocating points of high ground where men with telescopes would pass the word. Although his early involvement in telegraphy was overtaken by his interest in other things, the episode helps us to date the first stirrings of interest in practical telegraphy; as it happened, the new higher levels of image quality available from the Dolland telescopes more or less coincided with Edgeworth's interest in telegraphy. Due to considerable institutional obstruction (Edgeworth was an eccentric) and because in the England (and Ireland) of the time it was difficult to achieve anything of note without patronage, he was to suffer endless frustration; he did, however, recover his interest in telegraphy to become a pioneer of its application in Ireland after the turn of the century, but his ideas were never adopted in England.

There was, in fact, a telegraphic pioneer even before Edgeworth: in 1684 Dr Robert Hooke (1635–1703), distinguished chemist and physicist, published in the *Philosophical Transactions* of the Royal Society (of which he and his friends formed the first nucleus), a paper on a primitive sort of shutter telegraph, the idea of which, although it was never developed, was placed in the public domain and knowledge of it would naturally circulate in the scientific community. It is almost certain that Hooke's work influenced the early English telegraphers Murray and Gamble, and, because Chappe was interested in science and because scientists exchanged knowledge across borders, Hooke's work is likely to have been known by Chappe too; as we shall see, he also experimented with shutters.

In the late nineteenth century some previously private letters of Edgeworth's daughter Maria (1767–1849), an accomplished authoress in her own right, were published.[3] The correspondence was between her and another authoress who had made reference in one of her books to 'telegraphing by signals'. Maria Edgeworth wrote, 'This subject happens to be particularly interesting to me . . . My father was the first person after Hook [*sic*] who tried experiments . . . long before the French Telegraph . . . in the year 1767.' She had been a former neighbour in Ireland and a life-long friend of Kitty, the wife of the Duke of Wellington (the first British Army commander to use telegraphs in the field) and was obsessive about the French claim of priority over her father for the invention of the telegraph. She did her best to counter this. There is no doubt about the precedence of Edgeworth's 1767 work in relation to the bet on a horse race, but because that work was not further developed it is hardly a landmark. But Maria Edgeworth's claim of precedence over Chappe is not based solely on that, for, at about the same time as Chappe's early experiments, Edgeworth's interest in telegraphy was rekindled. He devised a unique apparatus – with nothing in common with the ideas of Hooke, Gamble, Murray or Chappe – with four separate pointers. As he described it:

> By day, at eighteen or twenty miles distance [29 or 32km], I show, by four pointers, isosceles triangles, twenty feet high [6m], on four imaginary circles, eight imaginary points, which correspond with the figures 0.1.2.3.4.5.6.7. So that seven thousand different combinations are formed, of four figures each, which refers to a dictionary of words.[4]

This was potentially brilliant. It was like a giant gas meter, and the scope provided by the extent of the potential vocabulary was enormous. Maria Edgeworth has asserted that experiments with this system predated Chappe, but the evidence to prove this is lacking. It may be said with more certainty, however, that Edgeworth's new telegraph was invented without any knowledge of Chappe's system, but by the time Edgeworth's trials took place in Ireland, the Chappe telegraph was public knowledge. Maria Edgeworth's further claim, that her father had successfully transmitted telegraphic messages across the Irish Sea is an extraordinary one; some have doubted its veracity, but the claim deserves to be tested. According to Clarke,[5] these experiments were conducted across the North Channel of the Irish Sea, between Portpatrick in Scotland and Donaghadee in what is now Northern Ireland, a stretch of water of over 20 miles (32km), a distance that was well beyond the operational range of any other visual telegraph. It should be noted that this is not the shortest distance between Ireland and Scotland, but the span of about 10 miles (16km) to the Mull of Kintyre would have involved trials in such an extraordinarily remote and inaccessible area that the idea can be discounted. Even so, there is no evidence which has survived to give forensic support to Edgeworth's claim of successful communication at a range of 20 miles. If it was achieved it must have been even more than usually vulnerable to atmospheric conditions, and the necessary scale of the apparatus liable to be the victim of the endemic windy conditions. It should be noted, however, that if it was made to work across such a distance, how much more efficacious it would have been at shorter ranges; this would have allowed some scaling down of the apparatus. Whether Edgeworth's design predated Chappe is moot, what is certain is that, although his telegraph was the first to be set up in Britain (the first since the Romans, perhaps more accurately), it was not the first to become operational, and therefore it becomes submerged under a tide of the success achieved elsewhere.

The issue of precedence, in relation to the lack of recognition, was really of interest only to the Edgeworth family, but the frustration felt by Maria on behalf of her father and expressed in such injured terms is understandable: on the evidence, Edgeworth's telegraph could have been an extraordinary achievement; that it was never given a trial against other system was unfortunate for the historian and may have been unfortunate for the country too because the French were going to beat us to it. That Edgeworth could not get anyone to take him seriously was not for want of trying or of need: Ireland was soon to be subjected to French invasion attempts. Throughout 1796 Edgeworth tried to interest the Irish administration (the union did not take place until 1801), but for no proper reasons the authorities took no interest.[6] He also tried to interest the authorities in England, but the Duke of York, Commander-in-Chief of the Army, took only an ephemeral interest. *The Times* of 7 November 1796 reported that two so-called 'reconnoitring telegraphs' invented by Edgeworth had been erected at some distance from each other in Kensington Gardens. The first message sent was: 'His Royal Highness the Duke of York arrived in Kensington Gardens to inspect Mr Edgeworth's telegraph at 11 o-clock this morning.' The reply was to hope that the Duke was pleased with the demonstration, which apparently he was; but no orders were forthcoming for Edgeworth's idea, at least not in England. During the peace that followed Amiens, he travelled to Paris with his daughter who wrote, 'the first object that struck us was the Telegraph [that is, Chappe's] at work'. While there, and no doubt bridled by the rejection of Edgeworth's own apparatus, they met telegraph practitioners from Sweden as well as France. When the war broke out again in 1803 Edgeworth was successful in being commissioned to install a telegraph line between Dublin and Galway, but when the invasion scare receded after Trafalgar, the Irish interest in telegraphy fell away. The frustration of the Edgeworths was, as we shall see, to be inflicted on other innocents: one is left wondering quite how Britain became the power in the world that she did when so much talent was wasted for lack of patronage or privilege. It is only with empathy that one can read Edgeworth when he wrote,

> . . . instead of labouring to show economy and disinterestedness, had I introduced my telegraph in the form of a lucrative . . . [racket] in which there might be rich pickings for others, I might have increased the number of my friends, and have gratified those who were in power, by an opportunity of increasing patronage.[7]

It was different in France. They had had their Revolution and cast such cant aside. As we shall see later, one of the gains of Revolutionary France was that it was much more accommodating to fresh ideas: men with new ideas such as Smith, Ronalds and Edgeworth, whatever their social background, would have thrived better there once the excesses of the Revolution had run their course, since, with a combination of the brilliant mind of Claude Chappe and a receptive bureaucracy (and to Maria Edgeworth's eternal chagrin) they developed the first operational telegraphic system – a thoroughbred system which was to operate not only for far longer than any other visual method anywhere, but which marked the true genesis of the telegraph age. But before we leave Edgeworth, we must consider his words, no less prophetic than those of any other brilliant mind of his day: 'I will venture to predict that it will at some future period be generally practised, not only in these islands, but that it will in time become a means of communication between the most distant parts of the world, wherever arts and sciences have civilised mankind.'[8] He was right: but his brilliance was not to be recognized.

## Chappe and the Revolutionary De-Christianization Period

Of all the names that the first telegraph age yielded up: Edgeworth, Gamble, Murray, Depillion, Popham and Pasley, it is that of Claude Chappe that is pre-eminent. He was the man who, with his brothers' help, caught the moment. Nothing can diminish the part he played in European political and military history, the story of the first telegraphs and his legacy to the nascent telegraph industry which was to transform world economic and social development. We must consider how the French Revolution first turned his life upside down and then brought him to fame, and ultimate tragedy. He was one of seven surviving children, born into a prosperous family (their uncle was the celebrated astronomer of whom we have already heard and from whom Chappe's passion for science derived) from Brûlon in the Sarthe region of France, about 25 miles (40km) from Le Mans. Chappe, like his astronomer uncle, had been educated for and had entered the Church; this gave him an extremely comfortable living and time to explore his love of science. The clergy were a rich and resented component of the *Ancien Régime*; together with the king and the nobility they owned half of the land of France. As for the poor, who often died of want unable to afford the marking of a grave, or as Arthur Young observed in *Travels in France and Italy* (1792–74), 'Poverty and poor crops' characterized their conditions, and in a retrospect on their plight before the Revolution, remembering that this was the time of the hated *Gabelle* – the salt tax which hit the poor hard:

> The abuses attending the levy of taxes were heavy and universal . . . But . . . what must have been the state of the poor people paying taxes, from which the nobility and the clergy were exempted? A cruel aggravation of their misery to see those who could best afford to pay, exempted . . .

The Revolution allowed the pent-up grievances of the oppressed poor to be vented in an orgy of destruction; writing in the same month on the Revolution, Young observed:

> Many châteaux have been burnt, others plundered, the seigneurs hunted down like wild beasts, their wives and daughters ravished, their papers and titles burnt, and all their property destroyed; and these abominations [if] not inflicted on marked persons, who were odious for their former conduct, . . . [were perpetrated in] an indiscriminating blind rage for the love of plunder.[9]

Aristocrats and the clergy alike were in grave danger: it was no secret at the time that the brazen ecclesiastics, serving neither the Church nor the state, were living in 'cultivated idleness'. A contemporary writer,[10] whose word pictures were woven into Dickens's *A Tale of Two Cities*, observed that: 'The teachers of morality never teach morality: they defy the anathemas of the ancient Councils, and in idleness enjoy the delights of the capital, and use up the funds given to them for the relief of their unfortunate flocks.' This was the scene, with Claude a young man of twenty-six, when the Revolution erupted in 1789 and he a part of the system which was so hated and now doomed. Commenting on the *Ancien Régime*, Geyl observed, 'The French had every reason to hate their history, which had nothing to offer them, no parliament like that of the British, no free cantons like those of the Swiss':[11] they were in the process of exchanging one absolutism for another, or, as Young put it:

> It is impossible to justify the excesses of the people on their taking up arms . . . But is it really the people to whom we are to impute the whole; or their oppressors who had kept them so long in a state of bondage. . . . and he who dines to the music of groaning sufferers must not, in a moment of insurrection, complain that his daughters are ravished, and then destroyed, and his sons' throats are cut. When such evils happen, they are surely more imputable to the tyranny of the master, than to the cruelty of the servant.[12]

It was not a good time to be explicitly Christian, and very dangerous to be part, as Chappe was, of the established Roman Church: the cross and the tricolour were incompatible, and Chappe was one of those who had to make a fateful choice; as we shall see, he chose the tricolour.

The fatal split between the Church and Revolution opened to an unbridgeable gulf: 'tragically, the first principle of the Revolution, *the sovereignty of the people*, was pitted against the basic conceptions of catholicity and tradition which Rome considered fundamental to the very essence of the Church as a spiritual society.'[13] The clergy who refused to subordinate themselves to the state were proscribed, driven into exile, clandestine ministry or counter-revolution; those who submitted to the Revolution resented the relentless demands on their conscience, and a crisis came when it became known that the clergy were implicated in the royalist rising in La Vendée. All were discredited as the enemies of the Revolution, and a hysterical attack on Christianity itself took place. From 1793 the process of de-Christianization saw Church treasure confiscated, bells removed and sent to the foundries, the ancient clerical monopoly on education swept away and general violence and destruction aimed at the Church was commonplace; Joseph Fouché (1763–1829), of whom we shall hear more, played a notable part in the process. In October 1793 the

Convention voted for the most anti-Christian act of the Revolution, the denial of Christ as the reference point for chronological time. As a benchmark of the Revolution, the start of the new calendar was backdated to 22 September, 1792: the start of year 1 would be marked by the date the Republic was declared.

The attack on Christianity began soon after the Revolution started. In fear of his life and robbed of his living, Chappe left the Church soon after the attacks began. His life would have to take a new direction: if it had not, he may have been one of the thousand who were condemned to death or of the 25,000 who were deported or sought exile abroad.[14] Chappe was not so much giving up Christianity as being parted from his comfortable lifestyle: an income from the Church while indulging himself in his scientific experiments. Returning to the sanctuary of a quiet life in his still comfortable parental home in Brûlon, where his brothers were also now in semi-exile, they could observe the dramatic events unfold in relative safety. It is likely that in the beginning of this period, Chappe had no greater ambition than to indulge himself in his interest in science, to keep his head down and await developments. But his development work on telegraphs was too insistent for him to remain at rest; by 1793 he was to be at the centre of the start of a new telegraph service in Paris and at the very heart of the administrative affairs of the Revolutionary government.

The king was temporarily reinstated as a constitutional monarch in July 1791, and with the Revolution showing signs of having run its course – in fact, its worst excesses were still to come – Chappe decided to go with the grain of French politics and attached himself with enthusiasm to the new Republican regime. Equally, his brother Ignace had by this time become a member of the Legislative Assembly and himself part of the revolutionary government. By the end of 1791 they were both in Paris. Events were now to take further dramatic turns. The revolutionary war started in April 1792 when France declared war on Austria for supporting counter-revolution and whose people viewed with dismay the de-Christianization that had turned Chappe's life upside down. With the first French Republic established in September 1792 and Louis XVI executed in January 1793 ('Frenchmen, I die innocent . . .'), with Robespierre's Terror and its ruthless and bloody centralized power in the ascendancy, and France having declared war on England and Holland in February, Chappe must have wondered where it was all heading. Fortunately for him, the meritocratic atmosphere among those who controlled the levers of power of France was conducive to their examining a newfangled telegraph. It was an invention which was ideally suited to the vitality of the times, distant communication at speed being a problem which was desperately seeking a solution. Chappe had the solution: it had emerged from his enforced return to Brûlon where he had time on his hands in which he could develop his ideas into a working system.

## Chappe's Early Experiments

During the early part of his enforced semi-exile in the Sarthe, when it was no longer politic to profess the faith ahead of the state, Chappe's mind would naturally have succumbed to the gravitational pull of his earlier scientific exposure, the seed of which had been sown by his uncle the Abbé Chappe d'Auteroche, who had written *Voyage en Siberie*, describing a transit of Venus observed in 1761. According to his brother Abraham, writing in 1805 shortly after Claude's death, 'Reading this book greatly inspired him, and gave him a taste for the physical sciences.'[15] We have heard already that Dolland telescopes were taken to California for a later transit of Venus and we can be certain that, through his uncle, Claude Chappe was introduced to the application of telescopes and was also probably introduced to the 'fine' Dolland versions that we have already heard about.

Chappe had an interest in science which dated from his religious training and he had come into contact with several like-minded men with whom scientific ideas could be discussed. He was intrigued by physics and had contributed articles to learned scientific journals at the age of twenty. Like Francis Ronalds, he too had experimented with electricity, observing that two soap bubbles, if charged oppositely, were attracted to each other and would explode on contact. Back at Brûlon and in collaboration with his brothers, also in enforced retreat to the family home during the early days of the Revolution, ideas for a telegraph were considered. Three emerged and he pursued each until the appropriate practical solution emerged. The first of these, being an audible system, was only practicable over short distances; recognizing that this was no solution, Claude Chappe tried to replace the audible signal with an electrical charge. Albeit with the understanding of electricity advancing at a rapid pace but with Ronalds's successful electrical telegraph experiments still over twenty years away, Chappe realized that, until the problem of electrical insulation had been solved, the practical method of distance communication which he wanted to give France now would be delayed too long (and perhaps elude him altogether) if he persisted with his electrical method. He therefore abandoned it, not so much because of disbelief in it as favouring less ambitious methods which he knew could be developed quickly. He considered two such systems, markedly different from each other.

His first experiments were conducted by communicating with friends who lived in Parcé, a little distance from the family home in Brûlon, a small town which stands on elevated ground above the Sarthe valley. From the family home, still in residential occupation as No. 1 Rue Claude Chappe, there is a clear line of sight to Parcé, some 8 miles (13km) away to the south on the Sarthe river. This gives rise to the intriguing question: was Chappe's interest in telegraphy induced by a boyish desire to communicate with his friend in Rue Vivier, in Parcé, or was it just amazingly convenient that the two terminal points of the first telegraphic experiments were 8 miles apart and available for experimentation? The distance proved to be a typical operational span for the visual telegraph, and with Brûlon being on elevated ground and the upper levels of the house at Rue Vivier giving a clear line of sight to the signals, it was a perfect location for the first experiments.

It is thought that Chappe's early ideas and his first experiments owed much to the earlier writings of Robert Hooke.[16] What is more certain is that the experimental communication of 2 March 1791 was observed by officials from the two towns, following which an affidavit from those at Parcé was sworn. This solemn document declared that many dignitaries had gone to a house in Parcé at the invitation of Claude Chappe to observe the experiment and that:

> First we were led into a room . . . and we found a pendulum clock, and a telescope pointing in the direction of Brûlon. Next . . . Chappe [announced] that his correspondent . . . would proceed by initiating a transmission that would be dictated to him by the municipal officers [at the other end]; . . . within the space of four minutes . . . the following [portentous] phrase was produced: 'If you succeed you will soon bask in glory.'[17]

The evidence of this message being received at the Brûlon end was corroborated by affidavit; the trial was repeated the same afternoon when the message sent was, 'The National Assembly will reward experiments that are useful to the public.'[18] Both messages were to be prophetic and, moreover, they reflect the attitudes of revolutionary France at the time. The pioneering telegraphic experiments between Brûlon and Parcé are memorialized with a museum at Brûlon and tablets at the terminal sites in the two towns.

Successful though this demonstration was, Chappe was not satisfied that it was good enough to move on to the development stage; but it was a major stimulant to achieve something that would work when scaled up. Confidence rose and Ignace Chappe was elected to the Legislative Assembly, while Claude set out to seek the support of the government for the further development of a telegraph line. Ignace was able to lobby support in Paris, but at first Chappe succeeded only in obtaining permission from the local commune near L'Etoile to erect a telegraph. These attempts proved nugatory, for the trials early in 1792 came to a riotous end when a mob (of a character that Chappe had sought to escape when he had given up the cloth) which had inflamed itself by a dangerous combination of hysteria and ignorance, convinced itself that the apparatus was subversive to the Revolution and thus summarily destroyed it. That was the end of another of the early Chappe systems, for nothing more was heard of it. Characteristically undeterred, Chappe was allowed to address the Assembly on 24 March 1792. He said:

> I have come to offer to the National Assembly the tribute of a discovery that I believe to be useful to the public cause. This discovery provides a simple method for rapidly communicating over great distances, any thing which could be the subject of correspondence . . . I can . . . transmit . . . the following or any similar phrase: 'Lukner has left for Mons to besiege that city. Bender is advancing for its defence . . . Tomorrow the battle will start.' . . . This discovery . . . offers a reliable way of establishing a correspondence by which the legislative branch of the government could send its orders to our frontiers, and receive a response from there while still in session. [Chappe here presented the affidavits and said with yet more prescience:] The obstacle that seems to me to be the most difficult to overcome is the popular suspicion that usually confronts those who pursue projects such as these. I could never have escaped from the fear that has overtaken them, if I was not sustained by the conviction that I should, as every French citizen, today more than ever, contribute to his country what he can. I ask, Sirs, that the Assembly submit to one of its committees the examination of this project . . .[19]

In due course Chappe would get the trial he wanted; he needed time to further develop his ideas for he had moved on from the Sarthe trial and the shutter system that was not unlike the systems that were later developed by Gamble and Murray in England (and which had been suggested by Hooke over 100 years earlier). Delay was assured in any case, for only a month after his appeal for a reconsideration of the telegraph, the government had new over-arching concerns: on 20 April 1792, France declared war on Austria and the French Revolutionary Wars began. Leaving aside the truce of the Peace of Amiens and the false peace before Napoleon's escape from Elba, France would now be at war until 1815.

After the hiatus caused by the outbreak of war, the Legislative Assembly reconsidered the telegraph and its fateful implications for prosecuting it. In September 1792 further trials were held on high ground (425ft [130m] above sea level) at Belleville to the north-east of Paris, but these suffered the same fate as those at L'Etoile. As Thomas Carlyle described it, the '. . . wooden arms with elbow joints . . . jerking and fugling in the air, in the most rapid mysterious manner', were for a new method of writing without postbags; the mob, however, thought it 'for writing to traitors; to Austria? – tear it down'.[20]

These were the most turbulent of times: to civil disorder was added the military threat from Austria: the black flag flew from Notre Dame and the Hôtel de Ville declaring: '*La Patrie en Danger*'. Volunteers had been called for to strike a blow for liberty and to defend France; the south answered the appeal for 'five hundred men who knew how to die'. On 2 July 1792 they had marched from Marseille and on the 29th they arrived in Paris where soon after the whole city was singing their *Marseillaise.* On 10 August a mob invaded the Palace of the Tuileries, the Swiss Guard was massacred and the king removed to the custody of the Tower of the Temple. As the glass in the windows of the Tuileries had shattered so had any hope of the survival of the monarchy; the king was doomed. Neither would any priest with an enemy be safe, he would be dragged to the dungeons. The odious Law of the Suspect was enacted: anyone with an enemy, priest or not, was in mortal danger of denunciation, followed quickly by execution. The people of Paris gave themselves up to lawless, violent anarchy; negligent of the reckoning, they gloated as the heads of a thousand counter-revolutionaries fell. These killings become a habit, and were the backdrop to Chappe's Paris trials, which took place in this dangerous atmosphere of doom. It was not merely from the guillotine that there was a suspended sentence, but in the east the ruthless Austrian invader, the sworn enemy of the Revolution, approached Paris.

Would Paris to fall to the Austrians? They were only 20 miles (32km) east of the Marne before they were routed at Valmy on 20 September. The Legislative Assembly was abandoned and replaced by the National Convention, the monarchy was abolished and a French Republic created. Ignace Chappe was no longer an elected representative in government, but he continued to assimilate himself among those in power Just how dangerous this would be can be judged from the fate of the Belleville telegraph trials. The mob, now fiercely anti-monarchist, thought that Chappe's telegraph was in communication with the king in the Temple and destroyed the apparatus in a frenzy. The crowd had no need for anything to justify its suspicion: the royal household had already had their tapestry equipment confiscated because anti-revolutionary messages had been woven into their work.

Claude meanwhile gained some advantage from the disaster of the September 1792 trials; he was now able to abandon all his previous telegraph concepts for a new semaphore system which would become the definitive one used in France. But first the new government, now on a war-footing, had to be convinced again. Chappe's latest ideas had been pigeonholed while the political cauldron bubbled and the Republic's borders were threatened; now they were handed to a committee and came to the attention of Charles-Gilbert Romme (1750–95), chairman of the Committee of Public Inspection. It was Romme who was to recommend the rejection of the Christian calendar, but, falling out of favour, as it was only too easy to do, he committed suicide in 1795 to cheat the guillotine. In 1793, however, he was sailing with the wind, oblivious of his fate while passionate in his espousal of Chappe's work. In April he addressed the Convention on the subject of the telegraph:

> Many memoranda on this subject have been presented to the Legislative Assembly, and have been delegated to the Committee for Public Instruction: just one of those truly merits attention. Citizen Chappe offers an ingenious method to write in the air, using a small number of symbols, . . . that can be executed rapidly and clearly over great distances.[21]

Here was the decisive moment when government sponsorship and protection of the trials could be obtained. Romme noted the importance of the invention for military purposes: France had declared war on England on 1 February 1793, and, in support of the Austrians, a British expeditionary army was now on the Continent; the urgencies of the war were mounting. He proposed that 6,000 francs be allocated to fund the trials. Three members of the Convention were appointed as official observers: Joseph Lakanal, Louis Arbogast and M. Daunou. The local authorities where the trials were to take place were instructed to provide security. Ignace Chappe, although no longer a part of the executive, was still able to lobby support for the project and its protection from the mobs. It was about this time that the word *télégraphe* was coined to replace the less elegant *tachygraphe*, by which name the Chappes had previously called their apparatus. The time for the crucial trials of the newest version of the telegraph was at hand. Chappe wanted to expand the scope of his Brûlon trials by having an intermediate station brought into use between the two terminal points: a successful correspondence between three stations would make the later extrapolation into a long-distance route the more credible; but where to place the signal stations?

As Chappe stood on the high ground at the Ménilmont Park in Belleville, now subsumed into Paris, and looked north, he was able to see two ranges of hills, apparently conveniently placed. On the far hills, about 16 miles (26km) away, was a town called St-Martin-du-Tertre; with his telescope he may have seen the watchtower perched on top, about 700ft (214m) above sea level. About midway to St Martin on a nearer hill, was the Chateau of Écouen, just above the town. On making an expedition to St-Martin-du-Tertre, presumably on a hired horse – the government issue of one to him came later – Chappe found near the summit the watchtower that he could see from Belleville; this was to prove most serviceable for his purpose. On climbing up the tower – an experience I have had in common with Claude

Chappe – he would have been delighted to find an astonishing 360° panorama. To the south there was Écouen, while beyond, with his telescope he could see Belleville and Montmartre (a century later he would have seen the Eiffel Tower); while to the north he would have seen hills at Ercuis, some 8 miles (13km) away, and destined to be the next station on the Lille telegraph line which, if his experiments were successful, he hoped would be ordered. But, for the time being, it was to be a trial between Belleville, Écouen (on high ground just above the chateau, probably on ground now occupied by the ruins of Fort Écouen, built as part of the defences of Paris in 1876–77)) and the watchtower at St-Martin-du-Tertre.

On 12 July 1793 the official trial was held:* Claude Chappe was with one official at Belleville; the two others were at St-Martin-du-Tertre, with assistants at an intermediate station at Écouen. The official observer at Belleville, M. Daunou, gave the message to be sent: 'Daunou has arrived here. He announces that the National Convention has just authorized his Committee of General Security to put seals on the papers of the deputies.' The twenty-seven-word message was transmitted in 11 minutes: 9 minutes later back came the languid reply: 'The inhabitants of this beautiful region are worthy of liberty by their respect for the National Convention and its laws.'[22]

Success, it worked! The officials concurred, messages could be sent and the first telegraph age had arrived. This brilliant data network, maybe not the first telegraph line yet but certainly the first network, was the forerunner of the electric telegraph, the telephone, radio, satellites and the internet, the world would change in a way which at the time could not be imagined; and Chappe's 'T'-type telegraph, as it was to be known, was destined to be the standard distance communication device in France for the duration of the first telegraph age, becoming obsolete only as the railways carried the electric cable.

Lakanal's report on the trials, submitted on 25 July 1793, was published[23] and is still available (untranslated) from antiquarian booksellers. Lakanal, who later was to live in the USA where he was president of the College of New Orleans (1822–23) emphasized the accuracy and security of the telegraphic transmissions. The next day, the National Convention, regarding the news as heaven-sent, decided to establish a French state telegraph service. It should be noted that, although three years later there was to be an

* The place where these trials were conducted is now commemorated (following the bicentenary in 1993.) by a monument at St. Martin du Tertre and a tablet in Rue du Télégraphe, Belleville, Paris. Curiously, the tablet refers to Lakanal and Arbogast, but M. Daunau is not mentioned. This omission is the more extraordinary because, not only did he attend the trial, but also his name appears in the first transmitted message.

English version of the telegraph, there was never a state telegraph service in Britain until after the electric telegraph arrived. The Convention was so impressed with the report on the trials, which coined the word *télégram* as the name for a dispatch by telegraph, and so mindful of the need for the fast transmission of orders to and of news from its armies at the front, that it allocated nearly 60,000 francs for the construction of the first line to connect Paris to Lille, and appointed Chappe, *Ingénieur-en-chef-télégraphes*, an office he was to hold for the rest of his short life. The successful trials in Paris marked the inauguration of the first telegraph age. There was another feature of this invention which should be noted, one not unconnected with the place of its invention: the telegraph was particularly suited, not just to a revolutionary government as quick to seize on the new as to destroy the old, but one with a highly centralizing tendency, one which, in due course, would be overthrown by a dictator whose disposition towards keeping control in his own hands and moving with his armies found in the telegraph a new method of giving orders and receiving intelligence which was most serviceable to his style. The revolutionary government would expand the telegraph in France; and then Napoleon saw to it that it spread not just within France but beyond its boundaries into conquered territories.

So, July 1793 was a momentous month for Chappe; they were momentous times and also very dangerous times. That year saw the king go to the guillotine, to be followed towards the end of the year by the queen Marie-Antoinette. This was a provocative act, not least because she was from the House of Habsburg and Austria, already at war with France, had been allied with England since February. We have seen how the mobs held dominion in their destruction of Chappe's equipment; these were no isolated acts of sedition. Violence was endemic at every level; we have also seen how the authorities executed those of Chappe's former profession; the executions without number were as frightening for their fickle, unpredictable character as for the fact of them. And now in July 1793, when Chappe had overcome all the difficulties that had so far been laid before him, the *Girondins* had been ousted from power and Maximillien Robespierre (1758–94) was elected to the so-called Committee of Public Safety, from which position he began 'The Terror'. In the next twelve months, during which the Chappes had to build the telegraph line to Lille, Robespierre's Terror was to make all the atrocities and injustices that had preceded it seem as a rehearsal; no-one was safe.

## The Chappe 'T'-Type Telegraph

We must now consider the characteristics of Chappe's telegraph. He had abandoned the principle of the shutter telegraph as advanced by Hooke because, as Shakespeare had observed, 'Things in motion sooner catch the eye than what not stirs', an elegant explanation of semaphore. The Chappe telegraph, the first, most famous and most extensive and longest-lived of the visual telegraphs, had, as its chief innovation, moving arms; this was semaphore even though the word was not coined until eight years later. Nothing like it was ever used in England; in 1924 Instructor-Capt Tuck described it thus:

> His invention consisted of a beam 12ft [3.7m] long pivoted at the top of a mast 18ft [5.5m] high; at the end of the beam were 3ft [1m] arms, movable about their points of attachment by ropes passing along the beam and down the mast. By the relative positions of the beam and its arms, sufficient shapes could be made to represent all the numerals and letters of the alphabet; and the motions were so simple and easily performed that any particular letter took only four seconds to set.[24]

Thus the essential variable components were the lateral beam, which was carried on the mast, and the two arms, pivoting about the beam. This format gave three different articulations: the beam could be horizontal or inclined up or down on each side; equally, the arms, or indicators, at the end could be set at different angles. The theoretical total of 256 positions was reduced to ninety-eight operational ones to avoid positions that might be confused. The counterweights at the ends of the arms would not be discernible at a distance. To reduce weight, wind resistance and reflections, half of the copper slats were placed in opposing orientation, and from a distance the black paint ensured a good discernible outline against the sky. Chappe needed help in the design of the rope and pulley mechanism which was required for manipulating both the beam and the two arms at its end. For this he turned to someone familiar with them, the well-known clockmaker of the time, Abraham Louis Bréguet (1747–1823) who helped to design the physical controls.[25] This relationship grew strained in later years and was the cause of much anguish to Chappe.

Even British commentators, writing after the last of the visual telegraphs had closed, considered Chappe's telegraph as the best: 'Various . . . telegraphs have at times been used, but the most perfect one in every sense of the word, as far as aerial telegraphs are concerned, was that which was invented and perfected by Messrs Chappe. . . .'[26] There was a fundamental difference in the way Chappe's system was operated (compared with what was actually used later in England). A cousin of the Chappes was on the consular staff in Lisbon and had been familiar with the sending of diplomatic traffic in code, unlike both Gamble's and Murray's shutter telegraphs, which were designed to transmit letters of the alphabet *en clair*, as was the semaphore system which ultimately replaced the shutter system in

England. Chappe's telegraph was refined, soon after it was introduced, to send coded signals the meaning of which could be looked up in a vocabulary. This had an advantage in addition to security: the encoding process allowed the message to be compressed (analogously to Popham's flag code which we shall be considering) which led to the shortening of transmission times for a message of a given length. The security aspect was soon recognized: soon after the first telegraph line opened, a member of the Convention noted that: 'The greatest advantage that can be derived from this correspondence . . . is that . . . [its contents] shall only be known to certain individuals . . . without any other person getting acquainted with the object of the correspondence . . . [and] without the enemy's being able to discover or prevent it.'[27]

For an account of the regulations for telegraphic correspondence of 1795 the reader should refer to Holzmann and Pehrson's book.

# 4
# The Development of the Chappe Telegraph

*Young men will go to the front; married men will forge arms, and carry food; women will make tents and clothing, and work in hospitals; children will turn linen into bandages; old men will be carried into the squares to rouse the courage of the combatants, to teach hatred of kings, and republican unity.*[1]

## The Telegraph Goes on a War Footing

Quickly after the July trials, on 4 August 1793, the Convention ordered the acquisition of the station sites which Chappe had identified for the first line between Paris, via Montmartre and the experimental stations already mentioned, and Lille to the north, near where the French army was in the field facing the Austrians. The Convention gave carte blanche to the Chappes to place their stations in any tower or other building of their choosing, as well as power to remove any trees that restricted the line of sight between stations;[2] local authorities were ordered to make available labour and materials. Church towers were easily requisitioned for churches now had no liturgical use, many had been converted to workshops and some even to taverns. Because Lille was in a war zone, there was the ever present risk of its capture by the enemy or of its being besieged; to accommodate this eventuality, and allow work to proceed in spite of a siege and to facilitate communication for the first time ever between a besieged city and its friendly forces beyond the besiegers, Claude Chappe sent his brother Abraham to supervise the works at that end of the line.

The distance was about 135 miles (217km), requiring sixteen intermediate stations, on average about 8 miles (13km) apart. The process of surveying the line to Lille – deciding which hills to use and where was the best line of sight – has not been recorded, but we know that good maps were available at the time. We have seen how in England the triangulation project had been achieved just in time through a French initiative. In France, the

European cartographic pacemaker,* they were already well ahead in such matters: the carte topographique de la France, which had been organized by the director of the Paris Observatory (the same Cassini who had proposed the Greenwich–Paris triangulation project) and financed by the government, began as early as 1750 and had been substantially completed by 1784, at a scale of 1:86,400.[3] Plainly, the provision of maps was not a difficulty to be overcome by Chappe, but there were others. The work on building and commissioning the first telegraph was taking place, as we have seen, during the Terror, the domestic situation in France was deteriorating rapidly, food shortages were appearing and the scourge of terror was creating paralysis. Thirty years later, Ignace Chappe wrote:

> It is remarkable how difficult it was to survive the second phase of our efforts [the first being the development work up to the successful July trials], the establishment and the organization of the line from Paris to Lille; how much energy, exhaustion, and resources we had to spend to overcome the unforeseen obstacles, returning endlessly, in a project of a kind that had never been attempted before; the fear and the worries caused by the uncertainty whether the project could succeed at all: the death of the project could always be read on everyone's face![4]

'The death of the project' – in the affairs of man there is no project having a modicum of complexity or creativity at the frontiers of knowledge which does not make the heart stop at some stage in its progress. There is no project where success, depending, as this one did, on the scaling up from preproduction trials to being operational, does not share a bed with the spectre of failure, of flawed economics or faulty design; there are a thousand plagues on a high-risk capital project which gnaw at the minds of its leaders. Claude Chappe and his brothers had confidence in their design and they had the skills required, along with determined bravery at a time when personal safety must have been a constant concern, to deliver one of the most remarkable developments of the age. It would have been a colossal achievement in peacetime, but they were operating in a war zone. Among all the difficulties were the instability of civilian politics, causing turmoil in the

*The most unalloyed legacy of the French Revolution is the metric system. In 1799 the French cartographers triangulated their way from Dunkirk over 700 miles (1,130km) due south down a meridian to Barcelona, and computed one ten-millionth part of the distance and called it a 'metre'. Representatives of Europe were summoned to the first metrical congress: 'to receive the metre from the hands of France'. But nowhere – not even in France – were the new units in daily use before the 1840s (Crawley, *The New Cambridge Modern History*, vol.9).

country, the requisitioning of horses for the army and the desperate state of the economy. In addition to all this, the military situation was tense too.

Less than three weeks after the Convention had ordered the telegraph line to Lille, another new and sinister aspect of the Revolution emerged: reflecting the increased scale of fighting and a threat to the French border, the army manpower had proved to be insufficient for the defence of the country. The voluntary system which had given France the *Marseillaise* and until then had been relied on to deliver the required numbers of soldiers had failed; the Convention ordered a *levée en masse* (wholesale compulsory enlistment): over 500 new battalions were to be raised.[5]

There was to be an unprecedented struggle; this was no war of princes but a people's war which had another twenty years to run. Chappe was near the epicentre of a revolutionary government in charge of the construction of the first telegraph line. Naturally there were difficulties with labour, the paralysis caused delays too in the arrival of funds, which the Convention had voted, at the point where they were needed. It became difficult to persuade workers to stay on the job when frequently they went without pay, sometimes for weeks on end.[6]

But in spite of the difficulties, by the end of April 1794 all the stations were built. Unlike the shutter telegraphs in England, the Chappe stations were built to permanent standards. The fighting with the Austrians was uncomfortably close at the time; Claude Chappe, who was based at the Paris end, received a letter dated 22 April 1794 from near the other end of the line, saying that '. . . every afternoon and all morning yesterday, the cannons fired constantly; we can hear them closely because the attack, we have been told, comes from Cambrai, which is no more than . . . [20 miles; 32km] from here.' Nevertheless, the training of operators was completed, the stations manned and commissioning work begun; by May the telegraph line was routinely transmitting texts of decrees from the National Convention.[7]

It would soon be time to declare the line operational; as the climax approached the process was conducted while not only the military situation was tense but Robespierre's Terror was reaching its crescendo. The civilian population recoiled at the retribution sought from any rebels; any royalist troops who were captured as the Austrians retreated to the Rhine and as their Prussian allies quailed, were executed by massacre. But eventually the job was done and the telegraph line was declared open on 16 July 1794. The first telegraph age had arrived; but it was in the hands of nihilists whose revolutionary zeal had lost its capacity to shock. At the same time as the telegraph was demonstrating its novel efficacy, another gruesome demonstration was at hand – in Paris two or three thousand heads were falling each month:

> . . . while in the provinces holocausts took place which made the blood of Christendom turn cold. At Nantes one monster massacred 500 infants, having first offered their mothers the choice of prostitution or death. Another sadistic scoundrel put more than five thousand people to death in Arras. Such men were as pitiless abroad as they were at home . . . [the Revolutionary armies] were followed by hoards of agents who bespoiled Belgians of everything but the barest essentials.[8]

The French revolutionary army was to operate on a new principle: they would live off the countries they invaded and make campaigns pay for themselves with booty: 'War must support war'. This upside-down world was the one in which the early work on the telegraphs was done, but there is a paradox which serves to show how elevated was Chappe's work considered to be, and, in a sense, how brave or naïve, or perhaps just determined he must have been. According to a definitive history of the period:[9]

> The scientific community ceased to exist during the Terror. Its members went into war-work or retreat, and in either case away from science. . . . In the opinion of the intellectuals of the 1790s, the creative period of the Revolution began, not with the Bastille . . . but with the fall of Robespierre.

The generality of this is secure, but it leaves Chappe's position strangely singular for he had gone into war work and, if not pure science, certainly the result of innovation. Chappe was the hero and he had praise heaped on him by the same government that created the environment in which to survive at all was the summit of most people's needs. Barely a fortnight after the opening of the Lille line, the murderous fever reached its peak in Paris: Robespierre's suspension of the last remnants of justice frightened the Convention into turning on him, for he was arrested, imprisoned in La Conciergerie in Quai de l'Horlage – the site of the earlier execution of Marie-Antoinette and twenty-one *Girondins* – and, before the mob could intervene, he was guillotined the following day, 28 July 1794.

With this relief came a reversal in military fortunes. As the revolutionary French armies overcame their unco-ordinated enemies, news of French victories came in to Paris by telegraph, or, at least, this is how it appeared. The French historian Gerard Contant has exposed as a myth in his *Claude Chappe et le Télégraphe Opticue* (1993)[10] the supposed first message being on 15 August when there came to Paris by telegraph, it had been said, the dramatic news that the French had captured Le Quesnoy, about 120 miles (190km) away in northern France. Le Quesnoy, 40 miles (64km) south-east of Lille was a medieval walled-town characteristic of many such towns in

France, the extensive ramparts exist to this day. It was said at the time that the news arrived in Paris about 10 hours faster than it could have arrived by horse; Contant asserts that the timing of the publication of the news was manipulated for political reasons. At its very birth, politicians realized the power of the telegraph: the new age was to give the holders of power the means of manipulating the distribution of news. Many a crooked government, and some not so crooked, has exploited this means of manipulation which the first telegraph ushered in. But in Paris in August 1794, in the way in which the news of this victory was announced, there could be no better demonstration to the revolutionary government of the utility of the new invention: red-hot military intelligence had come from the front at previously unknown speeds, the age of fast distance communication had been given to the world. Bertrand Barère de Vieuzac announced the victory at Le Quesnoy to the Convention:

> We seize upon this occasion to speak to you of a new establishment made under the auspices of the National Convention, of a machine by means of which the news . . . was brought to Paris an hour after our garrison re-entered the town. [Here he caught the moment when the world changed.] Modern peoples by printing, gunpowder, the compass and by the language of telegraph signs, have made vanish the greatest obstacles which have opposed the civilization of men, and made possible their union in great republics. It is thus that the arts and sciences serve liberty.[11]

If the equine scorekeeper was listening his heart-beat would have tripped when, marking his species' services to man across the millennia, he notched his talisman as the ranks of faithful horse-ghosts presented arms and saluted a new age.

Soon afterwards, the town of Condé-sur-l'Escaut (a short distance from Le Quesnoy, and another charming medieval walled-town) was also taken: the telegraph message received in Paris on 30 August was 'Condé is restored to the Republic. Surrender took place this morning at six o'clock.'[12] Some authorities have quoted the first message from the relieved town as 'Condé is taken from the Austrians': this is the statement that was memorialized on Chappe's tombstone. The prompt reply received at the front was, 'The fortress is no longer to be called Condé, but Nord Libre,[13] and the Army of the North deserves the gratitude of the country.'[14] Vestiges of the honour of the new name remain today in Condé-sur-l'Escaut. On the very same day, indeed, during the same session of the Convention in which the 'Nord Libre' message was sent and in a brilliant demonstration of the power of speed which they now held in their hands, back came the reply from Lille, 'The decree has arrived and has been sent by special courier to Nord Libre.'

Another courier had been sent from Lille with a duplicate of the dispatch about the surrender; he did not arrive (by horse) until twenty hours later.[15]

The excitement and the thrill as the impact of Chappe's telegraphic connection to Lille was absorbed can be imagined. These two messages, spreading with the rapidity of lightning, soon became known to all Paris, as well as to the Army of the North, and the victory and the telegraph were henceforth established as glorious facts.[16] The news of the fall of Brussels, the first of the foreign capitals to be over-run, went down the line from Lille, just over 60 miles (97km) away.

The extent of Chappe's enthusiasm for the Revolution (or disgust at its excesses) is unrecorded, but we are left with an impression that he was, and certainly became, a troubled man; but, in any event, work on the telegraph continued apace. The Paris–Lille line (which was to continue in operation until 1847, with a small break in 1802) was extended to the important port of Dunkerque in 1798 and to Brussels in 1803: the telegraph connection between Brussels and Paris lasted until 1814. The Lille line was extended further via St Omer to Boulogne in 1803, where, as we shall see, Napoleon waited with his flat-bottomed boats. This route was diverted to go by Calais in 1816, with an extension to Eu, south of Boulogne. The Calais station continued its correspondence with Lille until 1852. In its early days in France the telegraph was the exclusive province of the government. The immediacy, which was so attractive to a centralized power, was given an early illustration: a general in command of the Army of the Rhine was to telegraph in 1795: 'A battle took place [yesterday near Basel]. The fighting was heavy on both sides, but the enemy was completely defeated. He is now in full retreat and I am in vigorous pursuit. Their loss in killed, wounded and prisoners is huge.'[17]

At this early period of the war the British expeditionary force was mired in fighting a long way from home. Now that the French had their telegraph link to it is easy to see the strategic advantage they enjoyed when they could communicate quickly with their armies in the field, while the British commander might be a week away from London by horse and boat. Just as military messages had ushered in the telegraph age in France, so it was to be in its finale. In 1855 news of the capture of Sebastapol in the Crimean War arrived by telegraph:[18] it was one of the very last messages sent by the visual telegraph in metropolitan France. We can note here that, in 1801, Abraham Chappe devised a mobile field-telegraph and a dozen were made for the army. The machine was a smaller version of the standard design with hand-worked arms and mobility was achieved by the apparatus being mounted on a cart; these field telegraphs were used by the French army in Napoleon's time and in the Crimean War.

## Financial Difficulties

Following the successes of the French Army of the North in the late summer of 1794, by early the next year the First Coalition against the Revolution was breaking up; the British Army was evacuated from the Continent in April and all of France's enemies, save Britain, made their peace one by one; by midsummer the war in northern Europe was over. This changed the character of the war for Britain: following the fall of Holland, the enemy acquired control of a whole continental coastline and the Royal Navy became the last line of defence against Jacobinism. But on the Continent, following the Revolution's military ascendancy, a quiet descended over the previously violent scenes. But lest it be thought that, by their Revolution, the French had secured a method of government which was enduringly stable, the truth was the opposite: the Revolution had, in its haste, destroyed a considerable measure of economic resources, the country was becoming bankrupt.

War still had to be waged against England: financing such a war as the revolutionaries had embarked upon would have been an almost impossible task under the old regime, such were the fiscal demands. The new currency was the *assignat* and the government thought to solve its problems by printing them on demand. The corollary of inflation on an unprecedented scale was to be severe: the combination of the general mobilization that had taken men off the land and a series of bad harvests caused critical food shortages. The overthrow of Robespierre brought a general relaxation, but with too much nominal money chasing too few goods, it only brought about even faster inflation: by July 1795, the *assignat* had lost a crippling 97 per cent of its face value. Investors were ruined and workers were near to starvation because of the food shortages – a desperate situation made worse by a historically severe winter in 1794–95. Another change of government was inevitable, and, declaring virtual bankruptcy, the new one cleared the financial decks; by this robbery the peasants who had nothing anyway lost nothing, but the value of cash and debt was destroyed. But something else had changed: for the first time, the army had taken up arms against the general population. In Paris a young Gen Bonaparte, fresh from his relief of Toulon (previously captured by the British), led troops which were heartlessly to put down a mob of rioting, hungry Parisians. We cannot pursue this here, but what is relevant to our story is that this may have been the first time that Napoleon, called to Paris for the job, had observed the telegraph at work. Always quick to assimilate, he was to be alert to its importance to him, personally, in the future.

In 1794 the revolutionary government approved the adoption of the telegraph as a national utility and ordered the planning of suitable routes. We may observe here a difference between how the telegraphs developed differently in the two countries: in England they were to be (until 1825) an Admiralty monopoly and remained with the armed services exclusively for thirty years, but in France they were more widely appreciated as a utility to be exploited by government in the whole orbit of its role, mainly military, but not to the exclusion of civil matters of administration. Into the new, more peaceful conditions, and mindful of the financial difficulties, Chappe promoted non-military uses of the telegraph. He pointed out the benefits that would flow from using it for transmitting weather reports (the British Admiralty used theirs to report wind direction daily). But, attractive as it was to expand the telegraph network, new lines did not come cheaply; the financial difficulties of the government ensured that many of the expansion plans for the new telegraph, as it radiated out from Paris, were beset by financial problems. Chappe is recorded as having sent many letters pleading for the delivery of funds; two extracts serve as an illustration of the volumes of such letters: 'No more funds, we have lost almost eight days at an extremely important time . . . this situation makes me desperate . . .', and 'I do everything to assure the prompt success of the organization I direct; money or there will be no line to Brest.'[19]

Chappe, pondering on how to finance the expansion of the telegraph, suggested three ways of bringing cash into the service from commercial exploitation. First, he suggested making a charge for telegrams sent for private commercial and banking houses; next, an official journal (in much the same style as *Le Moniteur*, the official Napoleonic newspaper) for the telegraphic distribution of news summaries, as was later so successfully achieved by Julius Reuter and, in the 1850s, in taking news summaries off ships carrying the India mails at Marseilles and sending them more quickly to London via the telegraph to Paris and on to a Channel port; and, finally, for the operation of a national lottery. When the electric telegraph came in, such a broad use of the communication medium was not merely normal, it was central to its being. It was Claude Chappe who suggested the pan-European, commercial use of telegraphy when it was still over the horizon and out of sight to everyone else; but he was to be dead before his vision was realized. The new telegraph age, being the child of war and under the control of the revolutionary government in France, its capacity could not readily be turned over to private use, England still had to be beaten. However, the lottery idea, which required little telegraph capacity, was put into effect quickly. We have seen that gambling on horse races was the inspiration for Edgeworth's 1767 wager and, just as Chappe had intended, the use of the telegraph allowed the announcement of lottery winners to be made in the provinces on the same day that they were drawn in Paris. Just as Chappe had predicted it would, this paid for the greater part of the telegraph service. In 1799 the total operating costs of the telegraphs of over 400,000 francs were supported by a government subvention of only 15,000 francs.

The financial difficulties overcome, in part by plunder, Chappe was to see a huge expansion of the service with the laying of new lines. Probably due to the great distances involved in France and the great benefit to be gained from rapid communication with the armies of the Revolutionary War, further lines were ordered. Of particular note is that to Brest at the request of the navy, a distance of over 350 miles (565km) and with fifty-seven intermediate stations, which opened in August 1798 and which was completed in the remarkable time of only seven months. This line enabled communication with the French fleet where it lay close to the Western Approaches. By the turn of the century, Paris was connected to Strasbourg via Metz as well as Brest and Lille; this represented a total route mileage of over 800 miles (1,300km). The Strasbourg line consisted of fifty stations: in England the longest route – to Plymouth – was to have twenty-one. In 1800, with peace negotiations taking place with Austria at Lunéville, Napoleon ordered a new, small branch of the Strasbourg line through which communication was maintained in the period leading to the signing of the Treaty of Lunéville in February 1801 (further illustrating the different use made of the telegraph in France compared with that in England). As *Ingénieur-en-chef,* Chappe oversaw all these developments.

## Tributes to Claude Chappe

All suicides are tragic: if Claude Chappe's Christian faith survived the repression of the Revolution (we do not know whether it had) it was apparently not able to give the poor man the strength to ride out whatever torment he was being subjected to, nor to assist in any appeasement of that which he was unnecessarily inflicting on himself. Just how ill he was, and whether any of his brothers or other close family members (he had no wife) had noticed that he needed help is not recorded. He died on 23 January 1805, having found the courage to throw himself down a well at the telegraph headquarters in Paris. He had become ill during an inspection tour in the latter part of 1804 and suspected food poisoning;[20] other reports have mentioned a painful ear infection, which may have deranged his equability.[21]

Whether his physical condition was the cause of his suicide is more easy to doubt than the effect of the insidious attacks by others on claims for priority in the invention of the 'T'-type telegraph. It seems more probable that his mind, wearied by his bodily ills, became unequal to the struggle that was required to right the injustice of the claims against him, which, although perhaps true to a degree, were, it must be vigorously stated, certainly off the point. This whole question of priority, which we have seen was also exercising Maria Edgeworth's mind to her death in 1849, is not something that Chappe should have had had anything to do with.

Telegraphy was a concept, it was known in the ancient world and Hooke had announced it to the modern; the concept was not something over which proprietary rights could be acquired, such rights would apply to the mechanisms used to send the signals and any code which was used to encrypt them. Chappe's 'T'-type semaphore telegraph was the first developed, operational telegraph capable of unrestrained dialogue to be installed in the history of man – no qualification of this statement is required. Hooke conceived the modern telegraph, Edgeworth made one work, almost certainly before Chappe, but was it operational? No; did any aspect of Chappe's telegraph borrow a design feature from another? No. Maria Edgeworth's claims to priority (still being written about in 1897) were irrelevant. If Chappe had been goaded by any of this, his suicide was the more tragic. But something tipped the balance of his mind.

His suicide note, referred to by some newspapers at the time but not preserved, was more Delphic than illuminating: he had killed himself because he wished to avoid life's anxieties which were weighing him down ('*Je me donne la mort pour éviter l'ennui de la vie qui m'accable*'). Apparently, the only other clause to the one-sentence note (and this echoed the dying words of Louis XVI) was that, 'I have nothing to reproach myself for' ('*je n'ai point de reproches à me faire*'). It is these few words that give the clue to the needling to which he had been subjected. His brother Abraham, in a letter published in the *Journal de Paris* a few days later, observed, 'He is dead, like his uncle the Abbé Chappe, a victim of his passion for the sciences and his country' (the Abbé had died in California while on the transit of Venus expedition). This was no fraternal extravagance of phrasing, for his service to both the sciences and his country had been not just brilliant and monumental but immaculately timed to serve the interests of the Revolution. 'May their successors', continued Abraham, 'learn to imitate their example . . .'; this was probably a restrained sideswipe at some of those fellow Frenchman who had been needling Claude. The following day in the official French newspaper was the balanced observation that:

> M. Claude Chappe, the inventor and the administrator of the telegraph, died . . . at the age of 42; a true loss for the arts. It has been said with reason that the art of signalling existed long before him. But, in fairness, what he added was to expand this art into an application so simple, so methodical, so certain, and so universally adopted, that he can be regarded its true inventor.

This was the point, for it was Chappe, with his fraternal and other collaborators, who had assimilated everything that had preceded him through the ages, had added to it and conceived, developed and built an operating system fit for the times into whose service it was pressed. He designed the semaphore arms to secure the greatest visibility, strength, lightness, durability and ease in operation, and made it complete with a vocabulary code; it was an outstanding contribution to France and to the world. It had fallen to the Chappes to face administrative, political and military difficulties, and to succeed in circumstances of privation and grave danger. From beginning to end they were sustained by loyalty to France.

Claude Chappe had survived the attack on the Christianity; he had survived long enough to see the end of the Revolution; he saw the connection of Paris by telegraph to Lille, Brest, and Strasbourg and Huningue further up the Rhine near Switzerland; he saw the *coup d'etat* which brought Napoleon to power; his advance to dictatorship by his appointment as First Consul for life; he saw the politically convenient reversal of the de-Christianization policy by Napoleon's Concordat* with the Pope which restored Christian legitimacy; he had seen the defeat of Napoleon's continental enemies and the Peace of Amiens; he had observed the peremptory attitude of Napoleon, which hastened the collapse of the precarious peace; and in 1803 he was to build an extension of the Boulogne line to Cap Gris-Nez in order to telegraph across the Channel; and, just before his death, he saw the coronation of Napoleon as Emperor (2 December 1804) by the Pope in Notre Dame. Chappe's service to France, through all these events, which still have a resonance today, was unswerving.

In Abraham Chappe's letter in which he defended the reputation of his late brother, he referred to the accusations of those Frenchmen who had driven Claude to his despair; he had in mind Bréguet, Bétancourt and De Courrejolles, and possibly others. We have already come across Bréguet, who helped Chappe with the design of the semaphore arm control mechanisms; in 1796 Bréguet and Bétancourt started to advance their own competing design, but in the following year their attempt to have Chappe's design replaced by their own failed. Claude Chappe had participated in an exchange of correspondence conducted through the press, after the merits of the other system had been publicly advanced. Here was clear evidence of,

---

*The Concordat was reached in 1801: the French nation wanted its priests, its church bells and peace with Rome, and Napoleon had enough insight to grant it its wish; but with arbitrary administration of the law and with control over the press, the Concordat was intended not to save religion but to make it an instrument of government. To lull men's minds by fostering their interests while forbidding all criticism was Napoleon's method of securing a docile public. An alternative view is given by Georges Lefebre, writing over a century and a quarter later, 'At times he had a clear insight into the positive power of the spirit, even above that of the sword, and at the very beginning conceived of the Concordat as a means towards the education of the faithful into a willing joyful obedience.' *See* P. Geyl, *Napoleon: for and against.*

shall we say, a grievance. So it was also with the third known would-be claimant to fame; De Courrejolles, a captain in the French navy, had been unsuccessful in promoting his own design for a telegraph in 1783. It had been conceived and brought into use in a naval engagement in the Mediterranean against, of all people, Nelson, but he had been unable to persuade the Minister of War to adopt the system for the army.[22] He and Edgeworth had much in common, if not in their apparatus then at least their frustrated ambition.

History has been kind to the name of Claude Chappe. But by his death it was France herself who was robbed. We have seen already that Chappe had abandoned his early experiments with telegraphy by electricity because the optical one was more certainly deliverable for the urgencies of the moment. France lost a brain that might have alighted faster than others in France were to do on the potential of electricity to change the world of distance communication. As it was, his work had provided the first building blocks for the electrical communication industry that was to come. Ronalds's successful electric telegraph experiments were conducted in his Hammersmith garden in 1816; with the war by then finished it is impossible that Chappe would have remained ignorant of his work after the Admiralty had dismissed it. Ronalds published in 1823; Chappe would have become aware of Ronalds's successful insulation of 8 miles (13km) of cable: the very unsolved problem that led Chappe to abandon electricity. If Chappe had lived there can be little doubt that he would have continued the work of Ronalds, which he abandoned because he wearied of it, and the electric telegraph may have been introduced in France, with research and development sponsored by the Institut National de France before the railways allowed its exploitation in England.

In France, when ultimately the electric telegraph arrived, and before the Morse code was adopted, the telegraph needle at a receiving station would be propelled around a dial which had symbols which could then be interpreted. What were these symbols? They were none other than the semaphore attitudes of the Chappe 'T'-type telegraph, still in use all over France as electricity came in. Whereas in England there are no monuments to the pioneers of the telegraphs, save a modest tablet on Ronalds's house in Hammersmith, the work of Claude Chappe is celebrated in Paris. There used to be a model of a Chappe signal station at the Science Museum in Kensington, but it is no longer on display. In Paris, however, there is a fine display of a Chappe telegraph station at the Musée des Arts et Metiers and an exposition of the advances in communication illustrating the profound evolution of political, cultural and economic issues in response to the increasing speed of news transmission. There is also an example of the electric telegraph receiving apparatus showing the Chappe symbols on the dial. There are further tributes to Chappe's telegraph lines at the

Musée de la Poste. A Metro station is graced with the name Télégraphe, on Line 11, to the north-east of Paris, serving the area of high ground of Belleville. The station is on Rue du Télégraphe, which is close to the area where Chappe's telegraphic experiments were conducted. In this street, reflecting the role of the telegraph in revolutionary France and erected on the 150th anniversary of the Revolution, is a tablet commemorating the role of the telegraph in announcing the victories of the Republican armies. Nearby is a more modern commemoration of the site as the location of Chappe's experiments of 1792 and 1793, and the inauguration of the line to Lille, by which messages could be sent 'in three hours instead of three days'. These modern memorials were in recognition of the bicentenary of the trials in 1993. As part of the same celebration a special postage stamp was issued as a tribute to Chappe, along with several versions of a prepaid telephone card in honour of the man and his telegraph. At the first centenary in 1893 there had been erected a handsome bronze statue of Chappe and placed at the junction of the Boulevard St. Germain with the Rue du Bac.[23] Evidently the statue was a popular rendezvous, but, sadly and carelessly, was removed by the Nazis in 1942. It was the more sad because the monument had been entirely funded by subscription from employees of the state telegraph company. It should be held in mind that in 1893 the electric telegraph network, the origins of which lay in the work of Chappe, was at the zenith of its importance in the history of the world. Marconi had started his work on wireless telegraphy, but until radio came after the turn of the century, the telegraphic descendants of Chappe were pre-eminent. The statue, sculpted by Dame from a design by Farey, stood on a marble pedestal on which was a figure of Mercury lifted into the air by his flight and holding in one hand a letter, while in the other are the mobile arms of the telegraph designed by Chappe, who himself stands astride the pedestal with his telescope in hand, while behind him are the arms of his telegraph. On the face of the pedestal were the following fitting tributes:

> Claude Chappe presented the invention of the aerial telegraph to the Legislative Assembly held on 22 [*sic*] March 1792. He was named as *Ingénieur-télégraphe* by the National Convention on 26 July 1793. The first telegraph news was received in Paris several hours after the events taking place in Quesnoy [*sic*] and Condé on 15 and 30 August 1794.

It is convenient here to break with chronology and give a brief sketch of the later achievements of the other Chappe brothers. René had already been placed in charge of the Brussels line. Following the death of Claude, the brothers Ignace and Pierre-François were appointed jointly to the role of administrators of the telegraphs, and the fifth brother Abraham took on a military job close to Napoleon; his task was to translate messages from or to the Emperor from their telegraphic code and thus to have been a key part of Napoleon's control over troop movements. In October 1810 Abraham was sent to Amsterdam to supervise the extension of the Lille line, to connect the Dutch city with Paris, some 300 miles (480km) away. Ignace and Pierre-Francois were retired in 1823, but both Abraham and René had telegraph posts when, in 1830, following a new revolution, Louis-Phillipe removed them after a falling-out, but during the wars with England the Chappes' service had been both highly valued and continuous. When Ignace died in 1829, Claude was reburied next to him at the cemetery at Père Lachaise in Paris. In 1859 Claude's tombstone was removed to the headquarters of the Telegraph Administration at 103 Rue de Grenelle.[24] The efforts of Claude's brothers Ignace, Pierre, Abraham and René were also recalled on the statue of Claude referred to above.

# 5
# The Telegraph is Developed in England

*Be valiant and give signal to the fight.*
Shakespeare[1]

## The Chappe Telegraph Comes to the Attention of the British

When the telegraph was first developed in France, the Revolutionary War had only recently broken out, war having been declared on England by France on 1 February 1793, only six months before the successful Chappe demonstration of telegraphy from Paris. Even had the French authorities wanted to keep the innovation secret, it was scarcely possible with the public trials of it generating such interest and excitement, as they did. The telegraph towers with their weird moving arms were on full display in Paris and along the route; something strange had been going on in Paris since the first Chappe experiments a year earlier, and the news of the French victories, chattered out by the telegraph, was all round the capital in a flash. The maintenance of security over the existence of the invention was, therefore, impossible. While the vocabulary code remained secure, the visible workings of the device had been given to the world; moreover, in spite of the war, there was no shortage of refugees from the Revolution making their way to England to seek asylum and bringing their knowledge with them. In September 1794, only a month after the French victories were reported and talked about all over Paris, there appeared in the *Gentleman's Magazine* in London a report on this new-fangled contraption:

> . . . let persons be placed in several stations, at such distance from each other, that, by the help of a telescope, a man in one station may see a signal made by the next . . . he immediately repeats this signal, which is again repeated through all the intermediate stations. This . . . has been adopted by the French . . . [and called] a télégraphe; and, from the utility of the invention, we doubt not but it will be soon introduced in this country. . . . The machines are the invention of Citizen Chappe . . .

To this report was added in November, as well as appearing in the *The Sun*, a full drawing of Chappe's telegraph. In January 1795 an image of the telegraph was published in London by the famous contemporary caricaturist James Gillray (1757–1815): his allegorical cartoon was at the expense of the Whig opposition leader Charles James Fox (1749–1806), who made the political misjudgement of combining support for the Revolution with opposition to the war. Gillray lampooned Fox with his cartoon 'French telegraph – making signals in the dark': Fox was represented as a signal post standing in mid-Channel at whose base are the daggers of assassins; taking advantage of the blackness of the night, the hapless Whig chief is shown directing the French fleet to London, sleeping in supposed security. His body is contorted to simulate the pose of a Chappe telegraph, his hands and arms being arranged, signal-post style, with the rearward pointing to London while the front hand is holding a lantern to illuminate the scene for the French. The image, allegorically speaking, was predictive of the invasion scares which were to come, and of the strategic advantage then held by the French in fast communications technology.

From this journalistic coverage it can be seen that the existence of a telegraph system in France was given a good public airing in London. While presenting all this as news, the press demonstrated its freedom (in stark contrast to the censorship which was to be exercised increasingly in France, specially when Napoleon came to power); in private, however, the government and the military had already acquired a good knowledge of the new developments in France.

An early description of the telegraph, written by an eyewitness who had seen it working near Paris, together with working models, had been given to the Duke of York, Commander-in-Chief of the Army, which was on the Continent at the time. The Revd John Gamble (1762–1811), chaplain to the Duke, was a Cambridge mathematics scholar who was intrigued by the scientific developments of the age; he had taken an interest in signals and he it is who has explained how he came by a knowledge of Chappe's telegraph.[2] In August 1794 (a year after the Paris demonstration of the telegraph, and in the same month that the news of the French victories came to Paris by telegraph) a drawing of the system in use was found on a captured French soldier. The Duke was himself intrigued by the implications of telegraphy. Ordered to investigate, Gamble thought that Chappe might have been inspired by the evidence, which had existed for some time, of using the sails of windmills to send signals; he had himself seen such in Flanders when on active service with the Duke and it is likely that Edgeworth knew of this too when he carried out his abandoned trials in the 1760s. As Gamble tells us:

> If any apology were necessary for having written on a science apparently so little connected with the duties [of a chaplain] . . . I trust it will be found in my situation with an army . . . [in combat].

> When observing the great want of a system . . . [for] signals . . . a mechanical mind was naturally turned to . . . considering . . . a subject frequently the topic of conversation.[3]

This passage leaves us in no doubt about the perceived importance of the subject of signals to an army in the field. Gamble told the Duke that he thought that the Chappe telegraph could be improved upon. In his essay on the subject Gamble speaks of the 'inconveniences' of the French telegraph, and back in England he made a model which was seen not only by the military but by William Pitt (1759–1806), the Prime Minister. Here was something to be developed: an idea whose time was right and a solution to an obvious problem; if the French were to be beaten, an acceleration of the processes of commanding and controlling military units was urgent. The Duke asked Gamble to gather all the published knowledge on the subject; this gave rise to his first essay, which was published at the Duke's expense. It was issued widely to all who might have an interest in the development of signals technologies, including the Admiralty. Disregarding the empirical evidence of the French system, Gamble advanced a different one based on a number of shutters each of which would be manipulated by ropes: there would be only two states for each shutter – open or shut. The configuration of open and shut shutters would give a letter of the alphabet.

Although Gamble was in good company when he considered the shutter system an improvement over Chappe's, this notion can withstand neither analysis nor later empirical evidence in England. In the words of Geoffrey Wilson, '. . . the Chappe telegraph, in war and peace, would become the most famous, most widespread and longest-lived of all the visual systems of which it was the inspiration.'[4] Wilson was right, the Chappe system of telegraphy over land was never bettered by anything developed in England. What Gamble had alighted on was, however, a pragmatic method, for it was one that could be developed and built quickly and which, with the threat of invasion looming, had obvious attractions. In any event, Gamble was not alone in advancing the merits of a shutter system; in Sweden, telegraphic experiments by Abraham Edelcrantz (1754–1821) had followed quickly after the Chappe system had been exposed, even earlier than in Britain. In support of Gamble's view Edelcrantz had at first tried a version of Chappe, but this was replaced by a shutter system. Although the Swedish system was long-lived, it was never very important in historical terms compared with the experience of France and England because of its military use on land and at sea by them. Moreover, in the case of France, its use also as an instrument of government, even before the country became a dictatorship, gave it more historical importance.*

---

*For a masterly and highly recommended account of the contribution of Edelcrantz to telegraphy see G.J. Holzman and B. Pehrson, *The Early History of Data Networks* (1995); includes first English translation of Edelcrantz's *Treatise on Telegraphs*, written in 1796, just as the telegraphs were being developed in England.

Gamble proposed a simple system which could be built quickly, with stations from 6 to 10 miles (10–16km) apart. The base of the apparatus would also be serviceable, he noted, for quarters for the crew. It was, indeed, simple, but very serviceable, as we shall see, for the Admiralty's needs. But if Gamble allowed himself to imagine that fame and fortune beckoned, he could not have dreamt of the thunderbolt which was to strike him a little later. The military benefits of an acceleration of the transference of intelligence and commands were plain to see. In England, it was to be the Admiralty that was first able to exploit these in the war against France. As we have seen, it was entirely feasible to send a message to Portsmouth, the Navy's home port, via the Royal Mail, but it would be nearly a day's journey (a very fast time was four and a half hours) and this speed could not be materially hastened. With the Navy destined for the pivotal role in the defence of England against invasion and in the days of sail when catching a tide might be the difference between success and failure, a new method of communication which would take only minutes instead of most of a day to order the fleet to sea and to direct it was bound to get the attention of the Admiralty.

The simplest way of catching up with the leap that French signals technology had made would have been to copy its physical features (the code was another matter). Why should the Admiralty ignore that which worked and order something of which no operational experience existed? For strange as it is, this is what they did and to understand why is to understand how, ultimately, we inherited the semaphore line and the rich heritage of some of the semaphore stations which have survived to the present, unlike the non-permanent, shutter stations. The early Chappe system was much more complex in its workings than any of the later substitutes used in England and it had much more affinity to our semaphore system than our almost rustic shutter system. Here lies an important point: as we have seen, the French apparatus was usually placed on permanent, stone structures, either built for the job or existing buildings, often ecclesiastical; a chain of such structures would clearly take much time to build, and in England, unlike in France at the time, churches were still used for their Christian purpose. A simple system that was quick to build had obvious attractions for the Admiralty, for the demands of the war and the need for economy were urgent.

## The Shutter Telegraph Trials

Gamble's report was in the Admiralty's hands in April 1795 (the same month that the British Army quit the Continent). In August, with the collapse of the enemies of the Revolution, a temporary calm had fallen over the Continent. England was now alone, and Gamble was conducting a trial of his shutter telegraph, helped by dockyard officials, between Portsmouth and Portsdown Hill, some 5 miles (8km) away. The Admiralty had no previous knowledge of sending a message by spelling it out: the recently introduced coastal signal stations could send only pre-arranged messages. Wilson[5] described Gamble's equipment: it was a series of shutters working in a frame, pivoted about their horizontal axes, each board having but one movement, operated by a rope, and open or shut, in the manner of a Venetian blind, with two states on or off, as in the binary code of computers. When the shutters were open, their profile was so slight as to be indiscernible from a distance. Gamble's trial proved that it worked; it was a simple affair (too simple, as it happened) with five* shutters arranged one above the other and giving thirty-one effective combinations (the thirty-second position being 'at rest'), not many more than the letters of the alphabet. But if some symbols could stand for a word, as in France, the time saved by not having to spell out that particular word is plain. Nevertheless Gamble's five-shutter telegraph worked. In his essay, he tells us that his telegraphic signals, several metres high, were easily seen in Southsea, even from the Isle of Wight, some 14 or 15 miles (23–24km) away. However, although the trials had been a complete success, Gamble was destined for the worst of disappointments.

His had not been the only mind in London to be applied to the telegraph, for when Gamble returned from his trial in Portsmouth he found that a rival, another clergyman, the Revd Lord Murray (1761–1803) was attracting the attention of the Admiralty with a sixty-three-combination shutter system. Such is the nature of permutations, that given there are two states, the maximum number of settings is two raised to a power equal to the number of shutters thus: $2^5 = 32$ and $2^6 = 64$. Leaving one position aside in either case for 'at rest', Murray's essentially identical system gave sixty-three instead of thirty-one combinations. Murray's six shutters were arranged in three pairs, each above the other; this was the system which was adopted by the Admiralty. Although the stated defect in Gamble's model could easily be remedied, evidently he was not given the chance: the marginally greater simplicity of a five-shutter system could not compete with a six-shutter version with double the number of encryptions. There was no time for argument: the Admiralty was clearly in a hurry, for on 25 September 1795, only six weeks after Gamble's successful trial, the Admiralty ordered a telegraph line on the Murray model to connect London with both Deal and Portsmouth.

---

*Gamble had conceived of an even more simple telegraph with only four shutters: the halved number of combinations would have required some contortions with the alphabet, for instance, combining C with K; in this, Gamble was, I believe, going against the grain.

We must pause to make a few observations about the unfair treatment of Gamble: when he was peremptorily informed that an inventor, unknown to him, had exceeded his own efforts in a competition of which he was ignorant, his countenance, to borrow an expression from Dickens, must have been like a model for the bowsprit of a ship to be called *The Astonishment.* We have seen already that the Admiralty was to reject Ronalds's brilliant suggestion of an electric telegraph in 1816: that can be put down to bureaucratic stupidity; but the Admiralty's treatment of Gamble appears to be unforgivably duplicitous. Little is known about the circumstances, but how could it have been that Gamble could have remained in ignorance of the fact that he was in a competitive situation when he had been invited by the Admiralty itself to conduct the experiments at Portsmouth and had been assisted by naval personnel? The whole business of government practice was at the time riddled with patronage and nepotism. The Northcote-Trevelyan reforms which brought about the professionalization of the civil service were still fifty years in the future: government service had not yet reached the point where patronage would give way to a non-political administrative elite which was to emerge during the Age of Reform. Perversely, reform would have to wait until the French had been defeated. Both Murray and Gamble had patronage, but the absence of professionalism in procurement ensured that Gamble was dispensed with by the Admiralty. Having been treated appallingly by government, whether by muddle or conspiracy, Gamble did not give up on telegraphy, and, as we shall see in Chapter 7, he did some pioneering work for the Army and in 1797 he published his further refined essay on telegraphy, which can be seen in the British Library.[6]

Leaving to one side the Admiralty's treatment of Gamble, we have glimpsed the reason why the simple but crude shutter system was introduced in England and not a copy of the superior Chappe system. The shutter telegraph was installed at great speed, and, being regarded as a temporary affair for the duration of the war, it becomes clearer why it was decommissioned after the fall of Napoleon and the Treaty of Paris in 1814. Here is the point to grasp, for it explains how we were bequeathed the heritage of what remains of the semaphore line, for if the shutter line had not been temporary it would not have been so readily destroyed. And if Napoleon had not caught the Admiralty napping by his escape from Elba, there would have been no emergency to provide the urgency which a Britain at peace would have needed for the signal capability to be reinstated.

Amazingly, and with what resources is not recorded, in just over four months after the order was placed the line to Deal was opened in January 1796; the speed of this achievement is remarkable, for nothing like it had ever been done before. As Wilson[7] notes, the labour of seeking out likely elevated spots, some in remote districts, in all weathers, and then testing them and negotiating with landowners, some of them no doubt ill-disposed to co-operate, was considerable. But, as we saw in Chapter 2, at least topographical maps based on triangulated surveys had been drawn, just in time.

We have also seen that in France the government gave Chappe wide powers to requisition sites, including church towers, for the installation of telegraph stations. In England there was no equivalent power, not at any rate until the panic following the escape of Napoleon, when a Bill was rushed through Parliament giving government powers to acquire land compulsorily and to clear obstructions from lines of sight. So, in 1795, the task for the telegraph builders of first identifying and then discriminating among suitable sites for stations and dealing with landowners both to use their land and to clear obstructions must have been formidable; perhaps the atmosphere of an invasion alert helped. (We must assume that landowners were compliant with the needs of the Admiralty in supplying, on leasehold terms, access to and rights over their land in the midst of a national crisis in which victory was the only means of avoiding the Revolution's crossing the Channel; the aristocracy would have had no illusions about where their self-interest lay.)

In 1797, the first full year of the shutter telegraph in operation, the Admiralty's stock was high, for the year saw considerable action on the part of the Navy. None of the signals traffic content seems to have survived officially (but, as we shall see, some did in Norfolk), but in a year which saw the aborted French invasion of Ireland, their later invasion of Wales, the Battle of Cape St Vincent, with heavy losses to the Spanish fleet, the Battle of Camperdown, in which the Dutch fleet was mauled, as well as the rise to fame of Napoleon, we can be sure that the availability of telegraphy to the Admiralty was none too soon.

## Surveying the Shutter Telegraph Lines

A surveyor named George Roebuck, who became Superintendent of Telegraphs, was appointed by the Admiralty on 25 September 1795 to select sites for stations on lines to link London with Deal (and Sheerness) and Portsmouth; these opened in the following year. In October 1805, Roebuck was directed to choose sites for the Plymouth extension and in 1807, he was commissioned to survey a new route to Yarmouth, which was ready for use in June 1808. Little has been retained in the archives to expose the difficulties which Roebuck overcame in surveying and fixing the routes, all the stations of which are listed in the Appendix. In marvelling at the speed at which his task was completed, we can at least study the maps which he had available to him to facilitate his task, maps which, as we have seen, were informed by the triangulated surveys and other work conducted by Roy and his successors. Although the Ordnance Survey started in 1791 and was to become the official publisher of maps, it would be wrong to think that this brought the era of private-sector map-making to an end; on the contrary, there was a period in which the private sector was actively encouraged to take an area covered by Roy's primary triangulation, fill in the detail by a topographical survey and publish the results. Roy's primary triangulation of Kent had been completed sufficiently before the new war with France to assist the surveying of the Admiralty–Deal telegraph line in 1795–96. Another timely development was to play a key role in facilitating the surveying of the Portsmouth line, which was done quickly in 1796.

## The Maps of Lindley and Crosley

In 1789, two surveyors, Joseph Lindley (who had worked with Roy on the triangulation from the 'Great Base') and William Crosley combined in partnership to conduct a topographical survey of Surrey. It is interesting to note that before Crosley went to Surrey, he was surveying canals in Lancashire. Lindley and Crosley's work followed on from that of Roy and predated by over twenty years the first Ordnance Survey map of Surrey, which was not published until 1816. With Roy's encouragement, Lindley and Crosley took seven of his primary triangulation points in Surrey direct from his own work. These and the 'Great Base', the southern end of which lay just over the Thames from Surrey in Hampton, gave them reliable measured data covering the whole of Surrey. From this foundation of primary triangulation, they set about filling in the detailed topography within the eighty-five secondary and tertiary triangulations which they surveyed and recorded. Their new map of Surrey, on two sheets, was the first to be oriented to the Greenwich meridian,[8] and was much praised for its accuracy. Although there is no primary source to prove it, we can be certain that the map of Roy's survey of Kent and the maps of Surrey were on Roebuck's desk as he planned his routes to Deal and Portsmouth. In Surrey there was an added bonus: Lindley and Crosley had published detailed technical notes in a companion volume to the maps,[9] these showed, in meticulous detail for each of the seven primary triangulation points taken from Roy's work, the bearings for each of their own secondary and tertiary triangulations on hilltops, church towers or other structures.

From the detail that the two have left us on the points of secondary triangulations, we can see a remarkable correlation between the high points which they measured and the sites for telegraph stations used by Roebuck (and his successor Goddard, who surveyed the later semaphore line to Portsmouth). For example, one of these landmarks was Worplesdon church; later a semaphore telegraph tower was built next to it; this was the first station on the Plymouth branch after the junction was created at Chatley

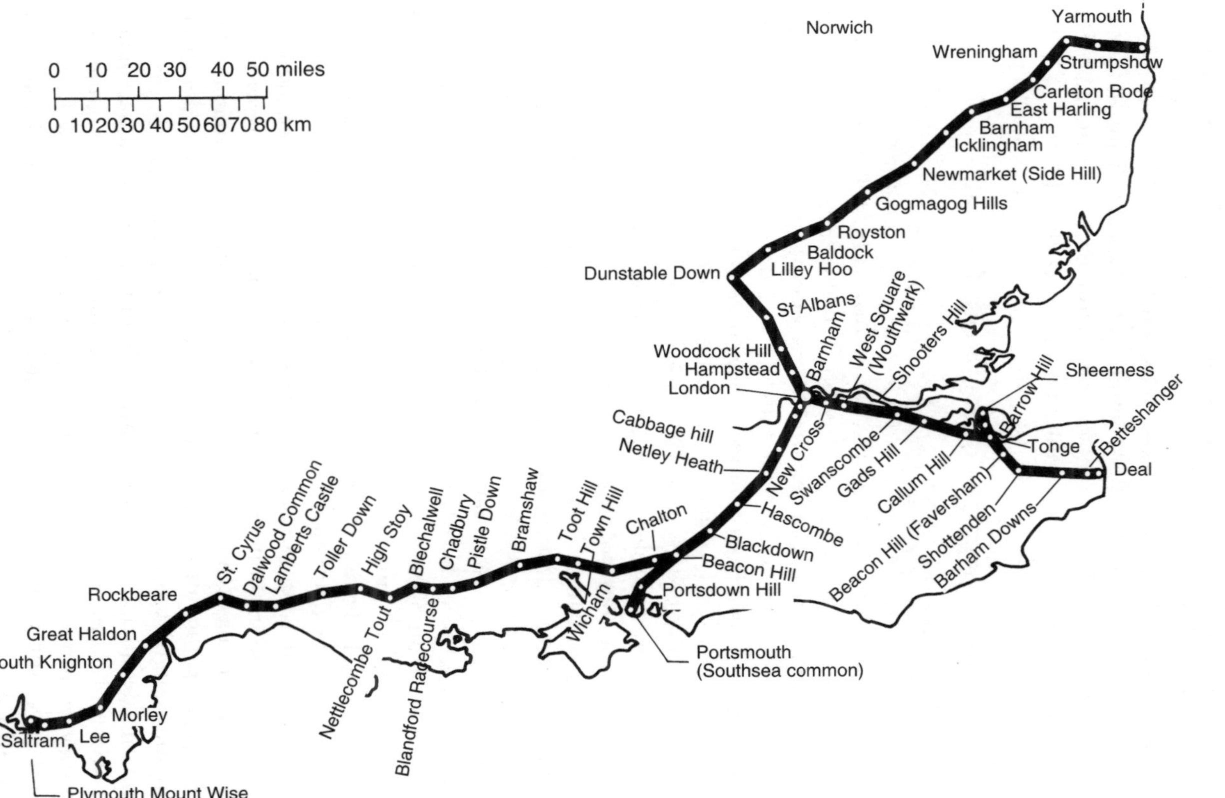


*The Admiralty Shutter Telegraph System, from Wilson 'The Old Telegraphs'.*

Heath, near Cobham. Other measured triangulation points in north Surrey surveyed by Lindley and Crosley were very close to both the soon-to-be-built shutter telegraph stations and those of the later semaphores. Near the shutter station of Cabbage (now Telegraph) Hill, near Leatherhead and the semaphore station on Coopers (now Telegraph) Hill in Hinchley Wood were Claremont House (and its Belvedere Tower) in Esher, a 'white house' at Barwell Court, Chessington, a house on Wimbledon Common, Esher church, Long Ditton church and Walton on Thames church.

## The Topography of South-east England

When Gen Roy wrote his *A Military Description of the South-East Part of England*[10] in 1765, he observed that there were three remarkable ranges of hills on the south of the Thames: the South Downs from Beachy Head to Winchester, the Middle Range, as he dubbed it, which starts near Hastings and ends at Hindhead, and the North Downs, from Dover to Farnham. Of course, Roy was interested in these hills not just from a general mapping point of view, but also from the point of view of their utility as points of advantage in the possible defence of London in the event of a successful enemy landing on the south coast. When Roebuck was appointed in 1795 he would have been able to examine Roy's observations and his military map of the whole of the south of England.[11] Informed by the information from both Roy's maps and his observations on the topography, as well as the maps of Lindley and Crosley, Roebuck would have been able to plan a route from his desk. Let us examine how the maps would have helped Roebuck: plainly if no maps had existed which showed spot heights, the whole process would have had to be conducted by empirical observations and interminable to-ings and fro-ings on horseback, of intermediate hills between the start and the destination of the route, a most daunting task. But as Roebuck sat with his maps, he would have in mind three factors as he gazed from the start point to the finish: first, that there was a restraint on how far apart the stations could be located; second, that a free line of sight had to be available between each station, and third, that each station and its reciprocating neighbour had to have 'sky-backing' behind each station's apparatus. This third one, in practice the most taxing, meant that the stations had to be planned in succeeding sets of threes. With a topographical map in front of him, a selection of likely hills which were within the range restraint could be identified, and, with the benefit of spot heights, perhaps aided by interpolation (for there were no contour lines), he may have been able to establish from the desk whether a free line of sight was available. It is unlikely that the sky-backing requirement would have been discernible from a map, because just a few feet could make the difference, but armed with a plan of where to put the stations and a back-up if they proved to be unsuitable sites, Roebuck could have set off on the arduous job of testing and retesting the route armed with a hypothetical one which required amendment only on the basis of field research.

We shall see later how critical to the defence of London were the so-called 'northern heights' at Hampstead. In an 1805 military map, *A Sketch of Highgate and Hampstead and Environs,*[12] the hills are shown with their hatching, but there are no spot heights; instead, each summit is numbered, not, as may be supposed to identify a hill, but as an expression of its relative height, that is, hill '4' would be higher than hill '3'. This style of map would have been most serviceable for surveyors of the later telegraph routes, to Yarmouth and Plymouth, giving, as they do, an essential guide to a route and leaving only the detail to be filled in by site-surveys. The early canal builders would have given anything for such a framework of elevations, just as the railway builders clamoured for relief maps a generation later when a large mileage of track was laid down. If the French Revolution had started two years earlier and the French astronomers had been unable to make the case for the cross-Channel triangulation because of the intervening war conditions, it is impossible to speculate about how much delay there might have been in providing maps with heights on them.

So, by means of the maps which were available to him, Roebuck would have established from his desk that the Middle Range and the South Downs referred to by Roy would not come into consideration for the route to Deal. In fact, once the telegraph line had reached the North Downs, which lie close to London, it would be a simple task of traversing the Downs until Deal was close, when the height already gained could then be lost on the approach to sea level. If this was ever considered easy by Roebuck, the route to Portsmouth was much more problematic: both the North and the South Downs had to be gained, and the Middle Range either exploited or a route taken through a gap in it. But the route to both ports would first have to gain the Thames Valley escarpment.

## Roebuck's Route to Deal

This took a short traverse of 1¼ miles (2km) from the Admiralty to the roof of 36 West Square, in Southwark, then to a hill of something in excess of 164ft (50m), 3 miles (5km) away at Nunhead, near New Cross. The next station, was 4½ miles (7km) away at Shooters Hill, which had sufficient height to gain the North Downs; the station was not on the summit of the hill about 460ft (140m) high, but on shoulder of it; not too high because sky-backing was required behind the next station, situated at a lower level, 10½ miles (17km) away at Swanscombe. Six and a half miles (10.5km) on, brought the line to Gad's Hill which, at about 330ft (100m), allowed the route to traverse the North Downs through Callum Hill, near Lower Halstow; Beacon Hill, near Faversham (which was the junction for the branch to Sheerness); Shottenden Hill, near Selling; then a span of over 11 miles (18km), and the longest on the Deal line, to Barham Downs, near Womenswold, then Betteshanger and on to Deal. Roebuck's route out of London ran along the Thames Valley escarpment and consequently suffered the consequence of the London fogs of which frequent reference is made in the novels of Dickens (and who, by coincidence, spent his final years living near the site of the telegraph station at Gad's Hill). When the experimental semaphore line came to be tried out, following orders given late in 1815 to run it to Sheerness, Goddard took the route more quickly out of London to the south via Chislehurst, thus learning the lessons provided by Roebuck's very fast surveying and commissioning of the Deal line.

## Roebuck's Route to Portsmouth

Roebuck's next project was the shutter line to Portsmouth, and we must consider the broad outline of how he gained the two or three ranges of hills that lay directly between the terminals. To gain the North Downs, the route picked up the Thames Valley escarpment at Putney Heath, and then south to a point further upstream on the escarpment, now known as Telegraph Hill, and about 3 miles (5km) south of Chessington (near the 'Star' public house). The view which Roebuck would have seen of the Thames Valley and London, and which can be seen still by any who venture there, is analogous to the view of Paris which Chappe saw of Paris from St Martin du Tertre: the whole London skyline can be seen, down to Canary Wharf and the Thames estuary. In Roebuck's day the view would have been all round, allowing a line of sight to the next station at Netley Heath, near Gomshall: this span to a hill about 820ft (250m) above sea level, allowed the North Downs to be gained about 30 miles (48km) from London. During the invasion scare of 1804 there were 190 soldiers billeted near Netley Heath with 170 horses, some of which were at a farm near Newlands Corner, a Surrey beauty spot on the North Downs with open views south to the 'Middle Range' of hills referred to by Roy. These soldiers were part of a force of 39,000 who were holding the North Downs from Guildford to Godstone; it is easy to imagine the puzzled excitement of these soldiers as they watched the shutters blinking their messages to the fleet.

The next station, nearly 8 miles (13km) away, was at Hascombe, south of Godalming on a hill of nearly 660ft (200m) in the Middle Range of hills. From there it was an easy lift to the next station at more or less the same height on the South Downs near Blackdown, the summit of which at over 900ft (275m) is the highest point in Sussex. The route could then run along the South Downs to Beacon Hill (Harting) before dropping down to Portsdown Hill, where Gamble had conducted his first trials of his rejected telegraph in the previous year.

## Plymouth and Yarmouth

The survey of the line to Plymouth, which was ordered in 1805, would have benefited from both Roy's military map of the south-east of England of 1765 and the 1796 extension of the Ordnance Survey triangulation to Land's End. The Yarmouth line (ordered in 1807) would have benefited from the northern extensions of the Ordnance Survey by which the whole country, excluding Norfolk, had been covered by 1809. In fact, Norfolk was not covered until later and many of the details of the stations there remain obscure. However, there is an intriguing aspect to the route taken to Yarmouth out of London.

By the time the Yarmouth line came to be planned, the evidence of the disruption caused to signal traffic by London's fogs was sufficient to point to the need for a new route to escape from the environs of the capital as quickly as possible. A direct route to Yarmouth would have taken the line close to the Thames estuary; this might easily have been able to exploit the existing coastal signal stations (Chapter 9) with all the speed and economy that would be achieved by it, but several of these stations would have been vulnerable to temporary obscurity through London smoke and Thames fog if the shortest route had been followed. Roebuck came up with the imaginative, inspired even, solution of taking the line quickly out of London by a counter-intuitive route. By taking a line at almost right-angles to the required route, on a north-by-north-west direction via Hampstead Heath and from there gaining the Chiltern Hills, he took the line via the clock tower in the High Street at St Albans to its summit on the Dunstable Downs, where it changed direction to regain a new bearing on Yarmouth. Inspired though this routing may have been, it did not completely eliminate problems with fog and bad visibility which were to be a persistent, endemic problem of the visual telegraphs in England, even with the better semaphore system which was brought in after the Battle of Waterloo. Through an intriguing and presumably irregular chance, parts of the journal of one of the shutter telegraph stations on the Yarmouth line have survived in private hands.[13] As an example of the difficulties caused by fog in interrupting signal traffic, the records for December 1813 and January 1814 are useful. In both months, fog prevented any transmission on seventeen days out of the thirty-one; there were two occasions when the inability to operate lasted for five consecutive days. This may go a long way to explaining why the telegraph was not considered for the dispatch of vital news such as Trafalgar (Chapter 8).

The impact of fog or bad visibility on the Portsmouth semaphore line is plain from evidence that arose nearly thirty years later. The following written response was given in answer to a Parliamentary question, in which the Admiralty was asked for a return of the number of days when the semaphore was not available by reason of the atmosphere.

| *Dates* | *Admiralty, number of days* | *Chelsea, number of days* | *Putney, number of days* | *Portsmouth, number of days* |
|---|---|---|---|---|
| From 1839–40<br>From 1840–41<br>From 1841–42 | 133<br>106<br>84 | 64<br>70<br>77 | 42<br>49<br>51 | 21<br>28<br>16 |
| Total Number of Days at each Station for Three Years | 323 | 211 | 142 | 65 |

*Note*: Whenever the working of the Semaphore at the Admiralty is prevented by reason of smoke, the state of the atmosphere to the eastward, or westward from the vapour arising from the water in St James's Park or other causes, messages are on such occasions, when of importance, taken to or from Chelsea or Putney stations, and generally effectually communicated from thence to or from Portsmouth.

(signed) Charles H. Jay, Commander
Superintendent

Clearly, the incidence of fog round London was severe: the reason for the Parliamentary question is lost, but we can suggest that it was a plant. The electric telegraph had already been invented and was in use on the railways, so was this a way of exposing the unreliability in our climate of the visual telegraph as a means of spiking the guns of potential Luddites who may have opposed the scrapping of the semaphore line and its replacement by the electric telegraph? The first part of the London–Portsmouth railway had opened in 1838 and clearly, at least to anyone who was alive to the way the world was changing, the combination of the railways and electricity was to create an irresistible force which would sweep the semaphores aside and bring the first telegraph age to its close.

# 6
# Telegraphy as it Developed at Sea

*Opportunity is of great advantage in all things, but especially in war; and among the several things which have been invented to enable men to seize it nothing can be more conducive to that end than signals.*
Polybius, 204BC[1]

*At this moment we are within four miles of the Enemy, and talking to Lord Nelson by means of Sir H. Popham's signals, though so distant, but repeated along the rest of the frigates of this Squadron.*
Capt Blackwood
HMS *Euryalus*, off Cadiz[2]

*. . . tomorrow will be a fortunate one for you young gentlemen. The 21st will be our day.*
Adm Lord Nelson, to a group of midshipmen
on HMS *Victory* before Trafalgar[3]

## The Early Days of Naval Signalling

Until the middle of the seventeenth century communication between ships in the English fleet was restricted to a few, simple, visual signals, sometimes backed up by the firing of a gun to draw attention to them. The first recorded use of a flag in the English seas is in the Bayeux Tapestry; it is thought to have been used as a flag of command to denote the ship carrying William the Conqueror.[4] The earliest surviving signalling instructions are contained in the *Black Book of the Admiralty*, dating from the middle of the fourteenth century. For example:

> Tis to be noted that at some convenient time when the admiral pleaseth to call the captains . . . together, to consult with them, he shall hang up in the middle of the mast of the ship a flag of council so that it may be known . . . [that] the captains . . . of the ships are bound without delay to come with their boats well manned on board the admiral's ship . . .[5]

By the end of the nineteenth century, flags were commonplace; warships used them to identify their nationality or to disguise it by flying false colours. Other simple flag signals, sometimes by knotting the flag in its middle, were specified such as for distress or enemy in sight. The main British flag was the ensign, but flags could also identify the rank of the senior officer on board and help to identify the place of the ship in its fleet. Some flags would be pennants, or long, slender streamers ending in a point, which were flown at the masthead. The dimensions of these flags and pennants were enormous, allowing recognition from great distances (if there was a wind): a pennant of a first-rated ship might be over 30yd (27m) long, and an ensign, perhaps 12yd × 6yd (11m × 5.5m). The signal flags which we are about to examine might be 8ft × 6ft (2.4m × 2m).

Simple flag signals were in use at the time of the Spanish Armada. Enhancements introduced later included a signal giving instructions as to how many ships should chase an enemy and then colour-coded flags for fighting instructions. But there was still no way of passing administrative messages other than, for example, a cask at the yardarm signifying a want of water or a tablecloth as an invitation to dinner.[6] The alternative would be to be obliged to sail close enough to be within earshot of a megaphone, or to put out a ship's boat if the conditions allowed it, but this would be hardly practicable in battle.

The main principles of the *Permanent Sailing and Fighting Instructions* were established for use as the eighteenth century began; improvements were incorporated throughout the century, somewhat haphazardly, because several systems and methods evolved as captains developed their own versions. By 1780 two different pathways had emerged: the *Permanent Instructions*, developed by famous sailors such as Adm Lord Rodney and Adm Viscount Hood. It was Adm Earl Howe (1726–99), however, who was to have a decisive influence in advancing both the efficiency and the standardization of naval signalling; borrowing on innovative thinking among colleagues and by his leadership of all the many thoughtful contributors of the period, his work led to the *Signal Book for the Ships of War*, issued in 1790: 'It was the long-delayed masterpiece for which the more progressive British sea officers had been waiting . . . all inhibitions were cast away and a true numerical system established.'[7] It remained the standard form for the Navy until it was expanded further, and Nelson had good reason to be grateful for it at the Battle of the Nile in 1798, after which he wrote to Howe to acknowledge the congratulations that he had been given on the victory; and said:

> By attacking the enemy's van and centre, the wind blowing along their line [while at anchor], I was enabled to throw what force I pleased on a few ships. This plan my friends conceived by the signals (for which we are principally, if not entirely indebted to your Lordship) and we always kept a superior force to the enemy.

The 1799 signal book contained some 340 signals, not a great number, so they were often added to by individual fleet commanders. Essentially it was a three-flag system by which each combination of flags had a meaning attributed to it in the vocabulary, or otherwise each letter of the literal alphabet had one or two flags allocated to it, to make the letter, and thus, somewhat long-windedly, spell out a word. Two events were to influence signalling practice before a new version of the code was issued in 1804, in time for Trafalgar. Because of a security breach in which the code was compromised by its capture by the French, a scrambling of the three flags in each part of the vocabulary was made; by confounding the enemy this merely recovered the position. The second event was more important: it was the work of Rear-Adm Sir Home Riggs Popham (a colourful man, an entertaining biography of whom has been written by one of his descendants[8]) who was destined not only to leave his mark on the signalling history of the Royal Navy but to have a major impact on land-based telegraphy as well.

## Popham's Naval Vocabulary Code

Two theories have emerged on how Popham came upon the idea for his vocabulary. In the *Gentleman's Magazine* for March 1799 there is an obituary notice for John Francis Callet, of whom it is stated that, in 1797 'he presented to the . . . [Insitut de France] a plan of a new telegraph, and of a telegraphic language, accompanied with a dictionary of 12,000 French words, all adapted to his telegraph'. This entry was spotted by a correspondent of *The Mariner's Mirror* in 1941,[9] who posed the question, did Popham get the idea for his telegraphic code from Callet's work? The answer is not recorded. Even if he did not, it seems clear that other brains, of which Popham had his own full supply, were at work on the problem. Equally up in the air is another contemporary theory: Capt Edward (Ned) Thompson (also known as Poet Thompson) contrived, while a lieutenant, a set of alphabetical signals which, according to a writer in the *Naval Chronicle* of 1812,[10] there was every reason to suppose furnished the idea of the telegraphic system ultimately developed by Popham. It was a crude system with a different flag for each letter in the alphabet. There was at the time evidently a double clandestine affair being conducted in elevated circles, and Thompson's flags facilitated a correspondence with which to conduct these intrigues, secretly from those not knowing the system.* The inference that the telegraphic signals then in use in the Royal Navy and

*I am reminded of when I and my brother were both familiar with semaphore signalling with flags or just arm movements; having learnt the system in the Boy Scouts, we could communicate with each other across the dining table, to the irritation of our parents, but in complete secrecy.

developed by Popham originated from Thompson's code is claimed from the fact that Popham was at the time a midshipman under him, as was a Capt Eaton, who preserved a copy of Thompson's signal code.

Popham's biographer says:

> Thompson may well have been responsible for Home's later interest in flag-signalling, for before they left Plymouth . . . [on a voyage in 1784 with Lt Popham on board], Thompson noted in a list of improvements which he considered necessary in the Navy, . . . [the need for him to] 'invent a new code of signals'.[11]

According to Hugh Popham, Thompson submitted 'a new code and mode of signals' to Lord Howe when he got home from the West Indies; Thompson died in 1784.

Popham's was not the only mind working on what must have been, now that the longitude problem had been solved, the most pressing intellectual problem of the Navy. Capt (later Adm) Phillip Patton (1739–1815) was also taking an interest. In 1784 he wrote to Charles Middleton (Lord Barham, 1726–1813), who at the time was Comptroller of the Navy, 'I have at last finished the signal book and shall send it to you at the first opportunity.' Evidently no copy of Patton's signal book has been preserved, but he refers to one of its advantages as being 'the small number of flags necessary'. And again two years later, 'Since I last wrote to you I have turned my whole attention to signals, of which almost every action in the last war proved [to be the subject of] miserable confusion and deficiency; and I have made some progress in making a very much-improved copy of my own system.'[12]

It is unclear whether Patton's flag signals were of the vocabulary type, as produced by Popham, or a refinement of the existing methods falling short of the conversational style that was to come. Wherever or however and by whom the idea was first conceived, Popham developed a word vocabulary in 1800 and put it into a practicable method of signalling which was to take best practice well beyond Howe's contribution. Grappling with the mathematics of combinations, Popham's first version contained about 1,000 words, and because he considered it likely to be widely attractive, he had the vocabulary privately printed; as his biographer points out.

'This vocabulary,' Home Popham wrote in his introduction to the original edition of his *Telegraphic Signals or Marine Vocabulary*, dated 1 November 1800, 'was originally made to facilitate the conveyance of messages from the *Romney* off Copenhagen, to Admiral Dickson off Elsinor [*sic*].' The occasion was that brief, bloodless browbeating of the Danes in August of that year, and *Romney* was having to pass on the Admiral's signals from Lord Whitworth, the Ambassador ashore, a task for which Lord Howe's *Signal Book for the Ships of War* had not been designed.[13]

Popham had invented a practical solution to a practical need – for a commander to be able to say exactly what he wanted, and not to be restrained by single-meaning, pre-arranged signals, which could not be qualified or adapted; as he said himself in presenting his vocabulary to the world:

> It is by no means intended to interfere with the established signals, as a single signal is certainly the most efficient for military evolutions [such as 'Close action']. It frequently however happens that officers wish to make communications of very essential moment far beyond the capacity of the established signals, and it is presumed that this Vocabulary will afford such convenience.[14]

Popham's solution to the problem was not at first applied universally in the Navy. Even as late as 1805 a story emerged of loss of life while urgent messages about the attempt of a French fleet to escape blockade had been taken by ship's boat. 'Had the Telegraph Signals been in use', Popham's correspondent assured him, 'the news would have been given three days earlier, without the drownings.'[15] Even before that incident Popham was not satisfied, for, in 1803, in addition to producing a version of his vocabulary especially for use by the ships of the East India Company, he published an expanded version with more words and some sentences. The flying of a 'Telegraph' flag signified the use of the code, and, although it involved the use of considerable quantities of bunting, it allowed a quite remarkable expansion of the speed and volume of signals traffic. As his biographer says:

> Apart from its remarkable range and flexibility – and in this, as in other respects, it was unique – Popham's elucidation of his system has an agreeable common sense about it. 'Prepositions and articles will be used as seldom as possible, and the sentences will be made short. In verbs, the number, the person, the tense, and mood, must be applied to the sense of the sentence . . .* But when it happens that the exact word is not in the vocabulary, one nearest synonymous will be adopted . . .'[16]

In 1805 Popham's telegraphic vocabulary was issued to the Navy officially, but, as we have seen and at the cost of some men drowned, it was not in universal use in that year. Nelson, however, was a great fan of the code and his employment of it at Trafalgar gave him an extra tactical advantage. Moreover, we can use his immortal message to illustrate not only the array of

*This practice became commonplace over forty years later when the electric telegraph demanded economy of words, not through any logical restraint, but simply through the imperative of cost.

bunting used to make the signal, in contrast to 'just four flags' which was to evolve later, but also the use of a 'nearest synonymous' word. In a work that does not include in its richness more than passing references to the telegraph, *The New Cambridge Modern History* does include a glowing reference to the suitability of the Popham's code to Nelson's style:

> . . . the tactical freedom which he enjoyed now that the old *Fighting Instructions* had been replaced by the new signal books (notably Sir Home Popham's *Marine Vocabulary*) enabled him to improvise brilliantly as he did at the battle of the Nile, or plan with minute care an unusual mode of attack, as at Trafalgar and Copenhagen.[17]

Popham was an enigmatic man whose character got him into scrapes regarding which his superiors were sometimes dismayed, and which his enemies enjoyed. But if the analysis of the Navy's contribution to the fall of Napoleon is correct – 'the far distant, storm beaten ships, always unseen by the Grand Army, stood between it and dominion of the world'[18] – Popham's contribution was truly momentous. But his *Marine Vocabulary* was not to be his only contribution, great as it was, to the first telegraph age. After Waterloo he was instrumental in devising a semaphore system of signalling after having studied the French *Depillion* system, which we shall come across later. Popham submitted a paper on the subject to the Royal Society, of which he had been elected a fellow in 1799, which appeared in the *Transactions* in 1816.[19]

## The Trafalgar Telegraph

The hero worship of Nelson after his death has achieved industrial proportions; on the centenary of Trafalgar a booklet was published[20] about the famous signal, giving authenticity to one intriguing aspect of it; Lt Col Baylis wrote:

> In 1846, as a member of the Royal Western Yacht Club, Plymouth, I had the good fortune to know John Pasco – Senior and Signal Officer of the *Victory* in the battle of Trafalgar (21st October 1805) – who kindly wrote for me the following letter at my request.
>
> I had the honour to suggest the substitution of the word 'expects' for 'confides' – Lord Nelson had chosen the latter – but, it not being in the vocabulary, must have been spelt, and have taken more time than could have been spared (as we were close on the enemy) and the word 'expects' only required one number. After it had been answered, His Lordship ordered me to make the signal (No.16) for close action, and keep it flying.
>
> (Signed) John Pasco,
> Senior and Signal Officer of the *Victory*,
> [on] 21st October 1805.

Nelson is reported to have said that he sent the message 'To amuse the fleet'. It is as difficult to understand what Nelson was trying to say, with the word 'confides' (he may have meant 'trusts'), as it is easy to understand why the abbreviated vocabulary did not contain the word. Pasco did Nelson a great favour in creating the memorable aphorism which lives today from an obscure, even unintelligible, meaning for the matelots it was aimed at. Even as it was, some historians believe that the cheers that went up from the crews as the signal was interpreted in each ship in the fleet were of derision, not hero worship (what else had they been doing for all the long months but their duty?). For our purpose, however, the story illustrates the constraints with which Popham's code had to operate and which would only be overcome when the 'four-flag' system was introduced later.

In all, there were thirty-one flags that had to be taken from the *Victory*'s lockers to get the message aloft in its hoist: quite a task for the 'bunting tossers' (as naval signallers were dubbed), specially when they were bearing down on the enemy and about to be fired on. The signal had the following flags for each component of it:

| *Message* | ENGLAND | EXPECTS | THAT | EVERY | MAN | WILL | DO | HIS | D | U | T | Y |
|---|---|---|---|---|---|---|---|---|---|---|---|---|
| *Number of flags* | 3 | 3 | 3 | 3 | 3 | 3 | 3 | 3 | 1 | 2 | 2 | 2 |

It is, perhaps, surprising that there was no code in the vocabulary for the word 'duty', but that the word needed seven flags, gives understanding to Pasco's suggestion of avoiding a many-flagged word such as 'confides' and using 'expects', which was in the vocabulary, instead.

Nelson himself had good cause to be grateful because of the intelligence he was given by telegraph of the movement and apparent intentions of the combined enemy fleet. Capt Blackwood, of the 36-gun frigate *Euryalus*, had been scurrying across the seas, gathering intelligence from outside Cadiz, and, by means of flag signals relayed by a chain of ships, had passed it on to Nelson who was cruising beyond the horizon. The log of *Euryalus* for 19 October 1805 tells us:

> At daylight observed the enemy's ships in Cadiz . . . At 7, saw the northernmost ships under way. At 7.20 dispatched the *Phoebe* to repeat signals between us and the English fleet. At 8, saw 19 of the enemy under way . . . The *Defence* in sight from masthead west. *Phoebe* WNW, firing three-minute guns. At 8.10, came within hail the *Naiad*, and ordered her to repeat as many signals as possible between us and the *Phoebe*. Made a telegraph message to the *Weazle*, [sending] intelligence to Gibraltar. . . At 9, ordered the *Pickle* [for

> which fame lay ahead] to proceed with all possible dispatch . . . and inform all ships that the enemy is out.[21]

It was all part of Nelson's conception for exploiting the advantage that Popham's code had given him. He had signalled on 4 October 1805 to Capt Duff in the *Mars*:

> As the enemy's fleet may be hourly expected to put to sea from Cadiz, I have to desire that you keep with the *Mars*, *Defence* and *Colossus*, from three to four leagues between the fleet and Cadiz, in order that I may get the information from the frigates stationed off that port as expeditiously as possible. Distant signals to be used when flags, from the state of the weather, may not be readily distinguishable in their colours [at too great a distance, in poor visibility the flags could be indistinct].
>
> If the enemy are out or coming out, fire guns by day or night, in order to draw my attention. In thick weather, the ships to close within signal [range] of the *Victory* . . . and I have desired Captain Blackwood to throw a frigate to the Westward of Cadiz for the purpose of easy and early communication.[22]

When Nelson knew that the enemy was out from Cadiz he knew that the battle, the outcome of which he never doubted, was about to take place; he was so pleased with Blackwood's work that he was summoned to the *Victory* so that he could be thanked for his services. Nelson, who now was able to combine his awesome penchant of close engagement of an enemy at sea with immaculate intelligence, had time on 20 October to say to his midshipmen in *Victory*: 'Tomorrow, will be our day'; he was right, and the day has been celebrated ever since, not, unhappily, as the French would have done, by a national holiday, but by British sailors everywhere. Meanwhile, Capt Blackwood, his work done until fate took a hand, had had time to write to his wife, telling her excitedly that:

> . . . though our fleet was at sixteen leagues off [40 miles; 64km], I have let Lord Nelson know of their coming out . . . At this moment we are within four miles [6km] of the Enemy, and talking to Lord Nelson by means of Sir H. Popham's signals, though so distant, but repeated along the rest of the frigates of this Squadron.[23]

The great merit of Popham's signalling vocabulary was that it allowed for a conversational style of communication, as distinct from a range of monologic commands. Popham had achieved the historic advance in

*he view north to the Clee Hills, The Wrekin, from the Worcestershire Beacon: in open country the range of a lltop beacon could be 40 miles (64km).*

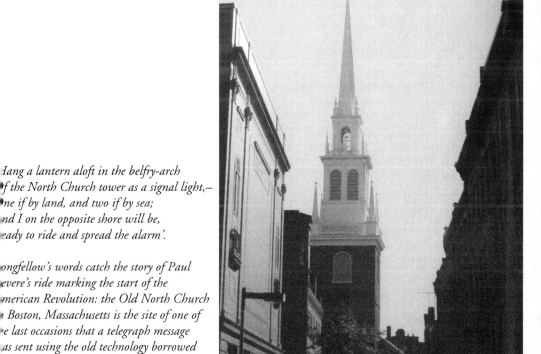

*Iang a lantern aloft in the belfry-arch*
*f the North Church tower as a signal light,–*
*ne if by land, and two if by sea;*
*nd I on the opposite shore will be,*
*eady to ride and spread the alarm'.*

*ongfellow's words catch the story of Paul evere's ride marking the start of the merican Revolution: the Old North Church Boston, Massachusetts is the site of one of e last occasions that a telegraph message as sent using the old technology borrowed om the beacons.*

*A nineteenth-century Dolland telescope with its carrying case (courtesy Jason M. Cinquino).*

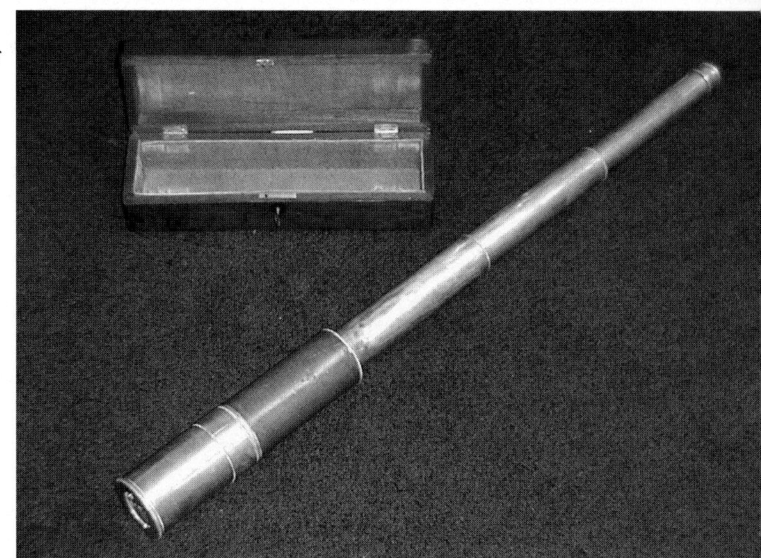

*Marker cannon at the north-west end of the great base in Neon Avenue, near Heathrow Airport.*

*The South Downs: Gen Roy identified this range of hills as a strategic defence line for London; the Portsmouth shutter telegraph line carried the summit of these hills at Blackdown.*

*Iodel of a shutter telegraph station: it illustrates how rimitive and temporary were these stations (courtesy oyal Signals Museum, Blandford).*

*A field version of the shutter telegraph; unlike Chappe's telegraph, this was never used in the field systematically (courtesy Royal Signals Museum, Blandford).*

*The shutter telegraph station at Great Yarmouth.*

*ortsdown Hill: site of Gamble's shutter telegraph xperiments, and penultimate tation on the Portsmouth ine.*

Published by P. S. & V. Lewisham.
Telegraph Hill Recreation Ground.


*Telegraph Hill Park, New Cross, London, c.1920.*

*Blackdown: the highest point in Sussex and site of a shutter telegraph station on the Portsmouth line.*

*Hascombe Hill: the site of a telegraph station, corresponding with Netley Heath and Blackdown, Sussex to the south.*

*St Alban's clock tower: one of the few remaining sites of the shutter telegraph.*

*Dunstable Downs was on the shutter telegraph line to Yarmouth.*



*Netley Heath, on the North Downs near Gomshall, Surrey: this site of a telegraph station corresponded with Cabbage (now Telegraph) Hill, near Chessington Zoo and Hascombe, near Godalming, Surrey.*

*The rededication of the memorial to Rear-Adm Sir Home Riggs Popham on 18 April 1999 in the churchyard of St. Michael and All Angels, Sunninghill, Berkshire (courtesy Catrina Popham).*

*Beacon Hill, on the South Downs at Harting, site of a shutter telegraph station corresponding with Portsdown Hill and Blackdown.*

*Shooters Hill: an early twentieth-century photograph of the site of a telegraph station on the London–Deal line; it corresponded with stations at Nunhead (New Cross) and Swanscombe in Kent.*

*The Admiralty office at Mount Wise, Plymouth, the site of the terminal station on the London–Plymouth line; this station was in use at the time of Napoleon's captivity in Plymouth Sound.*

*The three-armed Depillion semaphore; all later forms of semaphore signalling, whether by flags or mechanical arms, were derived from this French coastal telegraph system which was introduced during the Peace of Amiens as an attempt to gain tactical superiority over the Royal Navy. The Admiralty preferred a two-armed system.*

*The development of mechanical semaphore at sea by the Royal Navy originated in Depillion's development of the French coastal telegraph, but it was not introduced until much later. Considerable controversy was aroused as to whether the naval use was attributable to Rear-Adm Popham or Lt Col Pasley. The use of flags for semaphore was not adopted until the late nineteenth century.*

*The semaphore station at Chatley Heath, near Cobham, Surrey. This station, which has been restored by Surrey County Council, is open to the public. It is a rare example of a tower station on the Admiralty to Portsmouth line, which operated from 1822 to 1847. It superseded the previous shutter line, which was demolished, and ran further to the south; it carried the news of Waterloo to Portsmouth by telegraph after it reopened temporarily in 1815.*

*The military use of signalling by semaphore flags continued until the latter part of the twentiet[h] century; the US Navy continues to have a flag signalling capability but it is used 'only when we have to'.*

*Dawn: 21 October 1805 (Auguste Ballin, 1842–80). The calm was to be shattered by the Battle of Trafalgar, which was itself followed by a severe storm (courtesy of The Naval Club, London).*

*Pickle's Rough Trip Home: the schooner bui[lt] in Bermuda hastens wit[h] the Trafalgar news. Thi[s] contemporary artist captures the urgency of Pickle's mission (courtes[y] Geoff Hunt, RSMA).*

communication at sea – dialogue. Claude Chappe had achieved this on land in an vastly expandable way in 1793, nearly ten years before Popham did at sea. Although Popham's system of signals would not allow complete flexibility of expression – that was still to come from the mind of Popham, 'a damned cunning fellow' – this was achieved later, when he was to have a key role in the second phase of land-based telegraphy – semaphore.

## Tribute to Popham

Popham continued to develop his vocabulary code for use at sea, and, encouraged by an Admiralty committee in 1812, published his last revision of it.[24] The committee considered 'that its adoption will be of the greatest utility to the public service'. Several further revisions were made to Popham's code until, in 1816, it was issued as the first official Admiralty Signal Book. The logical constraints of any further development were too much for Popham and the elegance and economy of the ultimate, four-flag system were to escape him. He died in 1820, but not before he had made a major contribution to the semaphore method of signalling, on board ship and on land. In 1803 he had bought a house, now demolished, in Sunninghill, Berkshire, and when he died a memorial was erected to him in celebration of his life-time achievements in naval telegraphy and combined operations, a man described by his biographer as: '. . . one of the most intriguing naval officers of the period: a man of fertile imagination and restless energy; clever, plausible, a superb seaman, and a commander of whom one of his ship's company wrote: "No Captain ever left his ship more esteemed both by officers and men".'

The monument stands in the churchyard of St Michael and All Angels in Sunninghill still: a column with an immortal flame on top, standing on a square plinth; on one side, cut in relief, is an open vocabulary book of the type which might have been used at Trafalgar, a flag signal and a semaphore arm of the type used in a period later than the scope of this book. On another side is cut a globe, telescope and navigational instruments, reflecting his prowess as a hydrographer. The inscription of the names Copenhagen (where he first developed his vocabulary code), Buenos Ayres (where he had been when, to his chagrin, he missed Trafalgar) and North Coast of Spain (where he had supplied the guerrillas who were the scourge of the French in the Peninsular War), give some of the locations around the world where he served; we shall hear of St Helena later. When Popham's biographer, Hugh Popham, rediscovered the memorial, he found that time, wind and weather had erased all trace of the inscription to the man in whose honour it stood. He resolved to have the inscription recut, an ambition which was achieved posthumously, for, on 18 April 1999, a service was held to mark the repair and rededication of the memorial in the presence of Adm

Sir Peter Abbott, GBE, KCB, Vice-Chief of the Defence Staff, Mrs Mary Popham (the widow of Hugh) and other descendants of Home Popham, along with members of The 1805 Club, a voluntary organization dedicated to the preservation of Nelson-related monuments and memorials, and ratings from HMS *Collingwood.*

# 7
# The Revolution at War

*I am not at all afraid for England; we shall stand till the day of judgement.*
William Pitt

## The Characteristics of the Wars with France

Britain was at war with France, with two small intermissions, from 1 February 1793 until 18 June 1815 when Wellington (Arthur Wellesley, 1st Duke, 1769–1852) administered the final defeat. Although some agitators in Britain had hoped that the Revolution would be imported from France, this desire did not take hold and in general British opinion was hostile to the Revolution when the king was deposed in 1792. When he was executed in January 1793, and the French occupied Antwerp as a base from which to attack Britain, war became inevitable. Several countries were already at war with France at this point and Britain joined the first coalition against her. The twenty-two years of war which followed fall into three parts: the first, known as the French Revolutionary Wars, came to their conclusion in a sort of stalemate, in 1802 with the Peace of Amiens.* The next two parts, known as the Napoleonic Wars, had their first ending in 1814, after the French defeat at Leipzig in October 1813, following which Paris fell; Napoleon's escape from Elba followed, and after his acclamation in Paris on 20 March 1815 and his so-called 'hundred days', the war was renewed until Wellington closed the account. These wars were like nothing that had preceded them. The wars of the eighteenth century and before were limited affairs, conducted between kings. Something different was about to break upon the peoples of Europe: not because they were fought with any revolutionary weapons, but because they were to be wars not among nations but of them; total war. This was war on an unprecedented geographic scale, fought by armies of immense size.

Four things characterize these twenty-two years of war: first, Britain was the only country that was consistently at war with France throughout, apart from the pauses referred to. Second, the Navy was able to acquire

*By this treaty, Elba was ceded to France.

unchallengeable maritime supremacy. Third, were the ebb and flow, confusion would be a fair description, of which particular countries serving their own self-interests would, at one time or another, join the French against Britain: or, falling out with the French or seeing advantage in her defeat, become a member of one of the four coalitions which emerged against her. These coalitions always included England, which was the bulwark against which Napoleon always pressed in vain: 'All the evils, all the plagues which can afflict the human race', he wrote to Josephine, 'come from London!' Each of the countries of Europe which were, alternately, allies and enemies of France or Britain, had, according to Napoleon, its price – except Britain, which he could not hope to corrupt. The matter is so complicated as to defy brevity but suffice it to say that, at one time or other, most of the countries of Europe were engaged in fighting France, while many fought Britain.

The fourth characteristic was that, on no fewer than four occasions, England found itself fighting France alone.

## The Invasion Risk in 1797–98

To understand fully the atmosphere in the country in 1797–98, we must acknowledge the fear in people's minds, among both the common people and the ruling classes, of the threat of invasion, the perception of which did not go away completely until Trafalgar in 1805. There was no equivocation in England: Napoleon was an ogre, hated, feared, credited with nothing in redemption. Never mind that the age of reform beckoned, no revolutionary urge could be fostered in the breast of a people united in their determination never to yield dominion over themselves. Any reader who is unconvinced of the odious nature of the threat posed by Napoleon to English life might reflect on the words proclaimed by him on entering Cairo in 1798 and threatening India: 'Soldiers – you are going to undertake a conquest whose effects on civilization will be incalculable. You will strike the surest and most painful stroke possible against England until you can deal her the final death blow. . . .'[1]

In 1797 and early 1798 the French attempted a number of invasions of Ireland and Wales. They were desultory affairs, inadequately planned and led, but they served to make real the perceived threat of an organized invasion. By this time, Napoleon had established his reputation as a brilliant general after a series of victories in Italy in 1796–97, the news of which had broken in Britain and elsewhere like unexpected thunder. It was scarcely credible: Venice, a city-state of 1,400 years' standing, had been overwhelmed. After many centuries of success and with a system of government which was at the other end of a scale in terms of democracy from that which Napoleon was to create in Paris, her economy worn down over the centuries in disputing the east with Turkey, she had fallen meekly and without a fight to his generals.

One of Napoleon's first acts in Venice had been to throw open the gates of the Jewish ghetto, in accordance with revolutionary orthodoxy. In contrast, he plundered much of the art treasure (much of it itself previously plundered from Constantinople) and shipped it off to Paris – a process repeated in most of the cities he conquered, only to be reversed in 1814 or after Waterloo. As he swept through Italy, his ambition to seize power in France became clear, and, that if he did, he would seek to change the world and replace whatever government was in his way. The fall of Venice served as a stark warning which did not go unnoticed.

There was something else which did not go unnoticed: in Italy the wanton contempt with which the French army treated the churches and the clergy, aroused the indignation of a large part of the population of Lombardy. Such armed revolt as emerged was put down by Napoleon without mercy. The leaders were executed as if they had committed a crime in endeavouring to rescue their country from the arms of an invader. In one town, all the male inhabitants were massacred. That these bloody examples quelled the insurrections there is no doubt, but, as Lockhart[2] observed, 'the first dark and indelible stain on the name of Napoleon' had been fixed. The ruthless killings by a powerful invader were observed with foreboding across the Channel.

In England at this time the first shutter telegraph lines were being commissioned; Earl Cornwallis (1738–1805), who had served with distinction in the American War of Independence and was now the Master-General of Ordnance, was saying: 'It must be evident to every observer that Bonaparte has vowed the destruction of the British Empire, or to fall in the attempt. He only waits for a favourable opportunity to make his attack.'[3]

The development of telegraphy in England from 1796 was born into this national emergency and it goes a long way in explaining why the first lines were laid with such speed, helped, as we have seen, by the work of the Ordnance Survey but demanded by the exigencies of the moment. William Pitt, the Prime Minister, said, 'I am not at all afraid for England; we shall stand till the day of judgement', but the markets were not that certain, for the government's 3 per cent consols stock fell to its lowest level in history.

## The Defence of Southern England

In a secret document, Cornwallis marshalled his thoughts on the defence of southern England against invasion.[4] In it he invited acceptance of:

> . . . the supposition that the French will attempt to invade England with such powerful armies as those that they have sent into Italy and

> Germany, [and consequently] this country can only be defended and saved by the most decisive and vigorous policies – similar in many respects to those which were adopted with so much efficacy and success by America* in the former war and by France in the beginning of the present war.

He described the planning and execution of what became known as a policy of 'scorched earth': everything within 15 miles (24km) of the coast where an invasion had already taken place or was expected imminently and which had any potential to be of value to the enemy was to be removed or destroyed. Cornwallis's proposal became government policy on what should happen in the event of an invasion:

> If an enemy should land upon our shores, every possible exertion should be made immediately to deprive him of the means of subsistence. The Navy will soon cut off his communication with the Sea; the Army will confine him on Shore in such a way as to make it impossible for him to draw any supplies from the adjacent country. In this situation he will be forced to lay down his arms, or to give Battle on disadvantageous terms. But if unforeseen and improbable circumstances should enable him to make some progress at first, a steady perseverance in the same system will increase his difficulties at every step; sooner or later he must inevitably pay the forfeit of his temerity.

It was too evident, said the plan, to need any discussion of:

> How much the accomplishment of this object [of scorched earth] will be facilitated by driving away the livestock, and consuming, or, in case of absolute necessity, destroying all other means of subsistence, in those parts of the country which may be in imminent danger of falling into [the enemy's] possession . . .

Cornwallis proposed a census of the population, livestock and facilities in the invasion areas. Provided people's names appeared on the census (the routine population censuses did not start until 1801), they would be indemnified for all the losses occasioned by the scorched earth policy, one written in the finest of details, with planned rendezvous points and general procedures. In essence, women, children and the infirm were to drive the

---

*This is probably a reference to Gen Sherman's famous March to the Sea in 1864 during the American Civil War: the Georgia countryside had been ravished in order to deny it to the pursuing Confederate army, a policy executed with signal success.

cattle inland; carters were to report with their wagons and horses to remove stocks of food and anything movable inland; boatmen and bargemen were to report with their boats for public service, or else destroy them; millers and bakers were to feed the Army; those best acquainted with the countryside were to report on horseback to act as guides for it; able-bodied men were to report to the Army, with picks, shovels and axes to make road-blocks, and so on. A total of six routes of retreat through Kent and other southern counties were worked out through Stroud, Cobham, Aylesford, Maidstone and Teston Bridge, but 'the heights behind Lewisham and Sydenham are [to be] the ultimate points of retreat'.

Defiance and denial were the watchwords as Britain at bay contemplated the threat from France. Churchill caught the same mood in 1940 when he said in a world broadcast on 14 July, 'Should the invader come to Britain, there will be no placid lying down of the people in submission before him as we have seen, alas, in other countries. We shall defend every village, every town, and every city . . . .'

The detail of the routes that were laid down for retreating columns is astonishing for its exactness. It was set out in Gen Roy's *A Military Description of the South-East Part of England*[5]. In his report, Roy reviewed all the previous invasions of England: those of Caesar, Claudius, the Saxons, the Danes and, of course, William of Normandy. By examining the landing grounds which each of army had chosen and linking them with the routes taken as the invaders moved inland, Roy was able to give a strategic view on how best to organize a defence of southern England in the light of the lie of the land as he had surveyed it. As a single example of the detail in which the 1798 plan was all worked out and of the thoroughness with which the survey had been conducted by Roy, the following is indicative:

> Having crossed Bexley Heath, the column in its march from thence to Shooters Hill [where a telegraph station had been built] will follow the road on account of some extensive woods and other impediments. NB: the cavalry may retire by the road that leads from Crayford Church to the northern side of Bexley Heath and from thence by a communication [specially] opened for them bearing directly upon Wickham Church.

The strength of the Army deployed in the inland areas of the non-coastal counties was recorded at just less than 100,000 men.[6]

## The Defence of London

The defence of the capital was not neglected: a document[7] dated 31 January 1798 showed the garrison strength to be 5,400 infantry and 2,370 cavalry.

Any troops that fell back on London were to reinforce the established defence posts and the surrounding boroughs occupied, namely Hackney, Tottenham, Highgate, Hampstead, Hammersmith, Clapham and Camberwell. Moreover,

> On a critical emergency the troops must not be too much dispersed in quarters, but be assembled and accommodated in public edifices pointed out by the Chief Magistrates of the several districts and these should be previously known and arranged. One third of the effective numbers are always supposed to be on guard . . . and the whole ready to be assembled on the shortest notice. Detachments of artillery are to be stationed at certain points: at the Bank [of England], Somerset House – a battery of light guns to be formed at the Tower and one at Whitehall – small howitzers to be mixed with the guns.

The defences already noted to the south of London would be important if an invading force made a short sea crossing of the Channel, but if a landing were made well to the west and the northern heights of the Thames Valley were taken, London could be threatened from the rear. The French had drawn up an invasion plan of this character after the Seven Years War (1756–63). This intelligence had been acquired by the British years before, and, because a defending force with artillery would be able to bombard any enemy forces that had penetrated into the Thames Valley, the importance of the northern heights in the event of an invasion was not neglected. A *Report for the Defence of the Capital*,[8] considered that the Hampstead–Highgate ridge and the surrounding hills, when fortified, would be a 'citadel' which no enemy could afford to leave in his rear. Although the defences were never actually built, the positions of redoubts and of twenty-nine guns were marked on a map[9] and actually staked out on the ground. The defences were to be dug only after it was clear that danger was imminent. Arrangements were made with the civil authorities for the supply of labour[10] for this purpose and it was estimated that, with help from troops, the line north of the Thames could be built by 5,000 men with 300 horses in three days.[11] Plainly, the attention to detail in the defence plan was considerable.

## Gamble's Radiated Telegraph

Unperturbed by his shabby treatment by the Admiralty, Gamble, the unfortunate shutter telegraph inventor, continued to maintain his interest in telegraphy, but his contribution was becoming eclectic for he had invented a completely new type of telegraph. Writing in his 1797 essay,[12] and by now having been able to observe the telegraph of his rival Murray at work on the Admiralty roof, he concluded that the shutter system (both his own and

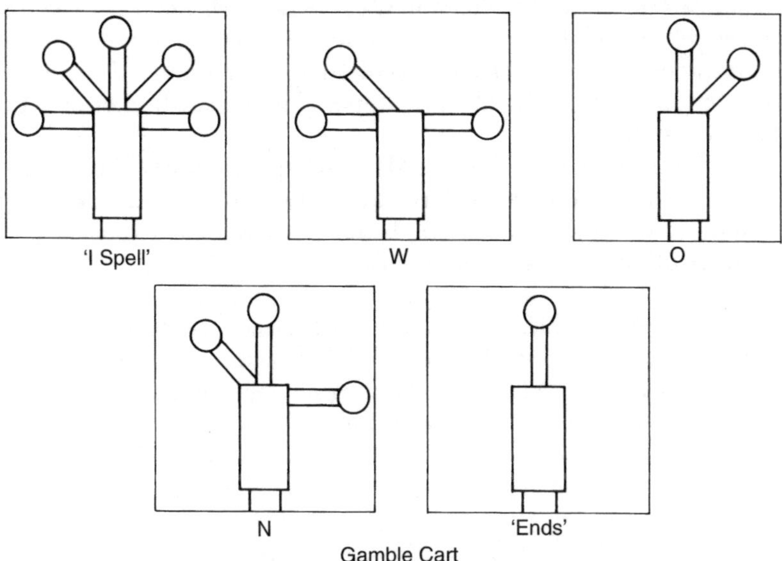


*An example of the Gamble Telegraph Code.*

Murray's) was not altogether satisfactory. In this he was, ultimately, to be proved right, for when a new semaphore system was trialled against the shutter in 1816, the semaphore's performance proved to be superior. What Gamble had developed in 1796, and written about in the following year, was what he called a 'radiated telegraph', which, even though the word had not by then been coined, was in fact the first semaphore (the word was devised in France to describe their coastal telegraph). Gamble's telegraph consisted of a single mast with five arms (or rays, hence radiated), all pivoted on the same axis. At the end of each arm was a disc to help the observer to discern its position. Each arm had five positions, which were, in clockwise order: horizontal at the left, diagonal at the left, vertical, diagonal at the right and horizontal at the right; this gave thirty-one effective positions. Gamble says that he was particularly concerned to design a telegraph suited for military use in the field and, one which could be fixed on a cart and hauled into position by a horse; in the portable version, the rays might be 5ft (1.5m) long. Because the telegraph was designed for use by the Army in the field, it would not always have been possible to achieve a good line of sight; Gamble accommodated this by having one side of the rays painted white and the other black. In this way the most suitable shade, according to the background, could be presented by changing the orientation of the cart.

Gamble, being Chaplain-General to the Duke of York, naturally brought his new telegraph to the Duke's attention. Shortly after, on 12 January 1798, the Duke wrote to the Secretary-at-War, 'Being well aware of the great advantage which in cases of emergency may be derived from immediate communication by means of telegraphs, I beg to recommend . . . that an immediate experiment be made on two portable (radiated) ones presented by the Rev Gamble.'

The trials duly took place and the Master-General of the Ordnance sent a report on them to the Duke and the Secretary-at-War. In contrast to the earlier blow to Gamble's self-esteem, the report on his radiated telegraph by a committee of top brass was full of praise:

> In the report which the Committee . . . have the honour of making . . . on Mr Gamble's Radiated Telegraph they have to express themselves perfectly satisfied with the ingenuity and simplicity of the construction, and also with the system of working the characters. . . . Telegraphs placed by Mr Gamble . . . [on the top of Woolwich Parish Church] admitted of a perfect communication by the help of telescopes between a radiated telegraph erected at Shooters Hill [where one of Murray's shutter telegraph was operating] at a distance of about four or five miles [6.4 or 8km] and with another on Blackheath . . .[13]

It is agreeable to be able to note that Gamble's new telegraph was seen operating side by side (or at least on the same hill) as Murray's at Shooters Hill. The offence given to Gamble by the Admiralty was probably well known; the report gave a tongue-in-cheek sideswipe to the Admiralty by suggesting that they might show some interest but they did not at the time; however, the first shipboard semaphores were plainly inspired by Gamble's concept. He applied to the Admiralty for a test of his radiated telegraph, of which he submitted a model. The Admiralty replied that they were well satisfied with the telegraphs erected under the direction of Lord Murray and that they did not think it necessary to make any experiments with the radiated form (and would he please take away the models and plans he had left at the Navy Office).[14] Gamble's radiated telegraph was a much lighter piece of apparatus than Murray's and had been shown to be superior in operation; the disdain which the Admiralty showed to Gamble is common in bureaucracies regarding something 'not invented here'.

In April 1798, during the invasion crisis, Gamble proposed to the Duke of York, as Commander-in-Chief of the Army, that telegraphic communication be set up with the east coast. The following month one of Gamble's telegraphs was erected on one of the towers of Westminster Abbey.[15] Whether a connection to the coast was ever made is doubtful, but in August *The Times* reported that 'a radiated military telegraph, the invention of the Revd Gamble, is to be . . . erected to convey intelligence to Windsor . . .'.

Also in 1798, on one of the Hampstead hills, known as One Tree Hill but later as Telegraph Hill, a telegraph station was built by the Army which put the position into contact with London. This Hampstead Heath site marked the first operational use of telegraphy by the Army. The same site was used in 1807 for the shutter telegraph line to Yarmouth. The London terminus of Gamble's radiated telegraph station was the 225ft (69m) north-west tower of the Abbey, completed some sixty years earlier. In 1798 the towers would have been the highest structures in London, except for the dome of St. Paul's Cathedral. The telegraph on the top must have been quite a sight, but surprisingly no artist captured it in any surviving picture.

There is one picture held by the Fogg Art Museum at Harvard University which supplies some evidence for the telegraph site on Hampstead Heath. The painting, by an unknown artist, shows plainly the arms of the apparatus and distinctly shows the disks at their ends, exactly in the Gamble form. Some writers have suggested that the painting is by John Constable, but he did not start painting Hampstead scenes until 1819, by which time the Gamble telegraph would have been long gone, and the shutter telegraph too.

No records have been retained, or at least so far discovered, which tell us what became of Gamble's telegraph, how long it was used, for what purpose and when it was closed down. It seems probable that the stations were dismantled as a result of the Peace of Amiens. After war broke out again, the War Office wanted a telegraph line from Shoeburyness to the Tower of London, at that time an important military depot. Whether the War Office were considering Gamble's system is not known, but a survey showed that it would be necessary for eight or nine stations to be built. Instead, the Admiralty co-operated with the Army to provide a stationary vessel midway between Southend and Sheerness to pass on military signals traffic via the Deal line.[16] The use by the Army of a fixed-line telegraph seems therefore to have come to an end with the Peace of Amiens; certainly neither Woolwich church nor Westminster Abbey was used as a telegraph station after 1802.

In 1797 British troops were sent to Portugal and took some Gamble telegraphs with them.[17] The government in France, chastened by Adm Jervis's victory at the Battle of Cape St Vincent, had pressed Spain to invade Portugal on account of the alleged help given to Jervis by a Portuguese ship. As we shall see later, the Duke of Wellington used telegraphs in the field during the Peninsular War, but it seems that Gamble's radiated telegraph was not used operationally. Unhappily, little is known about why the Gamble radiated telegraph fell into disuse in the Army, and there is no record of any trial being made of Gamble's system against any competing one after the 1798 experiments. It is sad to relate that, even though he was a telegraph pioneer, Gamble was never to have either of the systems he devised in an operational mode.

## Early Naval Victories

The French navy had suffered severe losses from the first years of the war. This attrition and the rise in the absolute as well as the relative power and effectiveness of the Royal Navy, gained by several historic victories, saved Britain's trade and protected her from invasion. Later in the wars this supremacy, in an epic illustration of sea power, allowed Wellington's armies in the Peninsular War to be supplied at will. The first of these naval victories was on 'the Glorious 1st of June' in the second year of war, 1794, just as the Chappes were commissioning their first telegraph line. In the House of Commons, a few days after the news reached London, the Secretary for War and Colonies, Sir Henry Dundas (later Lord Melville) said the victory was: '. . . so brilliant and so signal, that the enemy had not the pretence to say that they were overpowered by a superior force.' And another MP 'rejoiced in this victory . . . for it saved us from the possibility of an invasion by the French'. In fact, this was not so, for by the following year all France's continental opponents had suffered defeats and were forced to make peace. Britain continued the fight alone, and, as we have seen, made plans to defeat an invasion. But France had struck up alliances with Spain and Holland, both of which had strong fleets. However, before these fleets could be combined against the Royal Navy, it inflicted heavy defeats over the Spanish fleet at the Battle of Cape St Vincent (where Nelson was second in command) and over the Dutch at the Battle of Camperdown. On 14 February 1797, at Cape St Vincent off the coast of Portugal, the victory of Adm Jervis (later Earl St Vincent, 1735–1823) was to be exceeded in its brilliance and significance only by the those at the Nile and Trafalgar. In the Commons on 3 March, Dundas announced that Jervis's fleet had taken on and roundly defeated an enemy force twice its size. With only mild hyperbole (for the invasion threat was at high pitch), one MP thought that: 'One of the captured ships suggested a title appropriate to the character of the gallant Admiral, *Salvador del Mundo*.' Lord St Vincent's service to the Navy, at sea and at the Admiralty, was epic: if he was not quite the saviour of the world he certainly went on to command a navy that was.

## Egypt

Napoleon had taken no interest in the early skirmishes of the French invaders alongside the Irish rebels, and, as his power grew, he realized that the defeat of the Royal Navy was not immediately achievable; this may explain why he distanced himself from the Irish adventure. Instead, in 1798, noting that, 'If I remain doing nothing for long I am lost', he persuaded the Directory that he should sail with his army, neither for England nor Ireland but for Egypt. In this project, the Directory was actively canvassed by the foreign minister Charles Maurice de Talleyrand-Périgord (1754–1838), who, perhaps seeing a good opportunity to be rid of the ambitious General, extolled the benefits to France of new colonies, including Egypt.

Napoleon's fleet and nearly 400 transports with his army on board left Toulon and other Mediterranean ports undetected and continued to avoid Nelson in an extraordinary cat-and-mouse pursuit in the eastern Mediterranean. Nelson had no intelligence of Napoleon's objective, he could only surmise. Of all the objectives that his government and the Admiralty had guessed at, Egypt was not one. Nelson was a genius, what else took him east to Alexandria? In an extraordinary circumstance of being exactly right, but too soon, he contrived to arrive off Alexandria before Napoleon did, Napoleon's destination all along. There being no sign of Napoleon's fleet, Nelson left in search of it elsewhere. Thus was Napoleon able to get his army ashore in Egypt; had he been less fortunate and if chance had allowed Nelson to fall upon the French on the open sea, a holocaust of human loss might have occurred if the French had not first surrendered. This cannot be stated too strongly; it was not a question of firepower. Nelson was never cowed by an inferiority of weight of the shot that could be exchanged; it was a question first of the sheer quality of the seamanship throughout every level in the Royal Navy. From the lowest bilge-pumper, through every deck, the gun crews, the clearing of decks for action, the accuracy of aim, the rate of fire, the stowing, the riggers, the tacking, damage control and recovery, in every aspect of seamanship there were no crews on earth who could match those who manned the Royal Navy's ships, and the officers too.

If Nelson's fleet had fallen upon Napoleon on the open sea it would have been Trafalgar and Waterloo all in one day, an unspeakable catastrophe for France. With Napoleon killed or captured, his fleet destroyed and his soldiers drowned, the history of Europe would have taken an utterly different course from 1798: the later violation of Germany by Napoleon would not have taken place, there would be no reason for France to be hated by the Germans, no oxygen to make the flames of hatred erupt into the war of 1870 and the conflagrations of the twentieth century. Napoleon was lucky; through no skill of his, Nelson missed him and providentially for Napoleon, but not for Europe, his troops disembarked, together with his cadre of colonizing scientists and scholars – mineralogists, archaeologists, cartographers and naturalists,* and later achieved some military successes in Egypt and Asia Minor.

---

*This led directly to the later publication (1809–22) of a 24-volume work *Description de l'Égypt*, covering ancient history, the modern state, natural history, agriculture and commerce, and a topographical map. It also led to a preliminary survey for a canal, built nearly 70 years later, to join the Red Sea to the Mediterranean.

Napoleon's Egyptian campaign is not a subject we can pursue here for it does not connect with the telegraph story, except to illustrate, by its remoteness from France and the loss of the Mediterranean, Napoleon's difficulties of communication. There is just one matter to note in illustration of how Napoleon's wisdom would bend his policy to the wind of expediency. In Egypt Napoleon found it convenient to modify the licentious behaviour of his armies, as had been seen in Italy. In his general order before disembarkation, he included the exhortation:

> The Roman legions protected all religions. You will find here usages different from those of Europe: you must accustom yourselves to them. These people treat their women differently from us; but in all countries [and here he must have had his tongue in his cheek for he knew the free licence he had given his men elsewhere] he who violates is a monster; pillage enriches only a few; it dishonours us, destroys our resources, and makes those enemies whom it is our interest to have for friends.

Napoleon may never have realized how fortunate he was to get to get his army ashore unmolested, but his luck lasted less than a month. In a strange twist of chance, his survival of the voyage to Egypt and the destruction of his fleet soon to be administered indirectly led to his being able to seize ultimate power in France and to be the direct cause of seventeen more years of war and everything which would flow from them.

Nelson knew nothing of attrition: when the French fleet was found it could hardly be called a set-piece battle, for there was no planning of it. Without a pause, Nelson took into his mind the situation at his first sighting of the French at anchor in Aboukir Bay: they thought they were safe, protected by shore batteries and moored close to the shore, but not close enough for a daringly aggressive foe. Nelson, the master of manoeuvre, fell upon the hapless French; he attacked his quarry, just as light was fading, and telegraphing by flag signals, took part of his fleet between his enemy and the shore. This was a master stroke from which the French fleet could never recover. There had never been a battle like this before and there has never been one like it since; for the shock and the speed of delivering the rending stroke that, in some cases, literally blew Napoleon's fleet out of the water, there are no parallels. Not that the battle was one-sided in fire-power; the French were overwhelmed by manoeuvre, by skill and the will of the great sea commander. It was the opposite of El Alamein, fought less than 100 miles (160km) away nearly 150 years later: that was a turning point as was the Nile. El Alamein had the planning, a victory but no rout – the Battle of the Nile, with no planning was more than a rout, it was an annihilation, or as Nelson himself put it 'a conquest': only two French ships of any note escaped and all Nelson's survived. Save only for those which escaped (they were caught later), the whole French fleet was totally destroyed by Nelson on 1 August 1798.

When Nelson had entered the Mediterranean, having been hived of from St Vincent's blockading fleet off Cadiz on Pitt's initiative, Nelson's squadron was making a cheeky entrance into a French lake, daring to assail its master. After the battle, as dawn broke on the following day, the scale of the victory became clear. Nelson's ships could go as they pleased in the Mediterranean while Napoleon's army was marooned in Egypt. It is not going too far to say that this was the most decisive naval engagement in the days of sail; snuffing out Napoleon's larger ambitions in the east, it caused, at stroke, a strategic shift in emphasis back to Europe. Only Trafalgar can be considered in the same way as the Nile; the Battle of the Nile modified history, Trafalgar only confirmed it. We shall be observing how news of each battle arrived in London.

The loss of his fleet meant that Napoleon could not get his army back home, and in France events had turned against her as well; a second coalition of her enemies had formed which now threatened to invade. Napoleon's reaction, on hearing of defeats at the hands of the coalition, was to abandon his army in Egypt in August 1799 and sail for France. This dramatic act would either take him to the guillotine or to supreme power; but Napoleon had divined the nature of the French, they were tiring of defeats. Longing for a deliverer, Napoleon would appear to them as the heir to the Revolution. On the morning of 9 October 1799, having been lucky again in avoiding the ships of the Royal Navy, he made landfall in the Bay of Fréjus, to be greeted by local civil and military dignitaries who, paying no respect to quarantine laws, cried, 'We prefer the plague to the Austrians!'[18] And so to Paris: all the way the crowds rose in acclamation of a hero. Some stuffed-shirts called for him to be court-martialled for abandoning his army in Egypt, but Napoleon now had a hold on the imagination of the French and no move against him could be sustained in the face of public opinion being so strongly in his favour. Among those who could have stopped him, he captured men's hearts with:

> What have you done with fair France which I left so bright in your hands? I had left you peace, now I find war; I left you victories, now I find defeats! I left you Italy's millions, now I find nothing but predatory laws and poverty. What have you done with the hundred thousand Frenchmen whom I knew, who were my comrades in glory? They are dead.[19]

This eloquent, but disingenuous, charge was carefully rehearsed: it had scarcely been declaimed when Napoleon whispered to an aide that he himself need not take it to heart.[20] The grasping of power by Napoleon was to be no pushover, it was to be by the exercise of unbounded will. Blaming his admirals for the defeat at the Nile, a *coup d'état* was organized: Napoleon was appointed First Consul, confirmed by a manipulated plebiscite, and thus became, effectively, the sole ruler of France. Being alert to the power of propaganda and of the telegraph as a tool for its propagation, he dispatched a message with the words '*Paris est tranquille et le bons citoyens sonts contents.*'[21] The masses undoubtedly hailed Napoleon first and foremost as the man who would protect their country against an invader, which, indeed, he was, but they did not realize that, to accomplish it, the elective principle which had been introduced by the Revolution was to be suppressed. 'Napoleon was to become the agent of the greatest and most salutary Revolution mankind has ever known, at any rate since that of Christianity'.[22] But, even at the time, the young dictator's determination to do everything himself, his refusal to admit discussion, revolted his fiercest critic.[23] 'Under the pretext of saving France from anarchy, Napoleon's administrative law killed practically all local freedom.'[24]

As the people cheered their saviour, as they thought, they forgot that Napoleon inherited from the Revolution the conscription law, which served to fill his army during the whole of his reign. As the needs of the armies mounted with their losses, every male under 25 was liable to be called up, and the rules of substitution were drawn so narrowly that even the sons of the best families were forced to comply. The first conscription list for a year included all under the age of 21, but, if Napoleon needed more, resort was made to those who were 22, 23, 24 or 25. There was no exemption if arms could be borne: the only child of his parents, the young husband and father were forced to abandon whatever comfort they enjoyed and fight for France – not until the twentieth century would the generality of this be repeated. As Lockhart observed, writing in 1829:

> There is nothing in the history of modern Europe so remarkable, as that the French people should have submitted, during 16 years, to the constant operation of a despotic law, which thus sapped all the foundations of social happiness, and condemned the rising hopes of the nation to bleed and die by millions in distant wars, undertaken solely for the gratification of one man's insatiable ambition.[25]

The other side of this coin is remarkable too: Napoleon was to run a meritocracy. 'There never was,' wrote Lockhart, 'an army in whose ranks intelligence so largely abounded, nor in which so many officers of the highest rank had originally carried a musket.'[26]

The first years of Napoleon's rule saw some conspiracies against him and there was an attempt on his life in 1800. His reaction to this, there being no restraints on his power, was utterly ruthless: whatever his redeeming features, to which the English were in any event blind, Napoleon revealed in his grip on power the DNA of the tyrant. He took the opportunity to purge the opposition and forced through an extraordinary measure: 130 well-known republicans, called for the occasion 'terrorists', were proscribed without any legal process. Many of these were deported to Guiana, where most of them failed to survive the climate. Such unbridled power was anathema in Britain.

The title deeds of liberty had been wrenched from the Revolution by Napoleon: the beacon lights of freedom were held by Britain, but 'The obstacle is Britain,' said Napoleon, 'Britain must be overthrown, for otherwise the new order in France cannot survive, and then . . . Europe is ours. . . .'[27]

It is perverse that this great historic development – the grasping of power by Napoleon, which was to be unbridled, a bookmark in the history of Europe to the present day and ensured another sixteen years of war for Britain as the first dividend – sprang from the pulverizing defeat of Napoleon by the Navy at the Nile; but how was Britain now to be pushed aside? When Napoleon grabbed power he found the telegraph very much to his convenience: with Paris now connected to Lille, Brest and Strasbourg, news of Napoleon's appointment was sent down the telegraph networks. Within hours large swaths of France knew that their redeemer – or whom they regarded as such – was now in charge. Now the telegraphs in France would cavort to his tune, the greatest general the world has known, the master of manoeuvre, knew his moment had arrived: a great country, a great army and a great telegraph service were his. The speed of communication available to the nascent dictator, the first in world history to be able to operate by remote control, was one of the advantages which he held over Britain. The illustration of this is given in the next chapter where we shall see how slow was the travelling of the news of Trafalgar and the Nile.

# 8
# 'He Brings Great News'

*Give him tending; he brings great news.*
Shakespeare[1]
*As cold waters to a thirsty soul, so is good news from a far country.*[2]
*Was I to die at this moment 'Want of Frigates' would be found stamped on my heart.*
Nelson, contemplating how to send the news of the Battle of the Nile[3]

*[Nelson] . . . who bore the British Glory high,*
*and broke the naval power of France.*[4]

*The noblest sailor since the world began*
*Though in the hour of victory he died.*[5]

## Trafalgar

In the modern world there has never been anything, before or since, quite like the two-edged news of Trafalgar: it arrived in London like a bolt of lightning. Apart from the participants, and perhaps the grey-beards in Cadiz who watched Villeneuve's fleet leave harbour, and quite unlike Waterloo, no one knew that battle was about to be joined; or, if they did, they could never have known that a hinge-point in the century-long supremacy of the Royal Navy was at hand. No one knew either that another catastrophe like the Nile could be inflicted on an enemy; no one could dream that the perceived risk of invasion could be extirpated at a stroke; no population had ever ached more for a release from fear into joy or knew how to temper its joy with sorrow at the loss of their hero. The news of Trafalgar's triumph and tragedy was sublime, but it is relevant here for one outstanding reason: it was the last big news story to be promulgated with no help from the telegraph and a case study of something the world was leaving behind. What lay ahead, apart from naval supremacy, was the telegraph age. The most curious aspect of the story of how the Trafalgar news was conveyed is that the shutter telegraph from Portsmouth to London, which had become operational nine years before, was not used; moreover it was not even considered as a means of delivery by the Admiral to whom fell the privilege of sending the most important dispatch of his life. Here is what happened after Trafalgar.

## HM Schooner *Pickle*

The news of the victory off Cape Trafalgar on 21 October, 30 miles (48km) south of Cadiz, and of Nelson's death was carried by the fastest vessel in the fleet, the *Pickle*, until her landfall at Falmouth on 4 November, from where it was taken by successive teams of horses until its arrival in London in the early hours of 6 November.* The need for speed in the delivery of this news needs no amplification, the importance of the news is impossible to overstate. Nelson had died the death he wished for, in a battle which saw the annihilation of the enemy fleets, and for himself, and not to exaggerate, immortality:† and an escape from the social mire into which his relationship with Emma Hamilton was taking him. Additionally, Nelson's death and Trafalgar were to have great personal impacts and consequences on a vice-admiral and two of Nelson's captains. None could have imagined what the day would bring for them personally, even as the battle was at the point of being won. Vice-Adm (later Adm Lord) Collingwood (1750–1810), Nelson's second-in- command, had been in HMS *Royal Sovereign* which had headed the leeward of Nelson's two battle-columns; the first being headed by Nelson himself, in *Victory*. During the battle, *Royal Sovereign* received a terrible battering and had lost her masts and rigging. On Nelson's death, Collingwood became Commander-in-Chief of the British Mediterranean Fleet, but he was in a crippled ship: the stage was set for a moment of glory for Capt Blackwood and his ship HMS *Euryalus*. Collingwood, being unable to manoeuvre or signal:

> . . . called the *Euryalus* over . . . while the action continued, which ship lying within hail, made my signals [for me] – a service Captain

---

*By coincidence, this is the same date as the announcement of the news in 1942 of the victory at El Alamein. Although the news of the victory brought forth much joy, in the manner of Trafalgar, including the ringing of church bells for the first time since 1940, its impact was not of the same order because the battle was known to be taking place and hints of victory were also in the air.

†Trafalgar Square, one of the greatest architectural sites in London, was conceived by John Nash in 1828 but not built (to a design by Sir Charles Barry) until after 1840. Nelson's Column was added a few years later to give the site its permanent celebration of British sea power; that this was done over 35 years after the battle reflects how sublime his memory had become and remains. No one could have been ignorant of the celebration of the centenary in 1905, and, even today, his enduring valedictory exhortation 'England expects . . .' is still remembered.

> Blackwood performed with great attention: after the action, I shifted my flag to her, that I might more easily communicate any orders to . . . collect the ships . . . and . . . [tow] the *Royal Sovereign* out to seaward.[6]

## Lt Lapenotière

But, the most surprised captain of the hour was Lt Lapenotière (1770–1834). From a Jersey family and now master of the schooner *Pickle*, he it was who was tasked by Collingwood to make haste from Trafalgar to England and then London with the news of the great victory and the death of Nelson. Lapenotière would have seen the battle take place from a distance and have observed how Nelson's tactics were so successful, for *Pickle* was not built for fighting but (in Bermuda) for speed, and now Lapenotière was '. . . in the most important week of his life. . . . Events were whirling about him, or to phrase it more modestly, he was bobbing about in the thick of great events much as *Pickle* had bobbed about in the battle a week ago'.[7]

Lapenotière's instructions were explicit:

> By Cuthbert Collingwood
> Vice Admiral of the Blue [an organizational division of the Navy]
> Commanding a squadron of His Majesty's Ships off Cadiz
>
> You are hereby required and directed to proceed in His Majesty's Schooner [*Pickle*] under your command to England, and on your arrival at Plymouth [note: no mention of Portsmouth where the telegraph was] you are immediately to forward the accompanying Dispatches to the Secretary of the Admiralty, by taking them yourself express to him . . .
>
> Should you be prevented by Easterly Winds from fetching so high up as Plymouth, you are to make the first port you can in England, and act as is above directed, taking care to obtain a receipt for the dispatches, with which you are charged, and which are of the highest importance.
>
> As I trust you are fully aware of the great importance of these dispatches being forwarded as soon as possible, I rely on your using every exertion that a moment's time may not be lost in their delivery.
> Given on board the *Euryalus*
> Off Cadiz, 26 October 1805 Cuthbert Collingwood
> To Lieutenant Lapenotière,
> Commanding His Majesty's Schooner *Pickle*
> By command of the Vice Admiral
> If necessary, these Dispatches are to be thrown overboard, and for which you are to be prepared.

Lapenotière was delayed in his departure by a storm (which wrought much damage to the survivors of the battle) and it was 26 October before he set off. He made his landfall at Falmouth on 4 November, commemorated by a plaque on Fish Strand Quay, not far from the National Maritime Museum Cornwall, which reads:

> On 4th November 1805 Lieutenant John Lapenotière, Captain of HM Schooner Pickle, landed near here with official dispatches from Vice-Admiral Collingwood. These announced the victory at the battle of Trafalgar and reported the death in action of Admiral Lord Nelson.
>
> By noon Lapenotière had left by post-chaise for London where he reported to the Admiralty some 38 hours later. Normal stagecoaches took a week for this journey!
>
> J.R. Lapenotière, born at Ilfracombe in 1770, joined the Navy in 1780, rose to the rank of Captain and died in Liskeard in 1834.
>
> Erected by the Falmouth Civic Society
>
> 1982

## The Dispatches

Collingwood's account of the battle, written in the *Euryalus* on the following day, was to be published to the world in *The London Gazette Extraordinary* on 6 November 1805. Addressing himself to the Secretary to the Admiralty, he wrote:

> *Euryalus*, off Cadiz
> 26 October 1805
> Sir
> My dispatches containing the account of the action of the 21st inst, and detailing the proceedings of the fleet to the 24th will be delivered to you by Lieut Lapenotière commanding the Pickle Schooner, to be laid before the Lords Commissioners of the Admiralty, having no means of speedier, or safer Conveyance, with me at present. Duplicates* of the dispatches, and the necessary reports shall follow the moment they can be obtained.
> I am sir your most obedient humble servant.
> Cuthbert Collingwood

*Collingwood sent the *Entreprenante* in to Faro, in Portugal, with duplicate dispatches for the British embassy in Lisbon for onward transmission to the Admiralty.

## Why Not Portsmouth?

We do not know what time of day on 26 October the *Pickle* broke away from the fleet off Cadiz and made for Plymouth, but it was before noon on 4 November, eight days later, when she arrived in Falmouth, a distance of around 1,500 miles (2,400km): crudely, nearly 8mph (13km/sec) (disregarding any tacking that had to be done). Lapenotière and the *Pickle* had run a similar errand before; in February 1803, the favoured messenger had sailed from Malta in the *Pickle* with dispatches, arriving in Plymouth fourteen days later, where he also took a post-chaise for London. On this new voyage progress in the Western Approaches was very slow in spite of the *Pickle's* fourteen guns being jettisoned over the sides, and, in accordance with Collingwood's instructions, she put in at Falmouth instead of Plymouth. But the most important question is: what about Portsmouth? Why, in the space of eighteen months was *Pickle* twice carrying dispatches with news that had to be conveyed as fast as possible to London, tasked to Plymouth, and not Portsmouth where the shutter telegraph was located? It was as if the telegraph did not exist. Collingwood, apparently, never gave it a thought; but the telegraph had been opened in Portsmouth in 1796. Allen and Cross,[8] two present-day Nelsonic historians, are dismissive of the point; they concede that 'At Portsmouth there was a telegraph' but then somewhat weakly suggest that 'it was not sufficiently sophisticated . . . to have conveyed news of this importance.' Sophistication is not really the issue, we need some better understanding of why Collingwood, who must have been aware of the Admiralty's telegraph facility, in framing his particularly explicit and meticulous instructions did not even consider the Portsmouth telegraph. No contemporary source having been found to throw light on this, we can only conclude that the top Navy brass distrusted the telegraph because of its risk of closure, sometimes for days, because of fog; or, alternatively, was it a matter of professional pride, was this news just too hot to have anyone but the courier himself deliver it hotfoot? It remains a mystery, and a sharp contrast to the practice in France.

## The News Breaks

In Truro, only a few miles from Falmouth on Lapenotière's route to London, the *Royal Cornwall Gazette* had been published weekly since 1801. Although the first edition containing the Trafalgar news was not published until five days later, on Saturday, 9 November, the delay allowed for the coverage, not only of the news as Lapenotière passed through Truro, but of the London reaction to it, which had had time to come back to Truro by mail coach. When the first news of the victory at Trafalgar was celebrated in Truro, it was not saddened by the knowledge of Nelson's death; we can suppose that

Lapenotière shouted the news of the victory only as he sped through the town, certainly he was not in the business of stopping for a conversation. The *Royal Cornwall Gazette* claims, with justification, to have had the honour of being the first press recipient of the news, and Truro was celebrating the victory – indeed, had celebrated it – even as the metropolis was receiving it.

What the inhabitants of Truro heard first was not in the weekly newspaper, but by an illumination (a sort of nineteenth-century neon sign) announcing the victory outside the newspaper's subscription news-room. The scene was captured and published a few days later:

> At the moment we are writing . . . we are surrounded with shouts of exaltation and tears of sorrow. Our town is illuminated with a radiance worthy of its respectable inhabitants. The volunteers [the local militia recruited as a defence against invasion] are firing feux de joye in the Square. The town is crested with fire rockets and dazzling with tapers. [a description of the decoration of various private houses follows] . . . But the principal point of attraction is the Subscription News-room, in the square, where the British ensign waves in conspicuous pride . . .[9]

When the news arrived in Plymouth (not on the route out of Cornwall) – it probably came via Exeter – it was evening. A play was being performed at the theatre and one of the cast interrupted it as he rushed on to the stage with the news of the victory at which 'Hats, cloaks and doublets flew up and *Rule Britannia* was sung', but, after it became clear to the audience that the victory had been marred by Nelson's death, 'women sobbed and strong men's eyes were dimmed. The [play] . . . was abandoned, and the audience dispersed to mournful music'.[10]

The people of Penzance have always claimed that it was their town which heard and celebrated the news first. The story goes that *Pickle* chanced by a fishing boat off the Lizard, which returned to Penzance and gave the news to the mayor who announced it during a ball in what is now the dining room of the Union Hotel. This suggests that the news arrived in Penzance in the evening of 3 November; this is entirely compatible with *Pickle*'s arriving in Falmouth (to the east) on the morning of 4 November. No contemporary records are available to prove the story – the *Royal Cornwall Gazette* is silent – but the point of greater interest is that the story is still current nearly 200 years later. It is all part of the Nelsonian industry. According to a local history,[11] there is a banner dating from the time in Madron Church (the mother church of Penzance) commemorating the death of Nelson.

Lapenotière was not, of course, concerned with such matters. He arrived at the Admiralty in the early hours of 6 November, where he delivered the news, saying, 'Sir, we have won a great victory, but we have lost Lord Nelson.' One can almost feel the commotion which the news must have created at the Admiralty, and, as London woke, throughout the metropolis. The news, spreading like wildfire, would have travelled away from London at the speed of the first mail coaches to leave from dawn on that day. The same day as it arrived, the news was published in *The London Gazette*:

> *London, Wednesday Nov 6.*
> Between one and two o'clock this morning a Lieutenant of the Navy arrived at the Admiralty. As soon as his dispatches had been opened, expresses [urgent dispatches] were sent of to His Majesty, and to all the Ministers. At an early hour the Admiralty was besieged by anxious enquirers; it was known that intelligence of the utmost importance had been received.

There then followed what might be called a nineteenth-century press notice, shown in the box below.

*Admiralty, 6th November.*
Lieut. Lapenotière, of the *Pickle* Schooner, arrived this night with dispatches from Vice-Admiral Collingwood, announcing a glorious victory gained by His Majesty's fleet off Cadiz under the command of Lord Viscount Nelson.

On 19th October, the enemy's fleet, consisting of 33 sail of the line, four frigates, and two brigs, came out of Cadiz, and on the 21st at noon, were brought to action by the British fleet, consisting of 27 sail of the line, (seven having been previously detached under Rear-Admiral Louis) four frigates, and two smaller vessels. The engagement lasted four hours, and terminated by nineteen ships of the enemy's line striking their colours [surrendering], and being taken [into] possession, exclusive of one which blew up in the action.

Lord Nelson's ship being closely engaged with the *Santissima Trinidada*, and others of the enemy's ships, a musket shot, fired from the top, wounded his Lordship in the shoulder, and deprived him of his most useful life.

A gale . . . coming on next day . . . increasing in violence . . . [until] many of the prizes broke adrift, and being close to a lee shore, it is supposed that several of them must have been wrecked; and the Vice-Admiral had made a signal for destroying all that could not be brought away. Two ships, from which the crews could not be removed, made their escape into Cadiz.

The government, anxious as it was to spread the news to its allies, had 3,000 copies of *The London Gazette* announcement printed and sent by fast boat to the Continent.[12] It was as important to assure Britain's enemies as well as her friends of the scale of the loss that had been afflicted on the combined Spanish and French fleets. To make sure that the French civilian population learned the unvarnished truth, instead of a sanitized version which might be offered by their controlled press, an event took place which seems comic: an empty boat was let adrift just off Boulogne; the tide took it inshore, *The London Gazette* on board, and this is how the story, so enfeebling to the prospects of their navy, was announced to the French. As we shall see, this method of news delivery was to level the score, because just days before the French had announced their victory at Ulm by the same method.

As the news spread, 'It broke upon a London whisperingly aware of the victory, but unwilling to rejoice. Groups had begun to gather at the doors of newspaper offices in front of the Mansion House and Lloyds, and each shivering new-comer added his question to the rest: Is it true about Nelson?'[13]

The combination of jubilation and grief was difficult to handle, as *The Times* put it, 'We know not whether to mourn or rejoice. The country has gained the most splendid and decisive victory that has ever graced the annals of England: but it has been dearly purchased. The great and gallant Nelson is no more.'

## The Nile

The juxtaposition of how the news of the battles of Trafalgar and the Nile, seven years apart, arrived in London is fascinating. The news of Trafalgar arrived out of the blue only fifteen days after the event, with the telegraph playing no role in its transmission; the news of the Battle of the Nile took sixty-one days to reach London, preceded by false reports and rumours of the victory which had been carried by the Deal telegraph. Lt Thomas Bladen Capel (later Adm the Hon. Sir Bladen) was to play, in a makeshift way, the role of Lapenotière. But when Capel arrived in London on 2 October 1798, he had come, not from Falmouth, but overland from Naples. HMS *Leander* had been ordered by Nelson to take the news to England, just as the *Pickle* was to do seven years later, but disaster befell *Leander* after she had set out: Nelson's dispatch ended at the bottom of the Mediterranean weighed down with shot.

The battle had been joined at dusk on 1 August 1798; as the sound of the last shots died away, the remains of the French fleet littered the waters of Aboukir Bay. Probably no victorious fleet has ever been as isolated as was Nelson's as dawn broke the following day: the shore was hostile, for the French army held Egypt while at sea the atlas tells us how far away is the eastern Mediterranean, from Gibraltar even, let alone England: 'The nearest British warship . . . was 2,000 miles [3,200km] away at Gibraltar. At the most optimistic estimate it would take three weeks to get a message home . . . Nelson had no frigates to spread the news to friendly lands and was almost completely out of contact with the world.'[14]

The victory changed the course of history by bringing European affairs back to centre stage: India was saved, but because he had not been captured on the high seas, Napoleon's greatest days were ahead of him. As Nelson surveyed the scale of his success at daybreak on 2 August, and, having a wide-ranging strategic mind as well as a deep sense of duty, he had to look to both the east and the west to dispatch his news. To the east was India, the target of Napoleon's expedition – how was the news to be sent there? To have sent it by sea back to Gibraltar, round the Cape of Good Hope and through the Indian Ocean would have taken an age.

Nelson had himself been wounded and it was 3 August before he finished his main report to Adm St Vincent, who was somewhere off Cadiz. His need to know that the French fleet did not exist anymore and that Nelson's squadron lay damaged in the eastern Mediterranean was even more urgent than London's. Nelson's flag-captain from the *Vanguard*, Edward Berry, was chosen to play the role that Lapenotière was to take after Trafalgar, and the fifty-gun *Leander*, under Capt Thomas Boulden Thompson,* was dispatched to find St Vincent, and then, like the *Pickle*, take the news home. It was not to be: just twelve days out, on 18 August, the *Leander* had the misfortune to run across one of the few French ships to escape from the battle. The *Leander* first attempted to evade what turned out to be the seventy-four-gun *Généreux*, but, being slower, turned to face the enemy, and after an engagement which lasted over seven hours and after sending the precious dispatches over the side, the gallant *Leander* had to surrender when she could fire no longer; fame and fortune were not to be hers, nor Capt Berry's. In due course, after being released from captivity, Capt Thompson faced a court martial for losing the *Leander* but it concluded that he, his officers and crew had conducted a 'gallant and almost unprecedented defence . . . against so superior a force as that of the *Généreux*'† which was 'deserving of every praise his country and this court can give'.[15] Nelson spent much of his career in high office lamenting the shortage of frigates; after the Battle of the Nile his lack of them meant that he was unable to follow the desired practice of sending the same message in two different ships. The loss

---

*Capt Thomas Boulden Thompson had served alongside Rear-Adm Popham when they were both lieutenants on a voyage in 1784 under Thompson's uncle, Capt Ned (Poet) Thompson.

†The *Généreux* had its moment of glory in preventing the fast carriage of the *Leander's* dispatch to London, but the tables were turned two years later when Nelson captured her off Malta, to be followed shortly after by the taking of the last French survivor of the Battle of the Nile.

of the solitary frigate *Leander* meant that the vital news spread round Europe haphazardly, with the proper story often preceded by rumour. Moreover, and sadly, for historiography, there are comparatively few personal accounts of the Battle of the Nile because three bags of mail went to the bottom along with Nelson's dispatch.[16]

It was a French ship which was the first to give an account of the battle; having arrived off the Nile as the battle was raging and seen *l'Orient* blow up, the non-combatant transport made off and ended at the Turkish-held island of Rhodes. The Turkish governor sent a substantially accurate report to his government in Constantinople, where it arrived on 22 August, four days after *Leander* had surrendered. The British ambassador, Spencer Smith, was informed and sent a message overland to London and, separately, to the British ambassador in Vienna. The bona fides of the report remained unconfirmed, however, and Smith spent an uncomfortable two weeks before the story was verified to him.[17] In the meanwhile, the news, which by now had also been sent to the Russians at St. Petersburg, had set out on three of its many overland journeys, one of which was to India.

## The News Goes to India

The journey of the news to India gives colour to the task of messengers before the telegraph came to ease their toil. India, it will be recalled, was central to Napoleon's ambition in Egypt and its protection was the object of Nelson's ultimately failed attempt to intercept his invasion fleet. But even though Napoleon got his army ashore, it was marooned and could not be supplied; it was vital to let it be known in India that Napoleon had been thwarted. Nelson ordered Lt Duval of HMS *Zealous* to take his dispatches overland via Alexandretta in the north-east corner of the Mediterranean; he carried an open letter to any British representatives, seeking every assistance and a supply of funds on bills of exchange drawn on the East India Company. Duval left on 11 August in a local coastal craft, but, on arrival in Alexandretta four days later, he found that there was no British representation there. Instead, the news was given to the Turkish governor, who sent him off on the journey of a lifetime:

> . . . the lieutenant was dressed in Arab cloths and given a servant and two guards for the journey to Aleppo, some miles inland. There he was supplied with . . . camels and an escort of twenty-four Arabs for the journey across the desert. On 4 September they arrived at the Euphrates and on the 7th at Baghdad. . . . He was offered a boat to take him down the Tigris and on the 19th he arrived at Basra. There he found the *Fly*, packet boat, and was taken to Bombay, arriving on 21 October, after a journey of 10 weeks by land and sea.[18]

In a strange example of how variable could be the rate at which news travelled before the telegraphs, the Governor-General of India had had little time to react to and assess the new danger that had been presented to him by Napoleon's having landed in Egypt. If the Governor-General's period of nervous waiting was short, as we shall see, some of the great players in European politics had a longer period of anxiety to endure before relief came. Duval must have been one of the first Europeans to make the overland journey to India. Happily, Turkey joined the war against Napoleon on hearing of his defeat at the Nile and the Ottoman Empire controlled the land over which Duval had to cross, but he did not know that when he set out on his remarkable journey. This was to be the precursor of the established fast route to India. Decades later, but well before the electric telegraph connected London to India in 1860, there was to be developed an overland mail route to India to avoid the long haul round the Cape.

## The *Mutine*

Nelson, of course, knew nothing of *Leander*'s fate. Some ten days after the battle his fleet was joined by a number of frigates which, to the regret of their crews, had missed the battle: the business of naval warfare had a random ingredient in it – ships could pass within 25 miles (40km) or so of each other unknowingly, for the veil of the horizon was absolute. If the ship unseen were the enemy, an engagement would be postponed, or if the ship was friendly, the joining of a fleet would be postponed. It would take the invention of radio to overcome this fact of maritime life. A planned rendezvous on the high seas could be achieved only by ships sailing up and down an agreed line of latitude, for an agreed distance, until a sighting was made. But with the arrival of the frigates, Nelson had the opportunity to send a further dispatch to duplicate the *Leander*'s. On 13 August he ordered his Capt Capel to take the little HMS *Mutine* and 'proceed with all possible dispatch to some place in the continent of Europe, in the Neapolitan territories'.[19] The *Mutine* was a fast brig and Capel was setting out on a journey that fiction could not have invented; he left on 13 August and subsequently, approaching the tip of Italy, found two damaged ships, one under tow. This was the *Généreux* with the plucky but unfortunate captive *Leander*; unhappily for Capel, the *Leander* was not identified, she was mistaken for the *Guillaume Tell*, one of the other few French ships to escape from the Nile. How different Capel's story might have been if he had realized that the *Leander*'s dispatches had been lost; he would have taken his own to St Vincent in substitution of Berry's. In the days when there were no means of consulting superiors, ships' captains were expected to react to a new situation on their own initiative; if he had gone closer to the pair of ships and discovered that the *Leander* had been taken, he would doubtless have made straight for Gibraltar, then St Vincent and on to London. It was not to be.

As it was, Capel arrived in Naples on 4 September. The *Mutine* was observed entering the Bay of Naples by Miss Cornelia Knight, an Englishwoman and lady companion to the Princess of Wales, resident at the time with her mother. Her autobiography records how:

> Our telescope was constantly directed towards the entrance of the beautiful bay . . . I happened to turn my head towards the sea, and I thought I discerned a sloop of war . . . I consulted the . . . [telescope] . . . Presently we saw a boat pull off from the shore . . . [and the motioning of two officers suggested:] News of a victory . . .[20]

Capel reported to Sir William Hamilton, the British ambassador in Naples. This positive news of the battle, now over a month old, eliminated a lengthy period of intense anxiety for Hamilton. All that he had known for sure was that Nelson had gone in search of Napoleon's fleet, that it had been seen in Aboukir Bay had been known for only a few days, but what had become of Nelson? Had he found the French? Had battle been joined? What was the result? It was not since the end of June that Hamilton had had any certain news of Nelson, and in the meanwhile the agonies of waiting had been punctuated only with rumour or insubstantial reports. Now the news from Capel, a participant in the battle, broke like a thunderclap, 'I am totally unable to express the joy that appeared in everybody's countenance and the bursts of applause and acclamation we received', Capel reported. Miss Knight could scarcely contain herself as the news broke around her, she rushed into the apartment of her high-ranking Neapolitan neighbour, a general who was entertaining a party of officers, and broke the news; she wrote, 'Never shall I forget the shouts, the bursts of applause, the toasts drank, the glasses broken one after another. . . .'[21]

## Lt Capel's Overland Journey

After a little time to take in all the fuss around him, Capel set off on an extraordinary journey which was to end in London, via Vienna, where at the Admiralty he was able to confirm the news of the victory which had preceded him by rumour and an unconfirmed report by telegraph. At first he was taken by ship up the Adriatic to Trieste, and then the 300 miles (480km) to Vienna.[22] Reports of the battle had already arrived there on 8 September; this was the French report that had reached Constantinople via the Turkish governor of Rhodes. Capel reached Vienna on 19 September to confirm the reports.

> [Near] . . . Vienna, the great composer Joseph Haydn had been working at a mass since 10 July and completed it on 31 August. He could not have heard the news of the Battle of the Nile for at least a week after the completion but the work included a flourish of trumpets, which was appropriate to the great victory, and it soon became known as the Nelson Mass.[23]

Naples apart, Berlin was the only major court to receive the official news (on 23 September) in advance of the rumour, the British ambassador in Vienna, 400 miles (640km) away, having sent a dispatch. Capel, however, was London-bound; he reached Cuxhaven on the German North Sea coast on 27 September, only twenty-three days after he had arrived in Naples, and having covered over 1,000 miles (1,600km) overland from Trieste via Vienna. From there he was taken to England by the Royal Navy to Yarmouth (where the telegraph was not yet installed), and then on to London and the Admiralty on 2 October, having been dispatched from the eastern end of the Mediterranean on 23 August; this was two months before the same news was to reach the Governor-General of India.

Capel's arrival brought only confirmation of the news: to tell the evolution of the story as it appeared in London we must go back to 10 August, when French newspapers of 8 and 9 August had arrived. These contained vague reports of an action between Nelson and Bonaparte; these were probably based on false reports, but they were enough to set nerves jangling. The news on 21 August was grim: an official report coming overland from Turkey told of the evasion of attack on the high seas by Napoleon and his success in getting his army ashore in Egypt. Sir Henry Dundas, the Secretary-at-War and a director of the East India Company, not knowing that Duval was, at the time, somewhere between the Mediterranean Sea and the Persian Gulf, bound for India, was gloomy:

> Although the accounts from Constantinople are confused, I take it for granted that there is no just ground of doubt that Bonaparte has made good his landing with a large force in Egypt . . . I am always in hopes that we shall hear of Nelson doing something brilliant with regard to the fleet . . . [but the country has to come to terms with] . . . the misfortune it has undergone by the French with a large army getting possession of Egypt. The circumstance haunts me night and day . . .[24]

During the long month of September 1798 nothing of substance was received in London, except the confirmation that Nelson had (to the eternal fortune of Napoleon) not made an interception on the high seas. Some people started to reposition their attitude towards Nelson, lest he had sustained a strategic defeat. Earl Spencer, First Lord of the Admiralty, wrote to Nelson:

> You may easily conceive the anxiety we have been under about you and your operations and the distance at which you are really placed from us increased as it is by the present very inconvenient situation of Europe for communication [of which ample evidence has been given here] make it impossible almost to know what to write.[25]

This despairing note seemed not to have been assuaged by the unconfirmed report that had come in to the Admiralty by the telegraph from Deal around 20 September. Evidently, a neutral ship had come into Dover with reports from the French press of an action near Alexandria in which both sides had lost ships (untrue, only the French lost ships) but stating that the French flagship had blown up,* which, indeed, *l'Orient* had so spectacularly that during the battle it had 'silenced rage with awe'.[26] On 26 September the story that had travelled from the French ship that had observed the battle, coming via Rhodes and Constantinople, arrived in Dover. The Foreign Office took this as confirmation and wrote officially to the City of London. Parliament was at the time adjourned so no official account of the situation on that day was recorded there.

The news was all over London by the evening of 2 October. Lady Spencer, living with her husband at the Admiralty, was one of the first to hear it and had no inhibitions in expressing her emotions: 'Captain Capel just arrived! Joy, joy, joy to you, brave, gallant, immortalised Nelson.' Her husband, who had written so anxiously only a few days earlier, wrote more formally: 'Since my last letter . . . I have had the satisfaction of receiving your letters by Captain Capel and most sincerely and cordially do I congratulate you on the very brilliant and signal service you have performed to your country in the glorious action of the 1st August last.'[27]

Thus was the news of the Nile received in London. The news of its arrival in Paris is less well documented and, in any event because none of the detail was known to the French ship that had observed the battle and reported it in Rhodes, it could not arrive in a single report from the site of the battle. Moreover, because the press was censored and the release of bad news had to be managed, it was no doubt known in Paris well before it was generally released: it was not until 11 October (nine days after it was celebrated in London) that the news was carried by telegraph from Paris to Strasbourg[28] It was a fine illustration of bad news travelling slower than good.

---

*The poem 'The boy stood on the burning deck/Whence all but he had fled . . .' was inspired by the blowing up of *l'Orient*: the captain had died, but his son 'The boy' could not disobey his father's command never to leave the ship unless instructed to do so by his now dead father; hence the boy 'The noblest thing which perished there' was doomed (Lacheze, H., *The Nelson Dispatch*, vol.8, part 3 [July 2003]).

# 9
# 'There are Bitter Weeds in England'

*When Napoleon lay at Boulogne for a year with his flat-bottomed boats and his Grand Army, he was told by someone, 'there are bitter weeds in England'.*
Winston Churchill, House of Commons, 4 June 1940

*I do not say the French cannot come,*
*but I do say they cannot come by water.*
Earl St Vincent

## The Peace of Amiens

In 1800, having taken the field against the second coalition, Napoleon achieved such success that, by 1801, all the continental enemies of France had been beaten. All that had been expected from the coup had been delivered, save for the ruin of England and now for the second time she stood alone against France. There now took place, on 2 April 1801, a naval battle at Copenhagen in which Nelson was again victorious. Perversely, if there had been a telegraph link in place to transmit the dramatic news from Russia that she had reversed her hostility to Britain, a confrontation between Britain and Denmark, Russia's ally, would not have been necessary. As it was, the news arrived from St Petersburg at the speed of the horse and it was too late to stop an unnecessary battle taking place. If ever there were an illustration of how the world was changing and how vital it was for diplomats to have the fastest communication of pivotal news it was supplied by Copenhagen. British diplomats were slower to heed the lesson than was Napoleon. The victory, stunning though it was, proved to be a serious embarrassment to the British government because it should not have happened, and there was no benefit to be gained by making new enemies. In the new situation, the mood and the opportunity for peace conjoined.

By this time both the British and the French had grown weary of a war in which there seemed to be no prospect of a decisive result. Certainly the Navy had achieved a massive supremacy: during the eight years of war its capacity had grown, in spite of losses, from 135 ships of the line and 133 frigates to 202 and 277, respectively; against this the French navy had been reduced by half for by 1801 there were only thirty-nine battleships and thirty-five frigates left.[1] This was a tremendous absolute superiority of naval power, but, although Napoleon was never able to break it, Britain's sea power held no sway on the land mass of Europe. Napoleon's armies had overcome those of two coalitions against them and all of western and southern Europe was in Napoleon's grip. From this position, where the prospect of conquering the European mainland was as plainly beyond the British as was overcoming the Royal Navy beyond Napoleon, France called a halt. Worming and squirming his way through the peace negotiations, Napoleon's guile was disguised: he needed to draw breath before taking on the islanders again, his vanity would not allow him to be satisfied with what he had already achieved. Bryant described Britain, showing an impatience for peace at this time, as:

> A nation which . . . had temporarily forgotten what it was fighting for. The changes of the European scene had been so dazzling, the exhaustion of the war so great, that the British people were in a state of bewilderment.[2]

This harsh judgement, more properly reflecting Napoleon's misjudgement of a peaceable people, was not to be long in its reversal. But Napoleon had gained the initiative, a dictator can always outwit a democracy. This was the one thing that assured Napoleon's success, thought Edgar Quinet, writing in the 1860s:

> He perceived from afar the goal towards which he strove. Among the men of his generation he was the only one who had known for a long time what he wanted. While the others were running aimlessly backwards and forwards, he went straight ahead. Absolute power was his compass.[3]

One illustration of his guile will suffice, one which demonstrates again the power of fast information which was now becoming available more readily to Napoleon than to his opponents via the telegraph. Britain expected a French withdrawal from Egypt, where Napoleon had left his army in 1799, as part of the paucity of concessions he was to make in the preliminary peace negotiations; threatening to withdraw from them unless they were completed quickly, Napoleon tricked the British into concessions while knowing what the British did not. Thanks to his faster communications, Napoleon knew that defeat in Egypt at the hands of a British expeditionary force had delivered what the British negotiators thought they were extracting as a concession. In a further illustration of the power of speed of communication, in October 1801, a French admiral at Brest was able to send a letter under a flag of truce to Adm Sir William Cornwallis (1744–1819)*, whose fleet was blockading the port, informing him of a telegraphic message received that day, signed by 'A Chappe', to the effect that peace had broken out.[4] This news of the preliminary agreement which preceded the Treaty contrasts with the news of the Russian volte-face a few months earlier, which did not arrive in time to prevent the Battle of Copenhagen. If any illustration were necessary of the vital need for military and political leaders to be informed at least as fast of key events, if not faster than their opponents, here it was.

The preliminaries to the peace were signed in London on 1 October, and the Strasbourg telegraph carried news of it three days later.[5] Few good judges thought that the Peace Treaty signed on 27 March 1802 had actually settled anything, but the summer of 1802 saw England relaxing in the sunshine of the Amiens agreement. Wearied by nine years of strife, crushing taxation and starvation prices, the masses rejoiced at the thought of the return of peace and plenty.[6] But in political circles, except for Henry Addington (later 1st Viscount Sidmouth 1759–1844), the new prime minister following Pitt's resignation in 1801 and his appeasing political allies, there were few right-thinking or far-seeing supporters in England for the treaty. Whatever political will England wanted to exercise on the Continent, and at the least she wanted to restrain any further extension of Napoleon's dominion within it, the opportunity had been sacrificed by the treaty. It was for England (we should, of course, say Great Britain, for the union had been completed in 1801) that Napoleon maintained his contempt. Finding it inexplicable how the London press could be allowed, without implied government approval,

---

*Nothing has been heard in our story of Adm Cornwallis: it is only at this point that the story of the telegraph touches him, but he was a significant naval leader of the time; a great friend of Nelson, but opposite in character: Nelson, the pugilist, tearing into his enemies with no thought for anything but victory: Cornwallis with a peerless reputation as a tactician. After Pitt's resignation and the arrival of the Addington ministry in February 1801, the newly appointed Earl St Vincent selected Cornwallis for the key role of commander of the Channel Fleet. He flew his flag in the 110-gun *Ville de Paris* – a battleship which will reappear here – and took up the task of blockading Brest. Later, after war broke out again, Cornwallis was in the same job and is credited, by decisions he took in August 1805, with ensuring that when Trafalgar was fought in October, Napoleon was miles from the Channel and Villeneuve was heading for Sicily: in this sense it was Cornwallis, not Nelson, who denied the French the opportunity to invade England. As Andrew Lambert said (in P. le Fevre and R. Harding [eds], *The Precursors of Nelson*, Chapter 14, whom I acknowledge for this vignette): 'While Nelson might annihilate the enemy, Cornwallis was the Admiral who would not be defeated, and possessed the temperament and resilience for a monotonous, dreary and yet dangerous task [the blockade of Brest]. His selection was inspired.'

to offer such insults as it did as his treachery became exposed, Napoleon bridled, being unused to public criticism. In France the excesses of Revolutionary licence had been succeeded by a censorship more rigid, perversely, than that of the monarchy it had replaced. He returned every libel, as he described the press's jibes, with interest in what was described as 'reciprocal Billingsgate'.

Retaining by the treaty only her ring of salt water, and conceding French occupation of Belgium and the Rhineland, Britain's political effectiveness had been relegated, while Napoleon held much of Europe in his thrall; in large part this was with consent, in other parts less so. The dictator blustered and bullied for he wanted his way with Switzerland. From London the protests and diplomatic messages of Addington's appeasers travelled into Europe's capitals at the speed of the horse. Napoleon, whether from Paris or elsewhere on his telegraphic network, pulled the strings in his dominions at hundreds of miles per hour. Without allies and with no standing army of continental scale or ambition Britain was enfeebled in the face of Napoleon's power.

During the pause, Napoleon took the opportunity to have himself appointed First Consul for life (his first appointment had been for ten years). A plebiscite confirmed the appointment by a majority of over 400 to one. In the style of monarchs, he had himself referred to as Napoleon, his Christian name, while his surname Bonaparte was dispensed with as being the mark of ordinariness. In this repackaging of himself he was entirely successful: while still referred to as 'Boney' on the streets in England, he gave his name, nonetheless, to the Napoleonic legend, and the wars which began again in 1803 became known as the Napoleonic Wars.

## The Depillion Semaphore

During the peace one of Napoleon's dominating thoughts was the strategic advantage held by the Royal Navy and how it could be overcome in a new war. A new development in telegraphy was to give him the opportunity to gain an advantage. In 1801 an artillery officer turned inventor named Depillion promulgated a telegraph system which had advantages over the Chappe system, and which was, in fact, to be the forerunner of the our own semaphore system It was a three-armed affair, compared with the later, English two arms, when it was introduced twenty years later. One of the advantages claimed by Depillion for the new system was that it was particularly useful for ship-to-shore work; it was adopted almost at once for coastal signalling and it was installed along the whole of the French coastline from about 1803. Naturally, this new signalling device came under the observation of the Royal Navy; a captain wrote that 'This telegraph seems so simple, and at the same time so comprehensive, that I take the liberty of forwarding . . . a sketch for the . . . Admiralty.'[7]

In contemplating the problems of a cross-Channel invasion, Napoleon could hope for nothing better than to gain a tactical surprise over the Navy; an attempt to get his army across the Channel without interception might be made if the order to go could be informed by intelligence of the Royal Navy's movements. Napoleon could see that his coastal semaphore system would give some tactical advantage over their otherwise unbeatable opponent. One of the reasons why the English had gained such a naval supremacy during this period, apart from the Revolutionary purges having destroyed much French naval ability, was their blockade of French ports. This meant that neither the French navy nor that of any ally was able to leave port freely; in consequence, sea skills could not be practised and neither could battle-winning manoeuvres be developed; Nelson was the master of such tactics and was the most acclaimed practitioner of close-quarter engagements. The French coastal telegraphs were considered a sufficient menace for the English to use their sea power to land raiding parties to silence them; not only did this derange their signals advantage, but the French were also obliged to employ considerable numbers of troops in its defence: batteries sprang up at all points where the Navy could interfere with coastwise movements and every promontory bristled with guns. As well as fixed defences, detachments of field artillery were stationed at convenient junctions ready to rush to the scene when summoned by the telegraph.[8]

## The Rupture of 1803

Although Britain herself, as well as France, broke some of the terms of the Peace of Amiens, historians generally put the blame for the rupture on Napoleon, who, they assert, never regarded the settlement as anything other than a truce to allow him to strengthen his internal position and win time to consolidate his newly won mastery in Germany and Italy. He would be able to renew the fight with all the more vigour later. According to Geyl, the war with Britain in 1803 was willed by Napoleon; he wished only to give the French people the impression that he had wanted to avoid it.[9] One French historian, Frédéric Masson, an intense admirer of Napoleon writing a century later, saw it all as Britain's fault; he regarded Britain as the enemy throughout the period, since:

> Britain has always pursued her aim of world domination with cold calculation and unrelenting pertinacity, and for this purpose, while roaming the seas and conquering territories, has had to keep the European continent divided. France has no enemy as inevitable as Britain. Napoleon tried to hit her, first by an invasion project, then by unifying the continent. But Britain continued to foment division and to promote the formation of coalitions against the dangerous

> rival. Hypocritical Britain, who begins to call the slave trade immoral once she has no further use for it, but knows that abolition will cause the French West Indies to languish, who fights with the aid of mercenaries, or better still by subsidising rulers . . . Britain on whose account unhappy France has allowed herself to be trapped [a reference to the *entente cordiale* of 1904] into serving, with her blood and probably with her existence as a nation, against the new rival for world markets, Germany; this Britain it is who defeated Napoleon and with him the hope of a united Europe, and this Britain is for ever the enemy of France.

Geyl regarded this as appallingly crude, 'It is certainly only too characteristic of a particular French mentality, and it helps to explain by what ways Napoleon's imperial policy was able for so long to touch French hearts'; but as history, he said, 'it is childish'. 'Hatred of Britain, and the isolation and sterile rigidity of French culture were never so marked,' said Geyl, 'as when the French were poring over the whole continent of Europe,' as they were in 1803.

Geyl also quoted Georges Lefebvre, who regarded it more objectively than Masson:

> There has been passionate debate about the responsibility for the rupture. Bonaparte's provocations are undeniable, but it is no less true that England broke the Treaty and took the initiative for a preventative war, as soon as she could count on Russia. She tried to justify her conduct by pleading her concern for the European balance. But she would not allow the system to extend over the ocean, which had been created by the God of the Bible to be English. As between Bonaparte and England there was not really anything but the clash between two imperialisms.

## The Risk of Invasion in 1803–05

England declared war on France on 17 May 1803; being without allies at this time, Britain stood alone for the third time against France. A month later Nelson sailed from Portsmouth in *Victory*. Neither did it take Napoleon long to mobilize his plan of attack on England. The telegraph network had been expanded further, and, reflecting his ambitions across the Channel, Napoleon had ordered an extension of the Paris–Lille line to Boulogne, via St Omer. As we shall see, this would put Napoleon in direct communication with Brest, whether from Paris or as he lay at Boulogne with his invasion force. For, by 1803, Napoleon had reverted to the view that if he were to achieve the dominion he demanded on the Continent, he would have to remove the biggest obstacle to it, Britain. This would require at least a tactical mastery over the Royal Navy and the telegraph would, he thought, give it to him.

As war began again, Napoleon began assembling a huge invasion force all along the Channel ports and set up a camp for his Armée d'Angleterre, concentrated at Boulogne He decided to have a headquarters near the camp. In August he wrote to Adm Bruix, who commanded the naval force from Boulogne, 'I noticed two country houses near the signal tower on the way from Calais. These two houses seemed to be suitable [for a headquarters] to me.' This proposal was rejected because Napoleon, in fact, set up his headquarters in the château of Pont-de-Briques, about 3 or 4 miles (5–8km) to the south of Boulogne on the Paris road; although the chosen situation was not 'near the signal tower', it would be near enough for a courier to operate between the château and the terminal signal station located on the 'Boulogne belfry'. It did not remain here for long since in 1807 and again in 1809 it was struck by lightning, after which it was moved to the ramparts of the medieval fortifications.[10] In October 1803, with Napoleon's gaze set on England and in a bout of optimism for his invasion project, he ordered Chappe to build a further extension of the telegraph so that the cross-channel communication he craved could be achieved. To do this Chappe conceived of terminal points at a great height: Cap Gris-Nez probably to correspond with Dover Castle, which could easily be linked to Deal, where onward transmission could be achieved, albeit by a different technology. If England were conquered, London would, in theory, have been under Napoleon's remote control from many points in Europe, but visual telegraphic communication in an enemy's interior lines where guerrillas could operate while protected by a sympathetic civilian population was impossible, as Napoleon was to discover to his cost in Spain.

The 15-mile (24km) line from Boulogne to Cap Griz-Nez consisted of two intermediate stations – one at Wimille along the coast and a second at Bazinghen further inland, to gain a line of sight to the coastal cliffs – and was completed in 1805. Reflecting Napoleon's true intentions, the equipment for the future installation of Chappe telegraphs in England was stored in Bazinghen.* Communication was to be capable of day and night service. Experiments by Abraham Chappe (Claude was now dead) were conducted in night-use but the operation of the telegraph at night was not perfected before Napoleon marched east. In fact, it was not until the railways borrowed the semaphore concept for their own signalling needs some thirty years later,† that night-time use was developed into practical

*The linking of Paris to London would have to wait until 1850, when the two cities were linked by the electric telegraph.

†We may note here that the semaphore system of signalling remains in use, albeit on more remote railway lines, nearly 200 years since it was invented by Depillion.

operational deployment. Railway semaphore signalling operated at very close range – a few hundred yards (about 0.8km); it was the great distances that could not be overcome by Chappe.

While all this was going on, Napoleon's ambition was undimmed; declaring his intention with barefaced impertinence, he anticipated his successful invasion by having a medal designed for his '*Descente en Angleterre*', which was to be '*frappé à Londres en 1804*'.[11] But he had not reckoned on the islanders: there was no doubt that, from the king to the humblest peasant, the English intended to stop Napoleon and some French historians have, as we have seen, never forgiven England for it. The underwriters of Lloyd's opened a Patriotic Fund; 5,000 leading merchants met and declared that the independence and existence of the British Empire and the safety, liberty and life of every man were at stake:

> The events perhaps of a few months, certainly of a few years, are to determine whether we and our children are to continue free men and members of the most flourishing community in the world or whether we are to be slaves . . . We fight for our laws and liberties – to defend the dearest hopes of our children – to preserve the . . . [continuity], and existence of the country that gave us birth . . . we fight to preserve the whole earth from the barbarous yoke of military despotism![12]

The Lord Chief Justice spoke of the duty the nation owed to the world to save it from its degraded terror, while bishops exhorted the clergy to remind their congregations of the enemy's cruelty. 'Oh Lord God', prayed an aged nonconformist minister at Colchester, 'be pleased to change the tyrant's wicked heart or stop his wicked breath!'[13]

When the islanders realized that without the defeat of Napoleon there could be no peace, they once again responded as one with defiance. In May 1804 William Pitt had resumed office as Prime Minister, and, rising above petty squabbles, and in terms echoed by Churchill in 1940, focused the attention of the Commons on the real issue:

> We are come to a new era in the history of nations; we are called to struggle for the destiny, not of this country alone but of the civilized world. We must remember that is it is not only for ourselves that we submit to unexampled privations. We have for ourselves the great duty of self-preservation to perform; but the duty of the people of England now is of a nobler and higher order . . . amid the wreck and the misery of nations it is our just exultation that we have continued superior to all that ambition or that despotism could effect; and our still higher exultation ought to be that we provide not only for our

> own safety but hold out the prospect for nations now bending under the iron yoke of tyranny of what the exertions of a free people can effect.

What of the English defences? Adm Lord Keith (1746–1823) (formerly George Keith Elphinstone) had been appointed Commander-in-Chief, North Sea Fleet in 1803, and, while his more famous contemporaries blockaded the French in Toulon and Brest, Keith was in charge of defending the coastline from Selsey Bill in Dorset to the north of Scotland. Of the Navy's pivotal role Keith's assessment was:

> If at any time the British Navy was an object of more peculiar concern to the country than at another, it is at the present, when an implacable enemy threatens us with invasion, and possesses the means of carrying his threats into execution to a greater extent than the political state of Europe ever before allowed . . . According to the enemy, 'the line of coast hostile to Great Britain will soon extend from the . . . Baltic to the Mediterranean', and armies after armies are destined to perish till the Republicans triumph, and Britain is subdued.[14]

An 1803 cartoon caught the mood of defiance: 'Who is it dares interrupt me in my progress?' demands Napoleon as he sat astride a globe; from Britain, a tiny voice replies: 'Why, 'tis I, little John Bull . . . and damn me if you come any further.'

> The maintenance of the one, huge strategic advantage which Britain had at the time – sea power, required the ability of port admirals to be in communication with their home waters fleets. The first coastal signal posts had been established in 1794, before, it should be noted, the shutter telegraph was invented, and were progressively expanded thereafter; in 1797 the *Norwich Mercury* reported that the signalling stations in Norfolk were operating, following the establishment of a naval facility in Yarmouth for the North Sea Fleet in the previous year.[15]

After the Peace of Amiens the English coastal signal station network had been abandoned; but on the day that Britain declared war on France, the Admiralty wrote:

> We do hereby direct you to make immediate application to the owners of the land on which the signal posts are erected for permission to re-establish them, and you are to take the earliest means in your power to put them into a proper state for service . . .[16]

In the next two years there was a spurt of activity in re-erecting the coastal stations and building new ones. Their importance for the defence of the country can be gauged from Keith's order, now Commander-in-Chief of the Channel Fleet, that each station (perhaps fearing raids*)* should be defended by dragoons. Capt Hudleston discovered that the signalling method used on these stations was invented by a Mr Goodhew,[17] and plainly it derived from contemporary methods of ship-to-ship communication. Hudleston, writing in *The Mariner's Mirror*, explained:

> The code used by [the costal signal stations] . . . was one red flag, one blue pennant, and four black balls and contained 145 orders and instructions; and their object was laid down in the orders thus: 'You are to consider the great object of establishing these posts is that no ship or vessel of the enemy shall be able to approach the coast without being discovered . . .'[18]

The technology used by the Admiralty's coastal signalling system predated the first telegraphs (from the Admiralty to Deal and Portsmouth) which came into use in 1796; they had nothing in common with each other, the coastal signalling system being somewhat primitive. All the English land telegraphs (both the shutter variety and the semaphores which replaced them) worked by spelling a message out, letter by letter, and, technically, the coastal stations with their flag-and-ball system, held aloft on masts 20ft (6m) high, were not at this time practising what we should call telegraphy because a dialogue involving infinitely variable text could not take place. This raises the question of why the much better Popham vocabulary code (which had already been developed and which enabled an infinitely variable message to be signalled) was not used by the coastal stations. Hudleston surmises that there was a deliberate Admiralty policy to keep the Popham code exclusively for shipboard use where the risk of its falling into the hands of the French could be better controlled: the Popham code was too good to risk being compromised. We might also add that a flag-based method of signalling required a breeze to allow it to be seen; even at sea this was sometimes a problem, but on a static station, more so.

When the war resumed, the naval blockade of the Channel was reinstated and the Army took up again its role in the defence against invasion. According to Goodwin,[19] the Army opted for a telegraph system that was a version of the Admiralty's flag-and-ball system already in use for their coastal signal stations. In 1803 in a document entitled *Defences of United Kingdom 1803* the statement is made that signals are to be made on church steeples when invasion is imminent, 'by flags and balls'.[20] For whatever reason, Gamble's radiated telegraph, though it had proved its worth in trials, was never a contender for consideration after war began again in 1803.[21] Some have suggested that Gamble's mobile telegraph was used in the Peninsular War by Wellington; it is certain that he used signalling methods to convey messages over large distances during the campaign. We can also be certain that Wellington had an early exposure to the concept of telegraphy through his fiancée's close contacts[22] in Dublin with Maria Edgeworth. Accounts of which telegraph systems Wellington used in Portugal are confusing; he was working in close contact with the Navy, who were bringing him supplies by sea, and a version of Popham's flag vocabulary system was certainly tried; the stronger evidence is that a version of the flag-and-ball system referred to above was deployed.[23]

So, the coastal signal stations used Goodhew's simple, limited and indeed obsolete code, but no matter. These stations had a singular purpose – defence against invasion, and intelligence and orders could be dealt with easily within the restraints of a limited vocabulary. For instance, a message such as 'Enemy fleet sighted ten miles off Beachy Head sailing north-east' could easily be accommodated. As it happened, it was never to be tested because no invasion fleet attempted the forcing of the Channel; if it had been otherwise, Keith's plan was that the monitoring fleet should dispatch a frigate with the news of a sighting, 'The Commanders of any . . . ships . . . that may be cruising on the enemy's coast, who shall observe that the enemy . . . [is coming], are to dispatch a fast sailing vessel . . . to the nearest port anchorage or signal station to give notice of the same . . .'.[24] Keith's orders required that whichever signal station received intelligence of an invasion force being sighted promulgated the news fast, not only to naval units but also military command posts set up for invasion defence:

> The CO at each . . . signal station, is with all possible dispatch to communicate the intelligence to the nearest Commanding Officer of the Sea Fencibles [a sort of marine Home Guard, an idea successfully advanced by Sir Home Popham] – flag officer – General Officer – Lieutenant of the County [who had home-defence responsibilities]– and to the Admiralty by Dragoons or Express [dispatch rider] . . . If a well-founded judgement can be formed of the place to which the enemy points . . . a second dispatch . . . should be communicated to His Majesty's Officers and the Admiralty as before. Upon receipt of such information, the Commanders of His Majesty's squadrons . . . are immediately to get underweigh and proceed to meet the enemy as far from the coast as possible . . .[25]

'I do not say the French cannot come,' growled the old First Lord of the Admiralty, Earl St Vincent, 'but I do say they cannot come by water.'[26] Of course, there were false alarms. A diarist of the day (Mrs Elizabeth Fremantle) recorded seeing at Portsmouth 'a great concourse of people on the beaches, the Yeomanry out and the telegraphs at work', because, she was told, a flotilla had been sighted. Next day it turned out that the invaders were only a fleet of coasters becalmed off the Isle of Wight.[27]

Such scares would have sent both the Navy and the Army into high alert. Insufficient is known about how the Army intended to telegraph their orders in the invasion zones; it is likely that temporary signal posts were erected to correspond with the coastal signals, but this is speculative. In the absence of any Army standard at the time, in practice, it is likely that local commanders would have their own preferred method and this would, in some cases, if not most, have been the long-standing Army method – a written message taken on horseback by a dispatch rider. The other ancient, primitive method of the lighting of fire beacons was also part of the defence plan. According to Goodwin,[28] the county lieutenants in the littoral counties established a system of fire beacons to call out the Volunteers, but this was not a country-wide system intended to alert the whole civil population (as was to be the case in 1940 by the ringing the church bells). The beacons were part of an integrated military–naval defence plan, and they were to be used only up to 15 miles (24km) from the coast.[29]

Even though little is known about how the Army was to send messages over long distances during the period of invasion risk, we do know that there was an integrated naval–military approach to the problem.[30] Moreover, there had been a complete reversal of the scorched earth policy that had been put in place for the 1797–98 invasion scare. It was felt, on reflection, that the balance of profit and loss vis-à-vis the invader of a scorched earth policy was too unfavourable to the defenders. Moreover, it was now thought that such a method of warfare would promote confusion and despondency and encourage the French. Instead, no foot of ground was to be ceded that was not 'marked with the enemy's blood'. The enhanced coastal station network, which had seen several church towers pressed into service and joint working with the Army, would allow the enemy to be engaged either at sea or as he attempted a landing.

Some authors have gone to the trouble of exposing what they consider to be the myth, in spite of widespread references in the literature, of the use of church towers as telegraph stations in Britain: the dichotomy is semantic. It is true that there were only two examples in Britain of churches where telegraph facilities of the true character, that is, corresponding in dialogue, were ever placed on them: Westminster Abbey, which was in contact with Hampstead Heath during the invasion scare of 1797–98, and Woolwich Parish Church which was an experimental station of the Army, but never operational. All other references to church towers and telegraphs must be to the Admiralty's coastal signalling network, on which although scant records remain, those which exist are persuasive; for example, the *Norfolk Chronicle* reported in 1803 that 'Signal flags . . . were stationed around the coast, on all church towers, and other lofty edifices, to give evidence in the event of the enemy landings.'[31] This must be a reference to the flag-and-ball coastal signalling technology, which only required masts to be erected for it to be operational; to place these on a church tower was both easy and cheap because of the immediacy of the invasion threat, and, of course, the distant views available from church towers made it natural that so many of them should be used. Because the invasion threat was temporary, the improvised arrangements could easily be removed and thus no permanent traces were left. This would appear to be the story of St Peter's in Thanet, where there is well-researched evidence of the use of the church tower for signalling but no traces remaining.[32]

To return to the incoming invasion intelligence received at a coastal station, the first priorities were to make the landing as costly as possible for the enemy: troops were to be alerted, including those manning the floating batteries moored off the more vulnerable beaches (later replaced by the network of Martello towers). Also to be alerted were port commanders by signals drawn from the 145-message vocabulary, which would be sent along the coast. If there were any gaps in the signal station chain, for whatever reason, standing orders would have provided for the message to be carried by horse to the next station, and then on to Deal and Portsmouth, and later to Yarmouth and Plymouth. Having ships on fixed moorings in estuaries enabled transmission between some of the larger obstacles. Capt Hudleston tells us that, before the shutter telegraph line was extended in 1806 from Hampshire to Plymouth, communication could be achieved between the Admiralty and the Torbay squadron by means of the chain of coastal stations west of Portsmouth.

The signal stations at Torbay (Brixton) and Dungeness had standing orders to report all arrivals and departures direct to the Admiralty by means of the coastal signal stations and the a shutter telegraph station, from where it would be passed to the Admiralty. Thus the whole system was a hybrid consisting of simple flag-and-ball stations along the coast, which could communicate only predetermined messages and were dependent for their full effect on the shutter telegraphs converging on London. Before the coastal signal stations had the link to London, local commanders, in accordance with standing instructions or on their own initiative, would respond to the situation. But, when the link to London was made, it was to create new concepts of command and control: the shutter telegraph allowed senior officers in London to take control. In August 1796, just after the shutter telegraph to Portsmouth opened, the port admiral was instructed to 'use the telegraph on occasions of importance or when in want of immediate directions'.[33] The absolute delegation to local commanders of tactical control of their forces, which was as old as time, could never have survived the invention of the telegraph; this restraint over the discretion allowed to the likes of Nelson and Popham, at least while they were in home waters, represents a turning point in the history of how the Navy was commanded.

Notwithstanding the preparations being made to destroy the fleet that would carry it, Napoleon assembled his Grand Army at Boulogne. The invasion atmosphere rallied the British, the ruling classes and the common people alike; huge armies of volunteers were recruited. Napoleon knew that he could get his army across the Channel by only exploiting a few hours of tactical surprise during a fog or in a calm (by the use of oars); strategic surprise was impossible. The admirals kept the fleets on their mettle and the shutter telegraph lines from Deal and Portsmouth kept the Admiralty informed. In July 1805 Napoleon left Paris for Boulogne; he had a cunning plan. From Boulogne he telegraphed to his admirals in Brest, 'Let us be masters of the Straits for six hours and we shall be masters of the world.'[34] But a false move or a rush of overconfidence and he would have found his Moscow seven years earlier, his soldiers saved by drowning in the Channel waters instead or dying on the Kentish beaches. Thus Napoleon kept his army in Boulogne, on a chance on the weather. But now logistics played their part: the number of transports required to lift the army to the south coast of England was so large that an ominous fact emerged. When it became clear that the invasion fleet could not all put to sea on one tide (thus making detection and interception much more likely), Napoleon had to concede that his project was hopeless and would wither if the Royal Navy continued to command the Channel.

## The French Telegraph and Trafalgar

Although, as we have seen, the arrangements made to deal with an invasion attempt on England were considerable and the Navy's telegraphic capability, when coupled with scurrying frigates, allowed the Admiralty to control its ships in home waters, the main issue was that nothing should be allowed to weaken the ability of the main battle fleets to confront and destroy the enemy. Every officer of the Navy believed that the country's first line of defence lay, not facing Napoleon at Boulogne, but outside the enemy's ports: control of the Western Approaches was the key to survival. Away from home waters, the old regime of command and control held sway: with no ability to communicate with the Admiralty except by a round trip by a frigate, everything depended on the battle fleet commanders. Napoleon, however, with the ability to communicate by telegraph the 350 miles (564km) to the Atlantic port of Brest from Paris, or from Boulogne when he was in camp there, had a major strategic advantage: lesser admirals than Nelson and Cornwallis may have allowed him to take advantage of it. Even though the telegraph allowed Napoleon to restrain his own admirals' zeal from engaging in any battle whose outcome was secondary, he was not able to will away the exceptional fighting quality of the Royal Navy; under Nelson it was a killing machine.

The capacity to blockade enemy ports during the earlier war had been a major strategic weapon of the Navy and was to be so again. When Nelson was appointed to the Mediterranean command in 1803, famously flying his admiral's flag from the *Victory*, his orders were to make for Malta, to take command of a further squadron waiting there and then to keep watch over the French fleet in harbour in Toulon and to destroy it if it ventured out. Additionally, Nelson's Mediterranean command had to protect both Gibraltar and Malta from attack. If the French were to escape from the Mediterranean and were able to rendezvous with other enemy fleets in the French Atlantic ports, only the Navy's Channel fleet and the land defences would stand between Napoleon and an invasion. The strategic necessity therefore was to keep the French and the Spanish fleet from menacing the Channel from the Western Approaches. If a French Mediterranean fleet were to escape from that sea and sail for the Channel, the news would have been with Napoleon in Boulogne within an hour or two of the news reaching Brest, whereas news of a defeat of Nelson's Mediterranean fleet, assuming that there was a frigate standing off from the battle and able to bear the news, would have taken several days to alert the Channel command. This explains why the Royal Navy, if it was to be beaten, had to be beaten in distant waters: both Napoleon and Cornwallis knew this.

Nelson's fear for the escape of the French fleet from Toulon can now be imagined; but to bottle it up in harbour was not his style; he wanted to destroy it, and his special battle tactic was to 'engage the enemy more closely'. To achieve this he would have to allow the French out, by exerting a much less close blockade than was favoured by many of great admirals of the day. This approach, the quest for a decisive battle rather than an inconsequential skirmish, is illustrated by Nelson's order from HMS *Victory* on 5 December 1803 to the captain of the frigate HMS *Active*:

> . . . it is of the utmost importance that the enemy's squadron in Toulon should be most strictly watched, and that I should be made acquainted with their sailing and route with all dispatch, should they put to sea. . . Should . . . you obtain any intelligence necessary for my immediate information, you are to dispatch a frigate [to inform me].[35]

Nelson was communicating at the speed at which a frigate could sail, but Napoleon was operating with intelligence moving at hundreds of miles an hour across France; happily, the sheer quality of the Royal Navy's fighting ability could not be deranged by the French advantage in this respect.

As it happened over a year later, the French naval commander Villeneuve achieved a break-out from Toulon; in April 1805 the French left port undetected and escaped through the Straits of Gibraltar, free to sail as they pleased, until located again. When this news reached the London market, government securities fell. Informed by an intelligence source, as the French intended, that Villeneuve was bound for the West Indies, Nelson set off in unrelenting pursuit, expectation, frustration and then renewed pursuit. Nelson covered the 3,000 miles (4,800km) from the Straits to Barbados in little more than three weeks at an almost record average of 135 miles (217km) a day.[36] After fruitlessly chasing Villeneuve across the Atlantic and then back again, Nelson put into Gibraltar in July, being only too well aware that the French fleet was still at large and of the risks to England of its gaining the Channel; Nelson was distraught. Moreover, if such a fact can be conceived, when he put in to Gibraltar, he had not been ashore for over two years.

Meanwhile, in 1804 Spain had allied herself with France against Britain; but Napoleon's plan to avoid the Navy's interception of his invasion force by decoying it to the West Indies was about to fail. Although the combined fleets had chased each other across the Atlantic, Nelson was not outwitted. On 22 August Napoleon telegraphed from 'Camp de Boulogne' to Brest: 'I hope you have arrived in Brest,' he said to Villeneuve, 'leave immediately with the united squadron [that is, with the Spanish] and enter the Channel. Everything is embarked. Appear in 24 hours and it is all over.'[37] At that time the resources waiting for the signal to begin the largest invasion the world had ever known – would ever know until the Second World War – were 175,000 men and 2,300 ships of all kinds collected along the coast at Berck, Étaples, Boulogne, Ambleteuse, Wimereux and Wissant.[38] The next day Napoleon, having heard that Villeneuve was not at Brest, knew that his invasion was doomed and that he would have to abandon it. Abusing Villeneuve, whom he considered to be '*sans resolution et sans courage moral*', on 24 August, the first orders to break camp were given.[39] The French plan had failed; later the combined French and Spanish fleet, having ventured out from Cadiz, was intercepted by Nelson who, on 21 October, a day which dawned calm and splendid, entered immortality through his death while destroying the combined enemy fleets at Trafalgar. Never again would the Navy be challenged by Napoleon; Trafalgar postponed indefinitely the possibility of a successful invasion of England. But, strangely, Trafalgar settled nothing in relation to Napoleon because two months before his navy was snuffed out, he had realized that he could not dispute the Channel. As was the case with Hitler, even after our acquisition of total sea and air supremacy, the victory which would give finality against Napoleon could only be won on land; only his defeats in 1812–14 and the crushing eclipse of 1815 could settle things. In 1805 England still had her naval supremacy and Napoleon still had his army: something else would have to be tried. As Hitler was to do in reaction to Britain's defiance, Napoleon turned the gaze of his army about, and it fell on the east, where, in both cases, after initial successes catastrophe awaited.*

In early September 1805, well before Trafalgar, good tidings came to London, for it was learnt from a captured schooner that in August Napoleon's troops at Boulogne had broken camp and marched off in haste, 'because of a new war with Russia'. The army had begun its march and was halfway to the Danube. Napoleon, who had been at Boulogne since 3 August – his longest ever stay at the camp,[40] himself left on 2 September, the day Capt Blackwood of the *Euryalus* brought the news to Nelson at Merton that Villeneuve's fleet was back in Cadiz. Nelson's victory eliminated the enemy's naval menace, but the Navy remained on guard; the shutter telegraphs continued to chatter across southern England and the signal stations monitored the coast; the open seas allowed the safe arrival from India of a ship sailing safely through the Western Approaches. The sea now belonged to England, but what about on land? The ship was carrying the man who was to be the match for Napoleon on the field – Sir Arthur Wellesley, the future Duke of Wellington.[41]

At sea, Napoleon was never to hold the initiative and therefore his superior telegraphic communications never had a strong influence on affairs. But not so on land, however, where he was master; when Napoleon lay at Boulogne he was in contact with Paris by telegraph and, through that city, with much of France. This capacity can be related to the question: what was Napoleon's distinguishing mark as a great general? This is part of the answer provided by *The New Cambridge Modern History*: 'It was his ability to move very large armies, sometimes of 200,000 men and more, across great stretches of the continent at speeds far greater than had hitherto been thought possible . . .'[42]

In due course, as the Chappe network spread across the Continent, Napoleon's grasp of the importance of the telegraph, and Abraham Chappe's development of a field telegraph, helped to build on his existing ability to command movement. In his ten years as emperor, Napoleon was in camp

---

*In a book in which Napoleon is a central player the reader may become sympathetic with how difficult it is to extirpate references to Hitler, who shared his ambitions with Napoleon. Far greater authors than I have struggled with this problem. In an important book by Pieter Geyl, *Napoleon: for and against*, a wide-ranging review of nearly 150 years of writing by Napoleon's detractors and apologists, written during the Nazi occupation of Holland, he explains his problem thus. 'Between the two world assailants in question the differences, the contrasts, are such that, even when as in my case one had hated the dictator in Napoleon long before the evil presence of Hitler began darkening our lives, one almost feels as if one should ask the pardon of his shade for mentioning his name in one breath with that of the other.'

with his armies for only fifty-four days fewer than he stayed in royal residencies.[43] For a man who combined, among other things, a propensity to take sole charge and was often a long way from Paris, he could scarcely have operated in the style which he did without the telegraph. He was to berate Marshal Soult, who showed some reluctance to use the telegraph, for not doing so enough.[44]

Napoleon, having moved his army east in August 1805, began an astonishing period of success that was to find him at the peak of his power. Before following this epic period, it would be useful to review Napoleon's interaction with the telegragh, and to summarize his impact on its development. When he became First Consul in 1799, the Revolution had created telegraphic links from Paris to Lille, Strasbourg and Brest. But Napoleon was no stranger to the telegraph: he had been in Paris when the Chappe experiments of 1792 were wrecked by the mob (and when the Palace of the Tuileries had been sacked), and he had been in Paris in 1794 when the line to Lille had carried the news of victories in the north, and he was again in Paris in 1795 when he used force against the people in their Royalist uprising. There then followed periods, during his glorious Italian campaign of 1796–97 and in Egypt in 1798–99, of utter remoteness from the centre of power in Paris, when he must have been reminded almost daily of the slowness of his lines of communication because the telegraph did not yet reach beyond the borders of France. This was to change, as soon as Napoleon took power: we have seen how Boulogne was connected, then followed Brussels, Lyons and Dijon, Milan and Venice, Antwerp, Flushing and Amsterdam, and then Mainz via Metz. As he reached the peak of his power, a huge telegraphic network was created by his orders.

# 10
# From Boulogne to Elba, via Moscow and Leipzig

*If anyone wishes to know the history of this . . . [Peninsular War], I will tell them it is our Maritime superiority that gives me the power of maintaining my army while the enemy are unable to do so.*
The Duke of Wellington[1]

## Napoleon at the Peak of His Power

Following Claude's suicide in 1805, two of his brothers, Ignace and Pierre-Francois, succeeded him as joint administrators of the telegraph service in Paris. Another brother Abraham was attached to the Grand Army with the rank of colonel and a special uniform. His task was to translate messages for Napoleon and his immediate staff and to keep him informed of troop movements reported by telegraph, which, following the move east, were soon to be at great distances from Paris. The French telegraph network, always at Napoleon's command, was extended into conquered lands.

In October 1805, as Nelson was preparing for Trafalgar, Napoleon's forces were massing in southern central Germany. As his army marched east, Napoleon was in Paris; on 13 October he learned by telegraph that a Russian army under Gen Mack had crossed the River Inn and was advancing on Munich; Napoleon, ever the master of manoeuvre, had laid a trap into which the Russians were to be ensnared. He rushed from Paris to join the army, which had surrounded the Russians at Ulm, on the Danube about 60 miles (97km) west of Munich, and forced its surrender.[2] The news of the capitulation at Ulm would have gone to Paris by telegraph, via Strasburg:

> Like other provincials, the people of Strasbourg soon came to know that important news was passing when they saw the telegraph arms on their cathedral constantly agitating. Parisians learned of important telegraphed news through news bills posted up in public places. After . . . [1798] the Strasbourgois enjoyed a similar service

> with regard to messages relayed from Paris which the Prefect of Bas-Rhin deemed proper to publicize.[3]

(These last had included many victories of the armies, the taking of Malta by Napoleon, the preliminary treaty which preceded the Peace of Amiens and the signing of the Treaty itself on 26 March 1802.[4])

Trafalgar and Ulm were destined to have a connection with Napoleon's decision in August 1805 to abandon any attempt at an invasion of England. The evening before the surrender of Ulm, Napoleon said:

> Soldiers, a month ago we were encamped on the shores of the ocean opposite to England; but an impious league compelled us to fly towards the Rhine. It is but a fortnight since we passed that river, and the Alps of Wirtenburg, the Necker, the Danube, and the Lech; those celebrated barriers of Germany have not retarded our march a day, an hour, or an instant. . . . Soldiers, but for the army which is now in front of you, we should this day be in London; we should have avenged ourselves for six centuries of insults, and restored the freedom of the seas. But bear in mind, tomorrow, that you are fighting against the allies of England . . .[5]

It was an absurdity for Napoleon to assert that some event in central Europe had prevented him from occupying London; the reality, of course, was that even before Trafalgar, and especially after, Napoleon's admirals had trembled at the power of the Royal Navy. It is as true to say that Napoleon found it as difficult to comprehend sea warfare as he did to find an admiral who would risk a few ships in order to seek a victory over the Royal Navy. Throughout the period 1801–14 the strategic doctrine pursued from the Ministry of Marine in Paris, in spite of Napoleon, was to maintain a 'fleet in being' and, through a building programme, hope to wear the Navy down. After Trafalgar:

> No less than 83 [ships] of the line and 65 frigates were built [by the French], so that in 1814 the fleet consisted of 103 of the line and 157 frigates, in spite of the heavy losses suffered during the war. These losses amounted to 377 ships captured or destroyed in action, 24 by shipwreck. The equivalent British figures – 10 and 101– are sufficient commentary upon the nature of the war at sea.[6]

The strategic doctrine pursued by the Admiralty was blockade. Great though the strength of the Navy was, in relative and absolute terms, because the blockade was to be extended against Napoleon and the resources expended on it increased, the Navy's global reach was to become a burden.

The other side of this coin was that ultimately the great ports of Bordeaux, Nantes, Le Havre, Amsterdam, Bremen, Hamburg, Lübeck, Marseilles, Genoa, Venice and Naples were to face ruin. These fruits of Trafalgar were, however, quite irrelevant to the strategic position as Napoleon faced Ulm: Napoleon was a man whose military genius operated on a continental scale – leaving aside over 600 skirmishes, he led his armies in over eighty pitched battles[7] – and he was on a course in which, in spite of the primacy of the Royal Navy he would control a vast proportion of the continental land mass, over 500 miles (800km) of which he had just marched his army from the Channel. The Navy could avoid Britain's losing the war, but, as twice in the twentieth century, it could not win it for Britain.

The news of the dramatic taking of Ulm was brought to England, it is said, by a French fishing smack. As we have heard, this megaphone news propagation service was to be reciprocated shortly, with interest, with the Trafalgar news being sent the other way.[8] For those who got their news from a newspaper, which would be a small proportion because they were both rare and expensive, they would have read in the same edition the news of both Trafalgar and Ulm. To temper the joy of Trafalgar and to add to the gloomy price paid in Nelson's death, the readers of Portsmouth were offered the following chilling Napoleonic call to his army, one which served to remind Englishmen why they were fighting and whom:

> Soldiers, if I wished only to conquer the enemy, I should not have thought it necessary to make an appeal to your courage, and your attachment to the country and to my person; but merely to conquer him is doing nothing worthy of you or your empire. It is necessary that not a man of the enemy's army shall escape; that that government which has violated all the engagements, shall first learn its catastrophe by your arrival under the walls of Vienna; and that, on receiving this fatal intelligence, its conscience, if it listens to the voice of conscience, shall tell it, that it has betrayed both its solemn promises of peace, and the first of the duties bequeathed by its ancestors, with the power of forming the rampart of Europe against the eruption of the Cossacks. Soldiers, who have been engaged in the affairs of . . . [Germany], I am satisfied with your conduct. Every corps in the army will emulate you, and I shall be able to say to my people – 'Your Emperor and your army have done their duty.' Perform yours, and the 200,000 conscripts whom I have summoned [by telegraph?] will hasten, by forced marches, to reinforce our second line.[9]

There was not much room for compromise here: being served up with these outpourings, these croaks of a tyrant who could never deserve any fruits of wickedness, the islanders could only be yet more grateful for Trafalgar and stiffen themselves against any temptation to quail. But things got worse: shortly after Ulm the news of Napoleon's victory at Austerlitz in December brought a sense of doom to London. His entry into Berlin on 27 October 1806 was followed a month later by his 'Berlin Decree' by which he ordered a trade war with Britain; this was a period when the telegraphs were constantly transmitting news of his victories and his orders. The fall of Stettin and Magdeburg followed quickly after Berlin, and in the following summer Russia called a halt to hostilities with France. News of all this went down the telegraph.[10] Napoleon had his sights on Vienna, as he had foretold before Ulm. His command of movement and his use of the telegraph to achieve it, while being remote from the field, was achieved by extensions of temporary field telegraphs where the front became extended from the permanent stations; this is illustrated by the message telegraphed to his chief of staff Marshal Berthier:

> I think the Emperor of Austria is going to attack soon. Proceed to Augsburg to act in accordance with my instructions and if the enemy has attacked before the 15th you must concentrate the troops at Augsburg . . . and everything must be ready to march. Send my guard and horses to Stuttgart.[11]

Unhappily, this particular message also gives an isolated illustration of the fallibility of the telegraph. We have seen already that its absence caused the unnecessary Battle of Copenhagen to take place (Chapter 9); in this case the existence of the telegraphic connection between Napoleon in Paris and Berthier at the front was to cause a hopeless muddle. We have also seen that the English climate gave cause for dissatisfaction with the telegraphs because of their unreliability and problems also arose on the Continent, even though the climate is generally better. As Chandler[12] observes, 'the fog of war', as well as the foggy atmosphere, 'grew rapidly denser as apparently contradictory orders came from Paris to headquarters'. One such order from Napoleon, the one quoted above, was delayed in transmission for several days by fog, and as it happened a further order, written only an hour later and sent by courier who travelled at the speed of the horse, arrived before the telegraphic message. To compound the perversity, the interpretation that could have been put on the telegraphed command, received as it was in the wrong order, was capable of being misconstrued creating a trap into which the hapless Berthier fell. According to Chandler,[13] most messages were still conveyed on horseback by a military postal service running a relay of mounted messengers, as well as by the use of mail coach services. It would seem therefore that the telegraph was not regarded as sufficiently reliable to make the traditional methods redundant. We have seen a similar position in

England in relation to the Trafalgar news and we shall see it again when Napoleon was the captive of the Navy off Plymouth.

Nevertheless, we can see how the telegraph was manna for Napoleon. To his ability, his spontaneous capacity to control from a distance can be added – 'the eye for the key point, the capacity to read the mind of his opponent, the ability to take quick decisions, a personality powerful enough to impose an obedience, all these qualities Napoleon possessed in their highest form'.[14] It was not just that he was master of France – he was master wherever he was by virtue of his communications and the telegraph. One of his ministers said that 'he wanted not only to govern France but to administer her from his army camp, and during military operations he did actually do this'[15] for, even when he was away at the head of his army and getting further and further from Paris, where the telegraph often followed, he insisted on keeping his officials on a leash.

The line to Lyon, comprising fifty-nine intermediate stations, had been completed in 1807 and was to continue in service until 1852. The line was further extended to Milan in 1809 (requiring a further forty-six intermediate stations) and Venice (another twenty-seven stations) in 1810, over which the French had retaken control from the Austrians in 1806 after Austerlitz in December 1805. The distance from Paris to Venice covered by the telegraph was nearly 700 miles (1,130km), requiring amazing resources to support over 130 intermediate stations. Napoleon's telegraphic network radiating from Paris now amounted to thousands of miles in length (Toulon, on the Mediterranean, was not connected to the telegraph in Napoleon's time: the extension from Lyon was made in 1821 and continued until 1852). In England, the Admiralty pleaded poverty but the dictator had no difficulty, evidently, in funding his extraordinary network. To reach Milan the route had to cross the Alps, which was done by taking it through the Mont Cenis Pass between Lyon and Milan. The highest telegraph station was at over 6,200ft (1,900m) above sea level;[16] the atmospheric conditions here, and further west in the Po valley, and the frets of Venice must have made communication very vulnerable to the type of interruption so often suffered in London and which has been remarked on in relation to Ulm. Napoleon had shown great frustration at the delays to the opening of the Milan line: he needed communication time to be reduced in order to more readily exert his will. He wrote angrily on 16 March 1809 to the Minister of the Interior, 'I wish that you complete without delay the establishment of the telegraphic line from here to Milan, and that in 15 days one can communicate with that capital.'

His ability to give orders by telegraph gave Napoleon's power a new immediacy: we recoil when such orders were given peremptorily for an execution. After Vienna had fallen, the leader of a Tyrolean revolt, Andreas Hofer, was sentenced to death and the order for his execution went from

Paris by telegraph on the Venice line in February 1810.[17] The prisoner was in the hands of Napoleon's stepson, the Viceroy of Italy, in Mantua in the Po valley. Napoleon's instructions were: 'My son, I had commanded you to send Hofer to Paris, but since you have got him in Mantua, give instant orders that the military commission be set up to try him and execute him on the spot. See that this takes place within 24 hours.'[18]

Whatever the Anglophobic outpourings of later French historians, and there were many of them,[19] it was this sort of abuse of arbitrary power which the common Englishman would not tolerate and against which he would fight alongside, fight for even, the privileged aristocracy. Hofer died in the service of the Empress of Austria, whose daughter was now to be Napoleon's wife. Leaving aside the reaction in Britain, this death made a deep impression, as well it might, on German-speaking people. It was no isolated example: Napoleon dealt with all revolts with pitiless repression. 'My intention', he wrote to one commander-in-chief, 'is that the main village where the insurrection started shall be burnt and that 30 of the ringleaders shall be shot.' And later, 'at least 200' people, should be executed.[20]

The year 1807 saw the start of a new expansion in the telegraph network; it was also, and the circumstances are not unconnected, the year of fate in the reign of Napoleon. Here we see the first hints of the flawed fatality of Napoleon's inexorable advances. This was the year, with Berlin in his grip, that in his mind he could see Russia, presently his ally, overthrown. The amazing victory at Austerlitz had inspired the dangerous belief that his genius and the power of France were invincible, and it was to make him lose all sense of moderation.[21] At Austerlitz he had defeated the two other European Emperors, of Austria and Russia. He overthrew the eight-centuries-old Holy Roman Empire and took possession of his inheritance. He conquered Italy, and, like Charlemagne, came to own the iron crown of the Lombard kings. For a time he spared the Pope. And like Charlemagne, he was already extending his empire as far as the Adriatic and the Ionian Sea. He conquered Germany and became the patron of the Confederation of the Rhine, whose frontiers he brought down to the Elbe. He crushed Prussia, which had dared to oppose his imperial destiny. He restored Poland, under the name of Grand Duchy of Warsaw and made it into a military frontier of his empire.[22] At Austerlitz he had stormed the Bastille of Europe, the barrier against the Revolution.[23]

Being a Roman emperor, he wanted to rule over the Mediterranean, once a Roman lake, and for that reason he coveted the east. Aix-la-Chappelle he had, Constantinople he wanted to have. How could he have shared the Ottoman Empire with Russia? How could he have established a sincere and durable alliance with the Tsar, who also wanted to be Emperor of the East?[24]

'For these reasons, he stood apart from his period; that is why he himself was bound in the end to be broken.'[25] The ground covered in this campaign was to be covered again in 1812 on the way to Moscow and East Prussia was to be pillaged then for a second time. As a soldier wrote home in 1812, 'The country where we are was previously ravaged in 1806 and 1807 and almost all the houses have been rebuilt since then, and now destroyed again.' The wickedness of Napoleon's wars of conquest is demonstrated in the same letter:

> . . . Eastern Prussia . . . is a very beautiful country but it is time to leave it soon if we don't want to die of hunger; the food shortage is beginning to be felt in a rigorous way. . . . the horses lack their forage and we are forced to cut [growing crops] so that they may eat. The poor inhabitants are . . . much to be pitied, we will leave them nothing at all to live on; we take away from the animals all the grain of whatever kind can be found; their own horses are not spared, what will become of them? . . . May God preserve us in our country from the horrors of war; there is no scourge more horrible.[26]

The French population was able to remain in denial of all this suffering visited on conquered lands, for which Napoleon was alone responsible. Writing after the first abdication in 1814, F.R. de Chateaubriand was to observe that:

> It is the fashion of the day to magnify Bonaparte's victories. Gone are the sufferers, and the victims' curses, their cries of pain, their howls of anguish, are heard no more; exhausted France no longer offers the spectacle of women ploughing her soil; no more are parents imprisoned as hostages for their sons, nor a whole village punished for the desertion of a conscript.[27]

But what of England? By 1807, with Napoleon at the peak of his power, his Continental enemies defeated and Russia now allied with him, England found herself alone in the war against France for the fourth time. As Bryant explained, there was no shortage of Quislings:*

> Within a few years Napoleon had entered every capital in Christendom save Moscow and London, had incorporated Italy and a half Germany into his dominions and had filled the thrones of Spain, Holland Westphalia and Naples with his kinsfolk. As though this immense dynastic empire was not enough, he had buttressed it

*The word had not, of course, been coined at the time; it dates from 1940 when Vidkun Quisling (1887–1945), who had aped the National Socialist Party in Germany, served as puppet prime minister of Norway during the Nazi occupation, thus giving a name to anyone who becomes the political puppet of an enemy.

> round with a group of subservient Teuton princes, on whom, in return for unquestioning obedience, he conferred puppet crowns. It was all done, a wit explained, by their saying the Lord's prayer together; the Electors of the German States said to Bonaparte, 'Thy will be done', and the great man replied, 'Thy Kingdom come!'[28]

The expansion of Napoleon's ego was unbounded: 'To honour and serve our Emperor', ran the compulsory catechism imposed on schools, 'is the same as to honour and serve God himself'.[29] Lacking an heir, he divorced his now barren wife Josephine, and surveying the regal bloodstock of the Continent and, unmoved by the irony, he alighted on a Habsburg princess, Marie Louise, for his purpose, whereupon in 1810, 'the niece of Marie Antoinette was united to the heir of the Revolution amid the cheers of the Paris mob. The guillotine had been legitimized'.[30]

The Revolution had eliminated the hereditary aristocracy, only for it to be replaced by a vain man who, unrestrained in his power, found no paradox in wishing to found his own regal dynasty. On 20 March 1811, the news of the birth of his heir (the King of Rome) was telegraphed all down the network from Paris. This transmission of an identical text gives the opportunity to make some observations on security. One of the ways in which Bletchley Park was successful in breaking the Germans' Enigma code during the Second World War was by their transmission of the same message multiple times; for example, greetings sent on the tyrant's birthday, which gave an obvious clue to its coded contents. There is no evidence that the French telegraphic code was ever broken by an enemy; it was not until radio allowed the interception of telegraphic traffic in the safety of a home base that decryption became a fruitful activity, for there were no means by which a spy could send intelligence back to his controller in a useful time frame.

But there is evidence that the telegraph in France was used for successful criminal activity: when the great writer Alexandre Dumas famously wrote into *The Count of Monte Cristo* an exciting account of the engineering of a change in the sense of a message, this was achieved by corrupting an operator of a signal station and resulted in the manipulation of stock exchange prices. It is likely that this idea came into Dumas's mind following a case in 1836 on which the Dumas episode seems to be based.

Dumas overlooked the technical difficulties of perpetrating such a crime at a simple intermediate station where the operator would, in practice, be transmitting what looked like scrambled text which he would not be able to understand. The crime was possible because of a weak link in the line: at some divisional stations the incoming traffic would be decoded by a director, purged of errors, re-encoded and transmitted on its way; by collusion the fraud could be carried out during this process. The whole question of security over these early data networks, although it was a question which would be examined more closely by a later generation of criminals and security services, had not been neglected, collusion apart, by the French telegraphic bureaucrats:

> It is forbidden for telegraphists, at risk of dismissal, to allow any stranger to operate the telegraph, . . . without a written order from the inspector . . .
> The telegraphists may not allow anyone to enter their station while the telegraph is in use.
> Any telegraphist who operates the telegraph when drunk . . .[31]

Reverting to Napoleon, we must observe that at this period the French idolized him and the glory he was giving them. No government has exploited so systematically the national thirst for military glory. None has appealed more successfully to the material passions or has presumed with such hardihood and success upon the administrative timidity of the French, part inertia, part egotism, which is content to surrender the conduct of affairs in exchange for a quiet life.[32] Or, as Bryant put it, was the tyrannical unity that Napoleon imposed on mankind:

> Sweeping away the franchises, privileges and serfdom of bygone centuries, smashing outworn ideals and institutions, making new laws, roads and bridges, devising out of his sole, reason, codes and systems to last for all time, and imposing on all the rationalising, undiscriminating bureaucracy through which, regardless of race or prescriptive right, he made his will obeyed.[33]

It was by means of the telegraph, and his huge capacity for work, order and control, that Napoleon could be the first ruler of the modern era to enforce his grip on subjugated races. His advice to his vassal kings was characterized as: let them be given a good administration and the Code, suppress ruthlessly the first revolt, let them feel that they are powerless against the power of Napoleon, and they will see their advantage in the only course left to them – surrender and submission.[34]

While Britain harvested the fruits of Trafalgar, turning the Caribbean into a British lake, advancing its own empire in the Orient and Australasia, Napoleon ruled a huge land mass, most of a continent. No one but a great man could have administered such a state:

> But Bonaparte was a great man. He possessed the supreme quality of genius – inexhaustible energy. He could work eighteen hours a day and take in the most complicated document at a glance. His mind,

> which could turn swiftly from subject to subject, was almost as universal as the France he controlled. Out of the chaos produced by the Terror the long, wasting war and the corruption of the Directory, he constructed, almost single-handed, the rationally organised State strong in the allegiance of its members and capable of ensuring stress and storm. He endowed it is with laws culled from the best systems of the past and published them in a Code of more than two thousand articles covering every department of human activity. He gave France a new system of education. He enriched it with roads, canals, bridges, harbours and magnificent public buildings.

But, as Bryant observed, there were flaws in his genius:

> It was impossible for Napoleon to leave his conquests alone; he had perpetually to remould them to his will. He had found Germany divided, politically unconscious, and ready to subscribe to the revolutionary ideology of the Revolution. Yet within a year of his victory over Prussia, his incessant interference, extortion and military tyranny were already creating a dangerous German nationalism round a single point – hatred of himself and France.[35]

The dividend from this German nationalism and hatred of France continued to be paid into the twentieth century. Great man as he was, of immensely higher mental stature than the tyrant successor to the German nationalism, yet like him, Napoleon could support himself only by conquest. But for Napoleon the vexing question remained: he might hold the Continent, but how was he to subdue Britain? Realizing that some new strategy was required to isolate the power of the Navy, he resolved to overcome Britain by destroying her trade. He ordered all European countries to close their ports to the British: neutral ships which attempted to trade with Britain were to be liable to capture. Although this was a policy which caused discomfort, hardship even, to Britain, it was not one which could, in the long-run at least, overcome the British sea power being ranged against it. If it was to be blockade and counter-blockade, the Navy's counter-blockade would always be enforceable, unlike the French blockade where there were leaks.

## Plymouth and Yarmouth are Connected to the Admiralty by Telegraph

We must return to the home country to discover what developments in the telegraph network were taking place in the post-Trafalgar period. The divine deliverance from the risk of invasion, as it was thought to be, the extent of

France's defeat and Nelson's death gave his memory an industrial dimension. We have seen how the news of Trafalgar arrived in London, with the shutter telegraph playing no role in its transmission. The fact that Lt Lapenotière had to travel to London by horse to carry the news, nearly ten years after the first telegraph age had dawned in Britain, is remarkable: it exposed the limitation of the telegraph because Plymouth was not connected to it. During Nelson's chase after Villeneuve across the Atlantic, the Admiralty suffered not only the anguish of protracted ignorance and suspense, but the slowness of communications with Plymouth exposed the limitation still further. As Bryant has explained:

> On the night of 7 July 1805 a sloop from the West Indies anchored at Plymouth. All next day . . . her captain was posting up the Exeter Road. Towards midnight his post-chaise rattled over the Charing Cross cobblestones and drew up at the Admiralty door. He brought urgent dispatches from Nelson.[36]

With the French fleet at large, invasion feared daily and the important role of Plymouth in the overall naval defence plan for the Western Approaches, the Admiralty was concerned about there being no telegraphic communication with that key port. In October 1805 orders were given to connect Plymouth to the telegraph system. This was achieved by making a branch from the London to Portsmouth line from a junction at Beacon Hill, the penultimate station before Portsmouth, nearly 800ft (240m) up on the South Downs. The extension to Plymouth was brought into use in 1806; on 12 July the *Naval Chronicle* reported:

> The new telegraphs are nearly completed; . . . and the lodges for those men who work them are almost finished. A short message has been conveyed, and an answer returned from London, in a space of time from 10 to 12 minutes; . . . [a speed] of conveying intelligence hitherto unknown in this part of the country, and will be a great saving . . .[37]

This new speed of communication was clearly the source of some contemporary marvel in Plymouth. Shortly after Plymouth and London were connected, an excellent example was recorded of the impact of telegraphy on the acceleration of the receipt of and response to orders. Routinely, it took two days for postal dispatches to reach the Admiralty from Plymouth. When Capt Lord Cochrane made landfall in Plymouth on 19 March 1809 in HMS *Imperieuse* the fact was telegraphed immediately to the Admiralty; within the hour of his anchoring, orders arrived by telegraph for him to report in person in London.

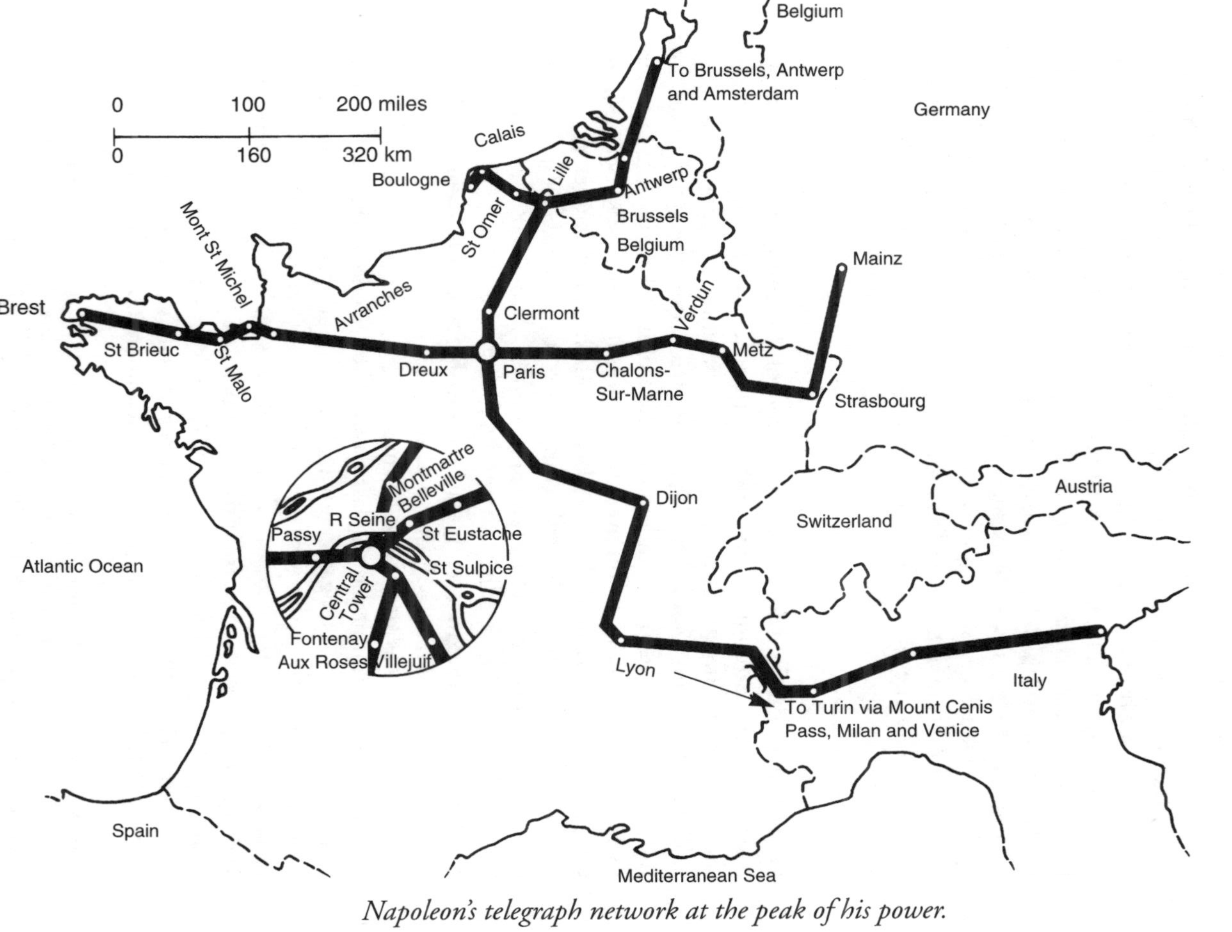


*Napoleon's telegraph network at the peak of his power.*

Cochrane was regarded as the greatest frigate captain of his day and the greatest and most daring fighting captain; he was in spirit a sort of nineteenth-century Viking.* His career was already alive with stories of deception, subterfuge and, significantly for our story, the shore-raiding of batteries and signal stations. We have already seen that the French coastal signal stations were considered a sufficient menace for the Navy to raid and destroy them whenever they could; Cochrane was a specialist, zealot even, for this type of operation. When he arrived in Plymouth he had just returned from the Mediterranean, where according to his autobiography,[38] he had blown up and completely destroyed the newly constructed semaphore signal stations on the coast near Marseille.

When Napoleon gave up his invasion attempt in 1805, leaving the Channel for his march east and the stunning victories at Ulm and Austerlitz, the defence of the North Sea and the Baltic came into sharper focus, and Yarmouth was the Navy's base for operations in those waters. The Admiralty had considered a telegraph connection from Yarmouth to London some years earlier, but the Peace of Amiens intervened before effect could be given to creating it. But by 1807, and with Napoleon sweeping all before him, the need for fast communication with Yarmouth became imperative. The shutter telegraph line to Yarmouth became operational in June 1808.

Even before this, while the Plymouth telegraph was being built, the Admiralty had decided to build an extension of it to Falmouth, a port lying some 50 miles (80km) to the west of Plymouth, which was itself a similar further distance west of Torbay. Being much closer, therefore, to the Western Approaches, a telegraph connection to Falmouth would be most serviceable if a fleet were to put to sea in a hurry. Adm Charles Middleton, a naval administrator credited with achieving the Navy's physical and administrative strength at the start of the French Revolutionary War, a friend of Pitt the Prime Minister and related to Lord Melville (the former Henry Dundas), was now Lord Barham and had taken political office as First Lord of the Admiralty, the last naval officer to do so. He was in office at the time of the Trafalgar campaign and, by adopting the principle of concentration of force, he has been credited with orchestrating its brilliant success.[39] We have seen already that Napoleon had gone east even before Trafalgar, but, even so, late in 1805 Barham wrote:

> The telegraph now erecting between London and Plymouth, is ordered to be carried to Falmouth, the importance of which will be

*Cochrane fell out badly with the British government: after the wars with France he served in the Chilean navy from 1817 to 1822 and later from 1823 to 1825 as an admiral in the Brazilian navy. In 1827–28 he was an admiral in the Greek navy. While in this post, the first naval engagement by a steam-driven vessel took place as well as the last naval battle in the age of sail, at the Battle of Navarino in 1827.

> very apparent, when the facility it will afford of a ready communication with a port so near the entrance of the Channel, is considered; thus affording a better opportunity of counteracting the operations of the enemy, than any reliance which can be placed on the blockade of Brest and such ports as Rochefort.[40]

This was no isolated reference to the Falmouth extension's being ordered, but all agree that it was never completed and for reasons which are obscure. As already noted, the attention of the Admiralty was to become more focused on the North Sea and the Baltic; this was perhaps a dividend from Trafalgar in that the risk of an invasion force entering the Channel from the direction of the Western Approaches had been practically eliminated. If this was the view that was taken it would, of course, release resources which could have been be diverted to completing the Yarmouth line. As a further twist, a week after Pitt died in office (on 3 February 1806) Barham resigned with the rest of the government; we now do not know whether it was Barham or his successor who cancelled the Falmouth extension.

## Napoleon Checked

One leak in the attempted French blockade of Britain was through Portugal, which refused to close her ports to British trade. With eastern Europe and Russia in his pocket, Napoleon was free to concentrate his entire force against the last remaining corner of the Continent where English merchants had a foothold. The Iberian peninsula, trackless and remote as it might be, was now at his mercy, he thought. But Napoleon's perverse logic was flawed, or else his problem was insoluble; of his fatal strategic blunders, his advance into Spain ranks high, 'in Spain he hit his head against the untameable resistance of an entire nation, and above all of the masses',[41] just the sort of romanticized resistance we English like to imagine awaited Napoleon if he had ever gained a foothold here.

As Napoleon sent an army towards Lisbon through Spain, Britain sent Wellington to assist the Portuguese. But there was to be no placid lying down of the Spaniards, the population rose as one and refused to admit to Napoleon's rule, appointing new leaders who were prepared to resist to the death. Spain joined forces with the Portuguese and the British. In this way the Peninsular War broke out and lasted from 1808 to 1814. This war was to be a running sore for the French; Wellington built up a magnificent army, supplied freely by the Navy and acknowledged by him as a war-winning resource, with which he was able, ultimately, to invade France from across the Pyrenees.

That Wellington was able to create in his mould a great and victorious army in the Peninsula was due as equally to his skill at arms as the fact that everyone knew where they stood with him. Even though this may not have generated enthusiasm, it certainly allowed a steady accumulation of confidence in him. His men did not love him in the sense that Napoleon could boast, but they relied on him; they knew that, while he commanded them, their sacrifices would not be wasted. No commander ever took greater pains to deserve his men's confidence. He was as frugal with their lives as with his words. He looked after what they most valued – their stomachs. 'The attention of commanding officers,' ran one of his bleak, laconic orders, 'has been frequently called to the expediency of supplying the soldiers with breakfast.'[42]

There were several ingredients to the French misery in Spain. Napoleon dared not go to the Peninsula himself, even though he had no other campaign on hand and all Europe remained in stunned peace in the early part of it. With his over-centralized state dependent on him for its smallest decision, he dared not bury himself in that medieval labyrinth of desert and mountain into which the telegraph could not penetrate. The terrain posed no technical problems that the Chappes could not overcome; it was the guerrillas which stopped the telegraph at the Pyrenees. The painful lesson had to be learned, for, just as it would be with the electric telegraph, the visual telegraph was useless if you could not control the ground over which it passed. The guerrillas were frightful, no Frenchman was safe. For nearly four years Napoleon's daily losses in Spain averaged a hundred. In the remote places – and there was no highway that did not run through or near one – the guerrilla forces at times grew into small armies. These were encouraged and armed by Wellington from supplies brought in by the Navy. The leaders – many of them men of the humblest origin – were as elusive as they were daring. The Spanish temperament, with its fierce individualism, heroic obstinacy and passion for revenge, lent itself to such warfare. The effect on French morale was grave and cumulative. Plunder, as their army had practised it all over the rest of Europe, ceased to be a pleasure; the mildest foraging expedition assumed the character of a nightmare. Every convoy needed a powerful escort, every village and town, if it were to be of the slightest value to the tax gatherers of Joseph Bonaparte (who had the misfortune to be placed on the Spanish throne by his brother), had to be garrisoned.[43]

It was not just the Spanish guerrillas who would attack the French telegraphs. The Royal Navy played a significant role both in destroying French telegraph installations north of the Pyrenees and supplying the guerrillas to the south on the Mediterranean coast.[44] In the absence of their telegraphs, their only response was to rely on the old methods – written dispatches, but, being vulnerable to guerrillas, the French had to build blockhouses along their communication routes to assist their troops, who were required in large numbers, to give some protection to the messengers.

*An early photograph of Westminster Abbey: the London terminus of Gamble's radiated telegraph, corresponding with Hampstead Heath, was located on one of the towers.*

*Hampstead Heath: site of Gamble's radiated telegraph experiments, corresponding with Westminster Abbey, and a telegraph station on the Yarmouth line corresponding with the Royal Hospital, Chelsea, and Woodcock Hill, near Borehamwood, Hertfordshire.*

*Woolwich Parish Church showing the Revd Mr Gamble's experimental radiated telegraph on its tower: correspondence was made with a similar apparatus on Shooters Hill, near the shutter telegraph station.*

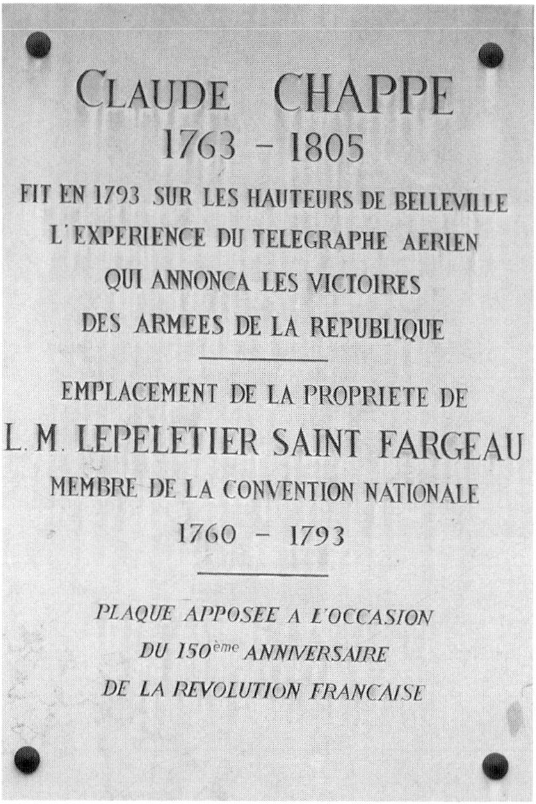

CLAUDE CHAPPE
1763 - 1805
FIT EN 1793 SUR LES HAUTEURS DE BELLEVILLE
L'EXPERIENCE DU TELEGRAPHE AERIEN
QUI ANNONCA LES VICTOIRES
DES ARMEES DE LA REPUBLIQUE
EMPLACEMENT DE LA PROPRIETE DE
L. M. LEPELETIER SAINT FARGEAU
MEMBRE DE LA CONVENTION NATIONALE
1760 - 1793
PLAQUE APPOSEE A L'OCCASION
DU 150ème ANNIVERSAIRE
DE LA REVOLUTION FRANCAISE

*Claude Chappe: 1763–1805.*

*A plaque to Claude Chappe's Belleville experiments erected in the Rue du Télégraph in 1939 on the 150th anniversary of the French Revolution.*

*No.1 Rue Claude Chappe: the Chappe family home in Brûlon.*

*Chappe-style indicators on an early French electric telegraph terminal (courtesy Museé des Arts et Metiers).*

*On the centenary in 1893 of the first successful telegraph experiments, a handsome bronze statue of Claude Chappe was erected at the junction of the Boulevard St Germain with Rue du Bac; it was removed by the Nazis in 1942.*

*A watchtower in St Martin du Tetre, near Paris, built near the site of a medieval tower used for defence but which in 1793 was the terminal station of the successful telegraph trials from Paris.*

*This 100 Franc Assignat was issued when the telegraph to Lille was being financed.*

*A junction telegraph station (courtesy Royal Signals Museum, Blandford).*

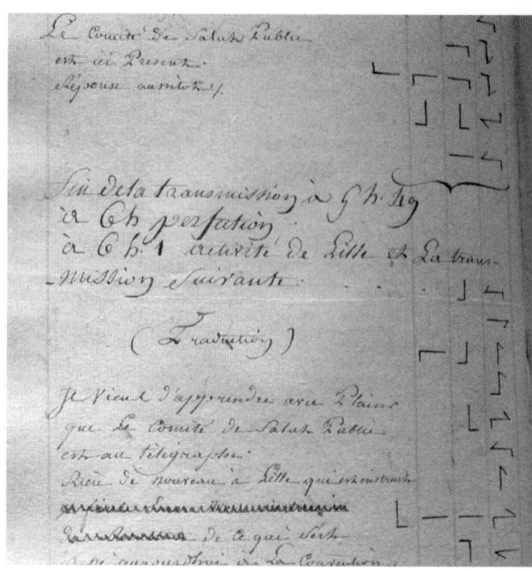

Le Comité de Salut Public
est ici Présent
Réponse aussitôt.

Fin de la transmission à 5 h. 49
à 6 h perfection
à 6 h. 1 activité de Lille et La transmission suivante.

(Traduction)

Je viens d'apprendre avec Plaisir
que le Comité de Salut Public
est au télégraphe
Rien de nouveau à Lille

*Extract from a telegraph station log book (courtesy Museé de la Poste, Paris).*

*The St Pierre telegraph tower at Montmartre in 1850.*

he St Pierre telegraph tower at Montmartre after its closure, showing the remains of the mast.*

*n early twentieth-century view of a French astal signal station at Cap D'Antibes; as these ations sprang up round the coast of France from bout 1802, they came to the attention of the oyal Navy. The semaphore arms (at rest) can be en against the mast; this station continued to e semaphore until Marconi's radio was troduced.*

N. G 23. ROCHEFORT-sur-MER. - La Tour des Signaux.


*The coastal signal station at Rochefort, originally of the Depillion semaphore type, grew into this dominating tower.*

*Cap Gris-Nez (with Cap Blanc-Nez in the background); this was the site of an experimental signal station designed in anticipation of a successful cross-Channel invasion, to correspond with Dover; it was connected to Boulogne, but never across the Channel.*

*Mont St Michel, Normandy: the site of a telegraph station on the route to Brest.*

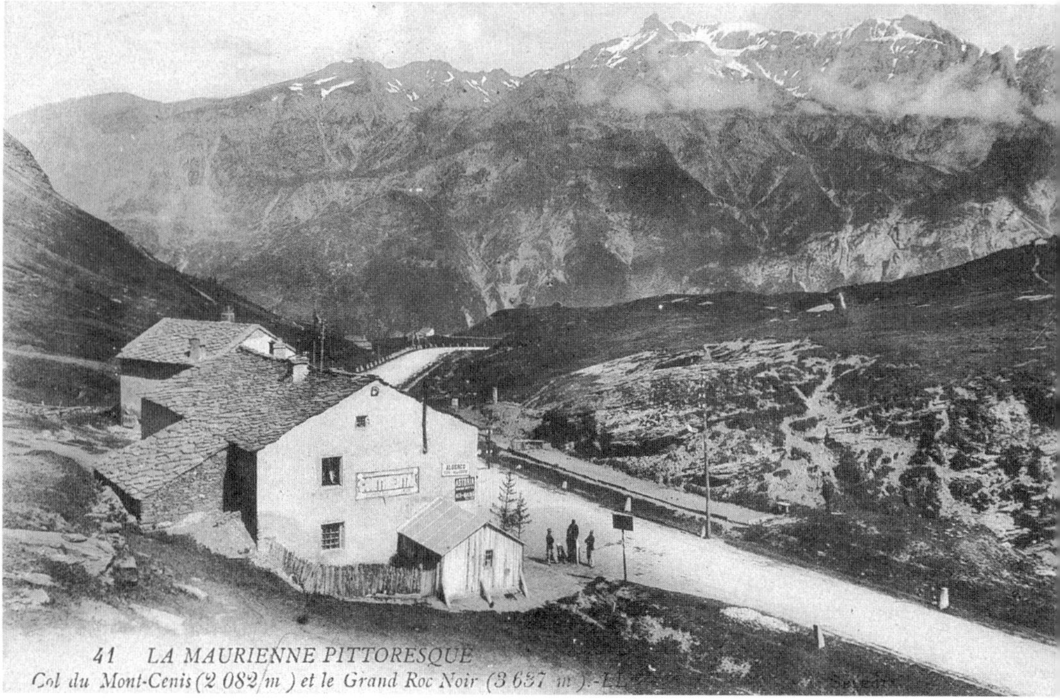

41 LA MAURIENNE PITTORESQUE
Col du Mont-Cenis (2 082 m) et le Grand Roc Noir (3 637 m). - LL

*To reach Italy the telegraph had to cross the Alps, which was done by taking it through the Mont Cenis Pass on the route between Lyon and Milan; the highest telegraph station was at over 1,900m (6,200ft).*

*enice was ordered to be connected to Paris by telegraph by Napoleon, the route via Lyon, Mont Cenis Pass and ilan reached Venice in 1810.*

*rench allegorical cartoon depicting the Chappe elegraph (courtesy Museé de la Poste, Paris).*

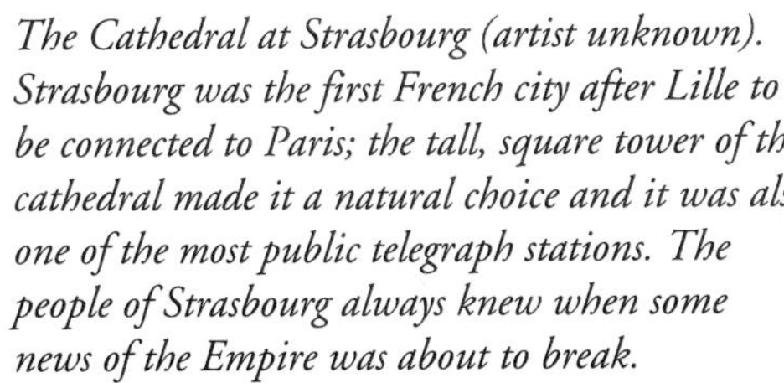

*The Cathedral at Strasbourg (artist unknown). Strasbourg was the first French city after Lille to be connected to Paris; the tall, square tower of the cathedral made it a natural choice and it was also one of the most public telegraph stations. The people of Strasbourg always knew when some news of the Empire was about to break.*

*The Chateau de Pont de Briques: Napoleon's residence during his Boulogne Camp.*

*An allegorical cartoon of rats leaving Napoleon, with a Chappe telegraph in the background.*

*As Blücher's armies moved west after Leipzig, the French telegraph stations fell into his hands; this photograph shows the site of one of them at Haut Barr in eastern France, its elevation above the surrounding countryside is plainly visible.*

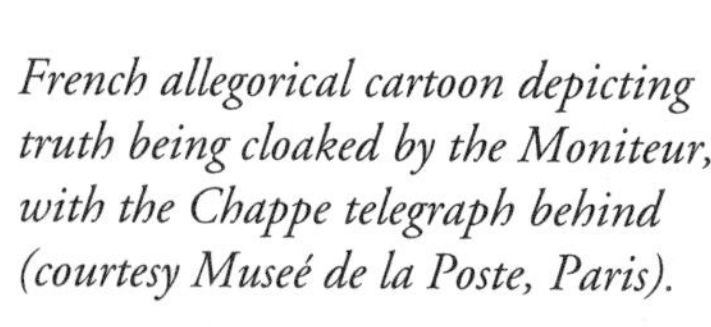

*French allegorical cartoon depicting truth being cloaked by the Moniteur, with the Chappe telegraph behind (courtesy Museé de la Poste, Paris).*

At one stage French communications became so acute that Paris might hear nothing from an expeditionary corps somewhere in the Peninsula or from Madrid for four or more weeks.[45] Such was the ferocity of the Spanish guerrillas that some would provide Wellington with the tribute of the decapitated head of a courier, along with the contents of his dispatch case.[46]

This severance of his communications was to be Napoleon's Achilles heel and it was as much a severe blow to his expectations, his assumption that his will would be able to overcome obstacles as it was militarily. In 1808 he had requested a report from the Minister of the French Navy on the instigation of telegraphs to the new war theatre:

> Send me a memo on the establishment of . . . telegraphs . . . so that I can learn in moments what happens in Toulon . . ., at Cape Finisterre [he already had communication by telegraph with Brest], and at Cape St. Vincent [on the Atlantic coast, north of Cadiz]. Make the memo short and clear, so that it tells me which new telegraphs you will have erected. . . . [I want to be able to] send via these telegraphs, an order to the squadron in Cadiz [Spain was nominally an ally] to perform a manoeuvre, or to prevent a squadron leaving Toulon or Brest.[47]

The references to Cape Finisterre and Brest are surprising, unless they were as an implied illustration of what he wanted: Toulon was not connected to Paris via Lyon until 1821. There was never any optical telegraphic connection of Paris to Cadiz; the guerrillas and the Navy ensured that the French telegraph could not cross the Pyrenees, but the episode gives great insight into Napoleon's grasp of the strategic and tactical opportunities afforded by his telegraph.

Wellington's communications, although far from easy, were at least not vulnerable to the excesses of the guerrillas. Command of the seas enabled Britain to dominate the coast of the Peninsula: her troops withdrawn from one coast could be moved more swiftly than Napoleon's land-bound legions to another. Communication with London by ship would typically be quicker than over the Pyrenees to Paris. Being the great commander that he was, Wellington was able to exploit his own advantages as well as making his enemy suffer from his own disadvantages; he even turned the tables on the French in terms of field telegraphs since, while the French had to operate without them, Wellington became the first British commander to use them in the field. Carefully he husbanded his own resources, never wasting his troops' lives and always precious with their welfare; gradually he allowed the French to be consumed by their shortages and their privations; Wellington never lost strategic control and at length wore the enemy down.

Another leak in the French blockade of British trade developed in Russia, when the Tsar allowed the import of certain British goods, an act which transformed Russia from the status of an ally of Napoleon to his enemy. Napoleon was in despair of the English: he could not break out of the cage that British naval power to the west and the south, and Russian space in the east and the north had made of Europe. He prepared for war with Russia, the defeat of which would have had severe consequences for Britain.

Regardless of the bloody lessons and the sinister warnings of history, he was planning to strike eastwards once more. England's dogged enmity had left him no other road to his destiny but across the wastes of Russia. Before the end of 1811 Napoleon had issued his orders for the mobilization of the Grand Army against Russia. Refusing to draw in his horns, a thing he now seemed incapable of doing, he left the Peninsula to look after itself while he directed his forces elsewhere. He did not abandon the Peninsula, he merely ignored it.[48]

As Wellington accumulated his strength against the French in the Peninsula, every road across Germany in the spring of 1812 was crowded with Napoleon's forces, horses, guns and wagons, with more than half a million troops, all facing east. Their aim was to drive back Russia into her Asian steppes and open a way to a world empire. The *Grande Armée* was the most concentrated instrument of power yet seen on earth. The restless energy of the Revolution, superimposed on the martial tradition of France, had been forged by the organizing genius of Napoleon into an irresistible weapon, in fourteen years it had entered every Continental capital except St. Petersburg, Stockholm and Constantinople.[49]

The scheming Fouché counselled against the Russian adventure, but Napoleon addressed him, 'You grandees are now too rich, and then you pretend to be anxious about my interests; you are only thinking of what might happen to yourselves in case of my death, and the dismemberment of my empire.' He went on, in justification of his expanded ambition in relation to Russia, 'There must be one Code, one Court of Appeal, and one coinage for all Europe. The states of Europe must be melted into one nation, and Paris be its capital.'[50] In a twenty-first-century Britain, this remark will cause a hollow laugh.

In June 1812 Napoleon invaded Russia with an army of 600,000; a soldier wrote home on 13 June:

> We have been almost continuously marching since I wrote to you from Torun [125 miles/200km west of Warsaw] on 25 May. We are here [Guerdauen, in East Prussia, 250 miles/400km from Torun] and the next letter which I will write will doubtless be from Russia which we are very near. We have to cross the Niemen from here in a few days; it is this river which separates us from the Russians, and they

> are waiting for us on the other side to defend their territory: it is probable that the artillery will decide the outcome.[51]

The distances involved in continental space are of a proportion that the inhabitants of our small island have difficulty in assimilating, distances which consumed Napoleon's army as the Russians retreated into their hinterland. We have seen already that there was no telegraph in Russia, which had allowed the Battle of Copenhagen to take place unnecessarily, neither was there one as the Russians fell back; the first telegraphs in Russia were not installed until the 1820s and the 1830s.[52]

Both sides suffered heavy losses at the inconclusive Battle of Borodino, before a further Russian retreat allowed the French to advance the 300 more miles (480km) to Moscow, itself being nearly 1,800 miles (2,900km) from Paris. The Russians exacted a ruthless policy of scorched earth as they retreated; it was given graphic, almost personal, illustration by a note found pinned to the gate of an estate whose splendid country house burned fiercely as the French arrived: 'I have for eight years embellished this residence, and lived happily in it with my family. The inhabitants of the estate, in number 1,720, quitted it at your approach; and I set fire to my house, that it may not be polluted with your presence.'[53]

Napoleon's nemesis followed the capture of Moscow and his lingering too long in a city which had been stripped of supplies and was soon to be engulfed in fire in the famously successful scorched earth policy. He had marched his army a distance we can scarcely bring to mind, into a hostile country, losing 200,000 men in the process, only to gain a ruin of a city, and the Russian winter was coming. Napoleon expected the Tsar to negotiate a peace but he wanted nothing but to be rid of Napoleon from his lands, saying 'I would go and eat potatoes with the last of my peasants rather than ratify the shame of my fatherland.' Less than two years later the same man had Paris at his feet.

With nowhere to accommodate them during the winter, the French began their retreat from Moscow in October. It was to be a catastrophe, for of the great army that followed Napoleon to Moscow only 20,000 stragglers emerged. The suffering of those poor men from disease, starvation and from cold cannot be conceived. The correspondent from whom we have already heard predicted trouble; writing in June he said, '[As we advance, the houses] will be emptied and I do not doubt that many inhabitants will die of hunger while waiting for the harvest.'[54] To die was to be the more likely fate of this French soldier. It was particularly a disaster for the Imperial Guard: an elite, self-contained force of all arms, its fighting ability and *esprit de corps* being of such campaign-winning quality and potential that it had been regarded as so valuable that Napoleon had refused to sacrifice it at Borodino; it was almost entirely destroyed in the snows in the retreat from Moscow.

Being rebuilt from the barest cadres, it was sufficiently restored to fight in the campaigns to come. 'In most battles', wrote Napoleon in 1813, 'the Guard artillery is the deciding factor since, having it always at hand, I can take it wherever it is needed', but it did not prevail at Waterloo.

Undaunted, in a manner incapable of comprehension by ordinary beings, Napoleon hastened back to France to raise fresh forces. On 3 December, Napoleon, in touch with Paris via courier and the telegraph at Strasbourg, announced to his marshals that the news he had received from Paris and the uncertain nature of his relations with some of his allies made it indispensable for him to quit his army without further delay. It was his business, he explained, to prepare at home the means of opening the next campaign in a manner worthy of the great nation.[55] But his blunder in Russia took its toll of him: one of his administrators noted that, after his return from Moscow, those who saw him observed a great change in his physical and mental constitution. The assembly of a fourth and final coalition against him made his final doom appear certain. All the great powers joined this alliance, Britain, Russia, Prussia, Austria and, finally, France herself.

On 13 March 1813, with the war in the east going badly, Napoleon ordered the Chappe brothers to build an extension of the line from Metz to Mainz, some 130 miles (210km) beyond. The first message on this line was telegraphed on 29 May that year.[56] The astonishing speed with which this extension was commissioned may have reflected the worsening military situation, for it was to operate for only seven months. Later that year, the Battle of Leipzig was fought:

> For on October 16th, 1813, three hundred thousand Russians, Austrians, Prussians and Swedes [later known as the Battle of the Nations] with more than 1,300 guns, closed in on a hundred and ninety thousand Frenchmen, Italians and Saxons under the greatest captain of all time. Three days later the battle of Leipzig ended with the desertion of Napoleon's last German allies and the utter rout of his army, scarcely a third of it escaping.[57]

This news reached London on 3 November, when in an extraordinary juxtaposition, the duplicate of the dispatch arrived first, to the chagrin of the bearer of the original. The *London Gazette Extraordinary* included the dispatch to the Foreign Secretary, Lord Castlereagh, from Lt Gen the Hon Sir Charles Stewart:

> EUROPE AT LAST APPROACHES HER DELIVERANCE, AND ENGLAND MAY TRIUMPHANTLY LOOK FORWARD TO REAP, IN CONJUNCTION WITH HER ALLIES, THAT

> GLORY HER UNEXAMPLED AND STEADY EFFORTS IN THE COMMON CAUSE SO JUSTLY ENTITLE HER TO RECEIVE.
>
> I wish it had fallen to the lot of a nobler pen to detail to your Lordship the splendid events of these two last days; but in endeavouring to relate the main facts, to send them off without a moments delay, I shall best do my duty, postponing more detailed accounts until a fresh opportunity. The victory of Gen. Blücher upon the 16th, has been followed on the 18th by that of the whole of the combined forces over the army of Bonaparte, in the neighbourhood of Leipzig.

This was no overstatement by Stewart: on the night before the battle, when Napoleon had made all his preparations, he visited every outpost and distributed Eagles to some new regiments which had recently joined him. According to Lockhart,[58] the ceremonial was splendid: the young warriors swore to die rather than witness the dishonour of France. It was upon this scene that the sun set, and, as Lockhart observed, 'with it the star of Napoleon went down for ever'. Leipzig, not Moscow, was the hinge of fate.

Leipzig was some 200 or so miles (320km) east of the head of the only recently completed fixed telegraph line at Mainz, which, leaving aside any field telegraphs he may have had, connected Napoleon to Paris via Strasbourg. But as the victor, Gen von Blücher (1742–1819) advanced to the west in 1814, the telegraph line fell into his hands. Wilson[59] tells us that some of the stations were the scene of bitter fighting. An interesting issue arises on account of the Chappe system of transmitting in code: each of the operators at an intermediate station knew only the service signals, that is, 'preparatory', 'end', for instance. Because the effective part of a signal was unknowable without the code (this is the aspect that Dumas overlooked in the Count of Monte Cristo's fraudulent manipulation of signals), the hapless operators at intermediate stations, when threatened with capture and destruction, were helpless in their inability to compose a signal to alert the rest of the line that they were under attack.

After Leipzig, the question for Napoleon was how to explain away the disaster to the French people:

> The fettered and paid scribblers who alone were allowed to write the news-sheets [for the *Moniteur*], were believed by nobody any more, had received instructions . . . as to how they were to represent the disasters of the campaign. The frost having done service as an explanation of the misfortunes of 1812, the defection of the allies was to make intelligible those of 1813 . . . 'He wants to sacrifice all

> our children to his mad ambition', that was the cry rising up from every French family.

In Paris he found the public profoundly cast down, almost despairing, and greatly incensed by his actions. His police, however zealously and arbitrarily they worked, could hardly prevent those widespread feelings from breaking forth. He had had a chance to make peace before Leipzig, and, because he rejected it, he was resented.[60] 'Every day Napoleon [had] packed the *Moniteur* with trumped-up diplomatic dispatches, fanciful news from abroad, debates in the Chambers edited to suit his purpose', wrote Pierre Lanfrey fifty years later. 'His Majesty's health has never been better' was the famous closing sentence of the bulletin in which the disaster in Russia was at last announced.

As Lockhart explained,[61] it was not by any means just the enslaved press; all the other evils attendant on an elaborate system of military despotism, of which only a few had any inkling in 1799 – conscription, heavy taxation, an inquisitorial police – all these were endured for so many years chiefly in consequence of the skill with which Napoleon knew, according to his own favourite language, how 'to play on the imagination' and gratify the vanity of the French people. In the splendour of his victories, in the magnificence of his roads, bridges, aqueducts and other monuments, in the general pre-eminence to which the nation seemed to be raised through the genius of its chief, compensation had been found for all financial burdens and consolations for domestic calamities. In defeat and the violations now inflicted on the families of those who had been violated, the people turned against Napoleon; he had brought rejection upon himself by 'an unendurable abuse of victory over a period of 15 years'.[62]

## The Errors of 1814

Napoleon had avoided capture when Paris fell in 1814, otherwise Blücher, the commander-in-chief of the Prussians, may have executed him summarily. The Tsar of Russia, in an act of magnanimity, which although well-meaning, proved to be a hopeless blunder, was determined to spare Napoleon on account of the problems which his death could have brought to the governance of France, now laid low, but although subdued, quite capable of a fast descent into chaos and anarchy. The vacuum which this would create, which any ambitious mind might try to fill, would not accord with the needs of the victors; they needed to make sure that the fulcrum of power in Europe had no avoidable leverage being applied to it by malcontents. Forsaking attempts to capture Napoleon and accepting his abdication at face value, the Tsar was content to see the Bourbon line, in the shape of Louis XVIII, restored to the monarchy and the deposed Emperor of

France installed as King of Elba, an island in the Mediterranean, out of the way, unmartyred still. But, as it turned out, still very dangerous. With the Tsar, the conqueror of Paris, now holding it in his grip, his influence could not be gainsaid; this is what he wanted for Napoleon and he only had to breathe the words to be heard. Even before he had taken Paris, he suffered, like all autocrats, from the fact that no one in his entourage could safely contradict him. He was unused to opposition and when he encountered it from his equals he reacted violently. He was unsuited to diplomacy, but events had only made it worse. Once he had taken the heroic decision to burn Moscow and see off Napoleon, the Tsar had marched from victory to victory. He had been at the head of his armies into Moscow, Warsaw, Berlin, Leipzig, Frankfurt and Paris. The lenient exile of Napoleon in Elba was to have undreamed of consequences; one of them was that the telegraph lines were closed down in England. Were it not for Napoleon's escape from Elba, this might have marked the end of the visual telegraphs in this country, the end, unless and until the owners of the country's vast merchant fleet found it in their interest to initiate their own telegraph system, as they did in 1826 when a semaphore was set up between Holyhead and Liverpool.*

The Treaty of Paris was signed on 30 May 1814, and the sovereigns and senior ministers of the governments of Europe went to London to celebrate. The Tsar and the King of Prussia arrived in London early in June, only six weeks after the last shot was fired. At the end of their summer of show and celebration, they were taken to Portsmouth especially so that they could be awed by the display of power by the Navy at Spithead. Wearied by the long years of war and the loss of treasure and blood, the peace was as welcome in England as anywhere. As later history has shown, great powers need to work at peace as hard and as well as at war. The first Treaty of Paris was botched; but even though the peace was to last less than a year, not even the biggest critics of the policy of leniency towards Napoleon could possibly have

---

*The Holyhead to Liverpool semaphore was the first and most important private sector telegraph to emerge during the first telegraph age. Operating from 1826 to 1860, making it the longest continuously serving telegraph anywhere outside France, it carried news of inbound ship movements, as vessels passed Anglesey, to Liverpool still some 90 miles (145km) away. A message taking minutes would beat the ship by hours, giving the owner of the cargo time to sell it or make arrangements for its transport or warehousing, and the ship-owner time to plan the next voyage. This was probably an example of greater utility than was achieved by the Admiralty to Portsmouth semaphore in 1822–47, which was probably much less used and its messages, if not banal, then not significant. It is a matter of great irony that one of the first messages sent from Holyhead was the reporting of the passage of the American ship *Napoleon.* For a longer account of the Holyhead to Liverpool semaphore line and other lesser commercial uses of the telegraph, see Wilson, G., *The Old Telegraphs*, 1976.

imagined his resilience and arrogance, in not just escaping from Elba, but raising an army from scratch on the way, one which, as it turned out, nearly won the day at Waterloo. These were events which no one had the ability to foresee; we should be less surprised by this than in awe of the power of Napoleon's personality and his abuse of his own capacity for greatness which he had, by steps, thrown away. In 1813, when retreating back into France, he could not bring himself to accept peace because it meant a retreat to France's old borders: regardless of the cost, he meant to win back all he had lost. He might lose his throne, he assured Metternich (1773–1859), the Austrian statesman, but he would bury the world, he boasted, more in posturing than prediction, in its ruins.[63] Had France been prepared to renounce the Rhineland, she might have prevented Britain from finding allies on the Continent to continue the war. The 'natural frontiers' were an article of faith for France. The whole drama of Napoleon's career up to the catastrophes of 1814–15 was impaled on the defence of these frontiers. 'The only peace consistent with his Roman conception of Gaul [it will be realized that, in Roman times, Gaul extended as far as the "natural frontiers"] lay in an empire in the Roman fashion, that is to say England subjugated and France supreme in Europe.'[64]

In 1814, however, with Napoleon out of the way, with the European powers about to adjourn from London to Vienna for the peace congress, and, in any event, with no naval force in existence which could threaten Britain, the Admiralty dropped its guard. In July it gave orders to close its four shutter telegraph lines from London and in November similar orders were given to close down its coastal signalling network. It had been by means of these networks that the Navy built its mastery of the Channel and seas. The shutter telegraph and coastal signals networks, for all their faults of vulnerability to bad weather, had enabled the Admiralty to feel able, and actually to be able, to react to an attempt at a cross-Channel invasion and to destroy the enemy on the high seas. On what basis can the Admiralty be faulted in closing the telegraph networks in 1814? They had waged a war at sea since 1793, they had taken on any force ranged against them and had proved themself to be a fighting machine of peerless quality. What did it matter that they could now revert to the mail coach for communication with the ports? Did it matter if a fleet missed a tide? Which nation was the enemy whose ships were to be reported by the coastal stations? It was the received wisdom that there was neither an enemy nor a match for the Navy. Moreover, now the war had to be paid for and the Admiralty, with no remit for advancing telegraph technology, had to make economies and so the telegraphs were closed.

Unlike in England, where the Admiralty was more concerned with economy than with exploiting the benefits to commerce (for which it had no brief), the French network was not closed down when Napoleon abdicated. The Chappe brothers continued to be held in esteem, even though the power base in Paris had been fractured and legitimacy had been transferred to the restored Louis XVIII and his government. No sooner than they had been restored than a situation report on the extent of the telegraph network was ordered; the king discovered that from Paris it radiated to Lille, Boulogne and Metz; Strasbourg, Lyon and Brest; a trunking of some 1,250 miles (2,010km). Such was the king's pleasure that he granted Ignace, Pierre and Abraham the rank of chevaliers of the Legion d'Honneur. These favours produced a culture on which the spores of jealousy could grow. There were to be rumours, after Napoleon's escape from Elba, that the Chappes were under arrest; this was a charge sufficiently credible for a denial to be published for on 17 March 1815 (just before Napoleon arrived and the king fled). The brothers had a letter published in the *Moniteur* pointing out that, while a military post had been established in the offices of the telegraph administration, it was to protect the telegraph and not to arrest the Chappes.[65] As already noted, probably because of the huge distances in France compared with those in Britain, the telegraph continued to be extended and exploited until the electric telegraph and Morse code took over. In 1846 the network had been extended to include Toulon, Marseille, Cherbourg, Bordeaux and Bayonne; Toulouse, Narbonne and Perpignan; Nantes, Orléans, Tours and Poitiers; a network of around 2,500 miles (4,000km), or from London to Edinburgh about six times.

# 11
# Napoleon: Escape

*And the King said: 'And how did you come by this dispatch?'*
*'By the telegraph, Sire'*[1]
As the news of Napoleon's escape from Elba arrived
Paris, 5 March 1815

*'You mean' [said the King, going pale with rage], 'that seven armies overthrew that man; a divine miracle replaced me on the throne of my fathers after twenty-five years of exile . . . only . . . for a force that I held in the palm of my hand to destroy me?'*[2]

## A Bill is Rushed Through Parliament

On 16 June 1815 a Bill was introduced into the Commons to which, during its passage through Parliament, not only was no amendment made, but also was subject to no debate. On 29 June the Bill, with all-party support, completed its stages, received the Royal assent and passed into law. It was *An Act to enable His Majesty to acquire Ground necessary for Signal and Telegraph Stations.*

Why did Parliament allow itself to be hurried? In an age when any interference with the individual and his private property was considered pernicious, why was legislation which gave the government power to requisition private land rushed into law in thirteen days with no objection? Why was there no opposition? Why should the government have been in such haste to take these new powers? Had they not only recently closed down their shutter telegraph lines? Had not the wars with France, which had lasted over twenty years, finished more than a year earlier? The answer to these questions is the same as the explanation of why in England and across Europe men held their breath: Napoleon was loose again, escaped from Elba and was regathering his army, bent once more on a final victory which would restore his dream of his single European state in his control. Hubris had not yet been turned to nemesis; who could say, as the Bill's passage was put on the fast track, that Napoleon's nemesis was at hand? Was he not a brilliant general? He may have been only one victory away, for all anyone knew, from the destiny he believed was his, 'to change the face of the world'. His dream had not yet been shattered at Waterloo, nor yet had he been cast into exile in the south Atlantic; that too, lay in the future.

## The Reaction to Napoleon's Escape

In order to capture the mood of the moment we must cast aside the fact that Napoleon was to be doomed at Waterloo: no one knew what was going to happen but the whole of Europe was making a reassessment following his escape from Elba. In spite of his capitulation in 1814, a page of history had not yet been turned after all.

In France, the Royalists were in the ascendancy again. The Restoration had destroyed the idea of Bonapartism, but evidently not the man. It seemed incredible that, only fourteen months previously, on 31 March 1814, the Tsar of Russia had led his troops victoriously into Paris after defeating Napoleon's army following what had been thought to be his final drubbing at Leipzig, a battle in which he had lost about two-thirds of his nearly 200,000-strong army. Was this not the man whose statue atop the triumphal column in the Place Vendôme had been toppled on the day of the Allies' entry into Paris, like any dictator who had become yesterday's man? Was it not the case that Napoleon, having abdicated not much more than a year previously, was banished to Elba in the Mediterranean? Had we not had the long dreamed of peace following the signing of the Treaty of Paris, much celebrated in London only the previous year, where all the leading statesmen and sovereigns of Europe gathered to mark the end, they thought, of war in Europe, one which had been waged, with only a small intermission in 1802–03, since France had declared war on Austria in 1792? Why, only in September of the previous year, 1814, the Congress of Vienna had assembled; this was to be one which was to see the leaders of the victorious European powers settle the peace and re-establish the balance of power in Europe. The news arrived in Vienna on the night of 6/7 March 1815 (the telegraph now stopped at the French frontier since its army had been rolled back) that Napoleon, wearying of his exile, had escaped. Until that moment, this once great man was merely 'King of the island of Elba after having been ruler of part of the world, [now] exercising sovereignty over [only] 500 or 600 souls, when he had once heard "Long live Napoleon!" from 120 million subjects, in ten different languages'.[3]

In a move which had no historical precedent, and which will doubtless always remain unique, Napoleon rejected his exile and attempted to regain his empire. Landing on 1 March with a small cadre of men near Cap d'Antibes on the Côte d'Azur, Napoleon headed for Grenoble, where he was welcomed even though the gates of the city had, on orders, been locked against him; the garrison commander was powerless to resist the acclamation with which the Emperor was received and the gates which had been barred for the protection of the people were opened at their demand. From

Grenoble his ever-growing band of followers marched to Lyon; here was located the most southerly reach of the telegraph link to Paris. It was from Lyon that the spread of the dramatic news accelerated:

> Paris heard the news of Napoleon's escape . . by telegraphed dispatch from Lyon at 11 am on 5 March 1815, four days after he had landed at Golfe-Juan. Three hours later the astounded Marshal Soult, [now] . . . Minister of War, telegraphed . . . Lyon for more details. Thereafter, the Lyon line was working constantly at pressure, with the King ceaselessly demanding information.[4]

The telegraph had been developed twenty-two years earlier for war and now it was to be used in war again; but in England the business of fast communication over land had been abandoned, consigned back to where it had only recently advanced. By a perverse regression, news travelled in England at the speed of the horse again, for the Admiralty had closed down its shutter telegraph lines in 1814. In France, Napoleon was now in control of the southern telegraph terminal and able to telegraph to Paris to anyone who would listen.

Napoleon remained at Lyon from 10 to 13 March; but this was no halt for rest and recuperation; taking control of the functions of civil government, he published several decrees – one, commanding justice to be administered everywhere in his name after 15 March; another abolishing all legislative bodies under the monarchy and summoning all the electoral colleges to meet in Paris, which they did at the so-called Camp de Mai on 1 June, and many others to regulate the transfer of power from the Bourbon government. It was when Napoleon was retaking the reins of command at Lyon that Marshal Ney famously volunteered to take charge of a body of troops headed south for the purpose of taking Napoleon prisoner. It was at Lons-le-Saunier, some 75 miles (120km) north of Lyon, that Ney's troops met Napoleon and his gathering army on the road. Famously, but to the cost of his life when Napoleon's power crumbled, Ney promised Louis XVIII to bring Napoleon back to Paris in a cage. In the event this was beyond Ney's power even if it were his desire: when the troops sent to capture Napoleon were confronted by him, any notion of detaining him dissolved; breaking ranks amid cries of '*Vive L'Empereur*', the would-be captors joined Napoleon's ranks, to be followed by Ney. After Waterloo, Ney having joined the losing side, was doomed: on 7 December 1815 the news of Ney's trial verdict and his execution were relayed down the telegraph network.[5]

One of the most remarkable truths about Napoleon is the power of his personality and the relationship he had with his soldiers: it was the former rather than a political cause by which he gathered an army as he progressed; it is more accurate to say that he regathered *his* army. During his career he achieved a spectacular kinship with his soldiers; by playing on the emotions of military glory and comradeship with evangelical zeal, he was able to create an unbreakable bond. In the hands of a genius with a more containable ambition, if such is not a contradiction, this power of inspiration could have led to a more benign but all-powerful conclusion. The spontaneous conversion of troops to Napoleon's columns, as happened with Ney's force, was no isolated incident: in *The Times* of 6 April 1815, in its *Telegraphic Dispatches* column, an item was reported that had been sent to Paris via the telegraph after the Lyon terminal was in Napoleon's hands:

> Telegraphic Dispatch from Lyons, 1 April 1815
> All the troops of the line of the garrison of Marseilles who had marched upon Gap [about 100 miles (160km) north of Marseilles, in Provence, and the first town to come under Napoleon's thrall], with the Marseilles volunteers, have joined the national guards, who went to meet them. The soldiers and the national guards embraced each other exclaiming '*Vive l'Empéreur!*'

As Napoleon advanced on Paris, the authorities had known by telegraph for more than a week of his new enterprise before the Paris newspapers, pondering which brew of lies and truth to retail, ventured to make any allusion to its existence. Then, echoing the word used in Vienna, Napoleon was declared an outlaw by a royal ordnance. Following this the *Moniteur* announced, in a passage at which even the most gullible would have smiled, that, 'surrounded by faithful garrisons and a loyal population, the outlaw was already stripped of most of his followers;  was wandering in despair among the hills, and certain to be a prisoner within two or three days at the utmost'. Once the veracity of the press has been impugned it is, of course, the devil's job to reverse public incredulity; as Lockhart observed, the *Moniteur* was in no better position to be believed in 1815, when Napoleon was in the ascendancy again, than it had been in 1814, when Napoleon's doom was at hand.[6]

On reaching Paris, Napoleon retook possession of the Tuileries on 20 March. In an attempt at atonement, but one which he was ultimately to regret, one of his first acts was to proclaim the freedom of the press. Being in control of the telegraph network allowed him to retain control over the terms of news dispatches. But it was not, however, in Napoleon's nature to be comfortable with criticism in a free press, for, in spite of the watchfulness of his police, neither he nor any other leader with unbridled power could ever bend to the wind of freedom.

In Vienna, even as Napoleon marched on Paris, the most powerful group of European leaders that had hitherto ever assembled in one place had reacted to the news in unanimity: this surely, was to be the foundation of

Napoleon's fall? How else could a coalition be forged so quickly, even if the spirit were willing? Napoleon had timed his escape from Elba badly. To have arranged such a meeting of statesmen such as that taking place in Vienna in the days when the horse governed the speed of travel and when France and Sweden were the only countries to have an operational telegraph would have taken weeks. As it was, the European leaders were there, on the spot, together, to lay their plans. Virtually as one they rose in agreement that the return of Napoleon to France was unacceptable; all Europe prepared once again for war. In consequence, three separate armies were assembled against him and he was finally defeated by Wellington at Waterloo, on 18 June. This defeat was just two days after the Bill to allow the construction of telegraph and signal stations was introduced in Parliament, and when the rebuilding of the telegraph network in London had already begun. The Admiralty still wanted their telegraph legislation; they could not allow themselves to be wrong-footed twice. Why did they persist? It seems plain that, although the Admiralty had been among good company, they had been badly caught out by the dramatic events following Napoleon's escape from Elba.

## The Admiralty is Not to be Caught Unawares Again

It did not matter that the war was finally over in 1815 and that there was no foreign navy to challenge them; the Admirals had heard the row in Parliament when news of Napoleon's escape had broken and were not going to be caught out again, they felt that they had to have something. And so, thanks to Napoleon, and the contemptuous dismissal of electricity, the shutter telegraph lines to Portsmouth and Plymouth were reinstated, at least for a short while, before the opening in 1822 of the semaphore line to Portsmouth.

Many had been made to look foolish by Napoleon's escape from Elba. There had, indeed. been a terrible fuss in Parliament: as a critic of the government remarked in a debate in the House of Lords in April 1815:

> There could not be a greater contrast than between the alarm which the escape of . . . [Napoleon] had created, and the efforts which had been made to prevent the return of that plague of Europe. You had at last delivered Europe [by the victories of 1813–14] – you had it in your power to make honourable and safe arrangements for peace – and you threw it away for the want of an act of vigour against . . . [Napoleon].[7]

What instructions, the Opposition wanted to know, had the government given to the Navy to contain Napoleon on Elba? This was a question for the Prime Minister, Lord Liverpool, an able man, the equal or better of all his colleagues, five of whom (Canning, Goderich, Wellington, Peel and Palmerston) afterwards became Prime Minister: Liverpool's answer to the question was:

> It was absurd to imagine that it was in the power of the Royal Navy to prevent Napoleon's escape. The greater part of the Mediterranean fleet had returned to home waters after the [first] Treaty of Paris, and the Navy did not have the resources to stop and search all the meanest fishing vessels.

'The Treaty was improvident', was the charge made against the government, because it 'afforded no security to Europe'.[8] The mistake, thought the Opposition, was on not insisting on custody for Napoleon. With the benefit of hindsight, this was self-evident and, although it was not to be a mistake made twice, it was a charge that the government was able to deflect. 'You saw the terms of the Treaty: you made no complaint then', Liverpool was able to assert. But this was not to say that the government was winning the argument.

The reason for the government's discomfort was their inability to speak plainly about the Tsar's mistake of being too lenient on Napoleon a year earlier. A new war against Napoleon was about to break upon Europe, a new alliance had been struck. It was only a month since the Declaration had been made on 13 March in Vienna by Britain, France, Russia, Prussia and Austria, with Spain, Sweden and Portugal joining in. The Powers had declared that Napoleon 'has placed himself in the pale of civil and social relationships, and that as an enemy and a disturber of the tranquillity of the world, he has rendered himself liable to public vengeance'. The inclusion of France in the list should be noted: this was Talleyrand's artful work.

This was no time for Britain to be upsetting Russia, she was an important ally; not only did she have a large army, but Britain's own could be only a shadow of it in its scale. Instead of poking the finger at Russia, Parliament went over the ground again to consider the situation after the fall of Paris in March 1814 and gave the government a ritualistic hard time. At the time Paris fell the government had not been in a position to insist on Napoleon's being placed in custody because it was 'treating with a man with arms in his hands'. At the time when the peace terms were agreed, Liverpool said for the government, Napoleon was not only still in control of his army, but his forces

> were in possession of every fortified town in France and Holland and a great number in Germany, including all fortified places on the Rhine, the Elbe and Italy. The Treaty had avoided all these places having to be taken by force with the risks attendant in the prosecution of the war against the advantages of peace.

The French did not break up their telegraph network in 1814, as happened in England; anyone in control of Paris in 1814, whether a benign new government or an occupying power, would be able to issue commands via its large domestic network. So, Napoleon, wherever he found himself in the field, would have been hard pressed to manoeuvre his troops in their scattered redoubts to make head against the armies that opposed him and could in large degree be manoeuvred by telegraph, which in any event held Paris in its grip). But the reason given in Parliament for not crushing Napoleon in 1814 was plainly just a cover for the real reason: the Tsar had been in control of both Paris and of the terms to be offered Napoleon. The Opposition could see through it:

> . . . so what that Napoleon had not been defeated in the field: he surely would have been! Was not the Duke of Wellington in control of the south of France, with his army freshly victorious from the Peninsula? It was plain that all Napoleon's power had dissipated and it was nonsense to suggest that Napoleon could not realize that he would be vanquished if he did not yield, for at the time of the Treaty, Napoleon had not much more than 20,000 men, while the allies had 100,000 infantry and 30,000 cavalry.[9]

Just so: on a division in the House of Lords at the end of this debate, the voting was *Contents*: 21; *Not-contents*: 53. This reflected the mood of the country.

While the government parried the attacks on it in Parliament for allowing the escape of Napoleon, the Admiralty sheltered from the storm created by their perceived culpability. It is easy to be critical of the Admiralty in their shutting down of their telegraph network, but it is only with 20:20 hindsight that this can be sustained. The Admiralty was not alone in thinking that the war was over in 1814; as we have seen, many people had been made to look foolish by Napoleon's escape, and no one had stood up and predicted his escapade before it had happened. To understand anything about the atmosphere in Britain in 1814, when peace had come, it is vital to appreciate how war-weary she had become and the great sense of relief that in Vienna the great statesmen were settling the foundations of a lasting peace, 'arrangements so extensive and important [which] had never before taken place in Europe',[10] said an Opposition spokesman, with no overstatement.

When Paris fell to Russian and Prussian troops in March 1814, Britain had been at war with France since 1793 with only a brief gap in 1802–03. With Napoleon utterly defeated and the coalition of his enemies bent on a peace which would maintain a balance of power in Europe, who could foresee a new war? And were not economies necessary to pay for the last one? The more one pauses to reflect on the bright prospects for peace as they seemed in 1814, the more remarkable becomes the extraordinary events of Napoleon's Hundred Days: unprecedented even by the standards of great men (or tyrants) of the past or since; it was beyond fiction, and, although Napoleon was an ugly menace to most of the European peoples of the time, he was worthy, not just by accepting his genius for generalship, of some acclamation for the sheer strength of his will and personality. It was by a great miscalculation that these strengths were contained by nothing more than 150 miles (240km) of the Mediterranean Sea.

## The Re-Establishment of the Telegraph Service

Little archival material has come to light which tells us much about how the Admiralty reacted to Napoleon's escape and of the new powers which had been granted by Parliament to re-establish the telegraph service and to set up new lines. The evidence that the lines were closed down in 1814 after the second Treaty of Paris has been widely accepted by writers on the subject: the shutter telegraphs were never anything other than temporary affairs. Most have left it at that, without exposing the fact that, after Napoleon's escape, some of the lines were reopened: Holmes,[11] however, is explicit and correct in stating that the Portsmouth shutter line was re-established. He does not say the same for the Plymouth branch, but there is irrefutable evidence to show that it was back in use by July and August 1815; this evidence will be covered in Chapter 12. I have found no evidence to show that either the Deal or the Yarmouth shutter telegraph was reopened; on balance, the lack of evidence to show that they were suggests to me that they were not. After 1814 the Yarmouth command reverted to the Admiral at The Nore (in the Thames/Medway estuaries), so it is unlikely that there was any operational need for a telegraph to Yarmouth after then, but immediately it has to be accepted that the Nore was served by the Deal line, for which there is no evidence of its use after 1814. There is neither contemporary nor later evidence yet discovered to explain why not.

Whether or not the new powers for entering land and reopening lines of sight were used to remobilize the Portsmouth and Plymouth telegraphs is not known; no freeholds had been acquired for any of the telegraph station sites and it seems likely that the leases on some at least of them had been turned back to their owners. If a surveyor were to have revisited a station site which had been closed down in 1814, he would have found in, say June 1815, much less than one full season's growth on the trees and probably no over-troublesome challenge to the sight lines. My speculation is that the Admiralty would have wanted to reopen all their lines, that they gave priority to Portsmouth and Plymouth, and then, with Napoleon in captivity, abandoned the telegraph line to Deal and, the least serviceable, to

Yarmouth completely. Of course, this was not the end of the telegraph story, for in 1822 a semaphore telegraph line to Portsmouth was opened, a line which took a different route from the shutter line and which was designed as a permanent facility with signal stations built on freehold sites. Being designed to last (which they were until the electric telegraph took over in 1847, many of the signal stations have survived to the present). But their story will have to be a new one. Now, the final chapters of the story of the shutter telegraphs have to be played out; Waterloo and St. Helena, anchored in history as they are, both touch the telegraph story.

# 12
# Napoleon: Defeat

*'There, my lads, in with you, let me see no more of you!'*[1]
Wellington to the Coldstream Guards, attacking at Waterloo

*Therefore, dear boy, mount on my swiftest horse.*[2]
Shakespeare

## Collision

It is scarcely possible to exaggerate what was at stake at Waterloo, not just two great armies coming together in a gigantic collision but two political systems, incapable of co-existence. One had to eliminate the other, each championed by its own army which were to pound away until a result was posted. A draw would not do, the business had to be finished at Waterloo, for Napoleon knew that, deep in the Continent, as arranged at the Congress of Vienna, the armies which had been mobilized by the sovereigns of Europe were bound for France. No official state of war existed; Napoleon, having been declared an outlaw by the coalition which included France herself – if not the nation, then some of her scheming leaders – knew that his defining moment was at hand. But France would unite behind him, and the weasels back in Paris would be eclipsed if he could beat Wellington and his Prussian collaborator Blücher. As Wellington himself was to observe later:

> I look upon Salamanca, Vittoria and Waterloo as my three best battles – those which had great and permanent consequences. Salamanca relieved the whole south of Spain, changed all the prospects of the war, and was felt even in Prussia. Vittoria freed the Peninsula altogether . . . and [its consequences] . . . led to Leipzig and the deliverance of Europe; and Waterloo did more than any other battle I know towards the true object of all battles – the peace of the world.

The Battle of Salamanca in 1812 had allowed the relief of Madrid shortly after; some thought that the battle raised Wellington almost to the level of

Marlborough. His prudence was well known, as well as his eye for choosing a position, and his skill in utilizing it, but at Salamanca he showed himself a great and able master of manoeuvre. Of Vittoria, as Viscount Castlereagh (1769–1822), the Foreign Secretary, was to say in the Commons: 'In the military annals of modern times, there never had been a train of successes on the theatre of war more glorious as those leading up to [including Salamanca] the final success of Vittoria.'

That Wellington's victory at Waterloo, his last battle, brought peace is inarguable, but there was more to it than that. There had never been anything like Waterloo before, and never anything like it since: the destiny of a continent was settled in an afternoon, for, as Victor Hugo said in his famous digression on the battle in *Les Misérables*, 'Waterloo was not a battle but a change in direction of the world.' For Hugo, it was not by Wellington that the victory was won, but by the intervention of the Almighty. He questioned whether there was a cause for the total collapse of Napoleon's army whose gallantry had astonished the world:

> Yes. The shadow of a momentous justice lay over Waterloo. It was the day of destiny, when a force greater than mankind prevailed. Hence the terrifying bowing of heads, the surrender of so many noble spirits. The conquerors of Europe were stricken with helplessness, unable to say or do anything as they felt the weight of that terrible Presence . . . On that day the course of mankind was altered. Waterloo was the hinge of the 19th century. The great man had to disappear in order that a great century might be born. One who is Unanswerable had taken the matter in hand, and thus the panic of so many heroes is explained. It was not merely a shadow that fell upon Waterloo but a thunderbolt; it was God himself.[3]

According to Hugo it was not in the true sense a victory, but a lucky throw of the dice, one won by Europe:

> It was the strangest encounter in history. Napoleon and Wellington were not enemies but opposites. Never has God, who delights in antitheses, contrived a more striking contrast or a more extraordinary confrontation. On the one side precision, foresight, shrewd calculation, cool tenacity, and military correctitude; reserves husbanded, the way of retreat ensured, advantage taken of the terrain; warfare ordered by the book with nothing left to chance. On the other side intuition, divination, military unorthodoxy, more than human instinct, the eye of the eagle that strikes with lightning swiftness, prodigious art mingled with reckless impetuosity; all the mysteries of an unfathomable nature, the sense of kinship with Destiny . . . Faith

> in a star mingled with military science, enriching but also undermining it. Wellington was the technician of war, Napoleon was its Michelangelo; and this time genius was vanquished by rule-of-thumb.[4]

For Hugo, had Napoleon won Waterloo it would have been counter to the tide of the nineteenth century: it was time for the great man to fall. More analytically, the *Cambridge Modern History* asserts that his efforts to reduce Europe to a single unity under his dynasty ran counter to the aspirations of the leading nations; his legacy was to incubate the seed of the growth of nationalism in Germany and Italy, but 'A united Europe could not be built by one man's will, or without the wholehearted support of most of its inhabitants'.[5]

It seems that this lesson of history has still not been learned. But we cannot dwell on that truth here. Whatever, Waterloo was the assertion of the Divine Right of Kings: conservatism had prevailed over the heir to the Revolution. Reform, overdue already would have to wait, for, although following the battle there was a degree of liberalism, and a grudging constitutionalism emerged from it, large numbers of men had suffered and died to maintain or restore, perversely, the aristocracies. Hugo is disparaging of the English for this; writing a generation and a half later, and with a certain canny perception of the English:

> . . . they still cherish their feudal illusions. They believe in heredity and hierarchy. They are a people unsurpassed in power and glory, but they still think of themselves as a nation, not as people. As people they willingly subordinate themselves, accepting a lord as a leader. The workman lets himself be despised, the soldier lets himself be flogged. We may recall that after the Battle of Inkerman [in the Crimean War] a sergeant who had it seems saved the army could not be mentioned in dispatches by Lord Raglan because the English military hierarchy does not allow any man of less than commissioned rank to be named in a report.[6]

Napoleon, had he struck his invasion medal, would have changed all this, for it is recognizable still today where, for a Frenchman to be a waiter is a respected profession, but is inextricably associated in the Englishman's mind with subservience. But the lowly Englishman cared only that by Waterloo the status quo had survived, dictatorship was stopped and Waterloo had put an end to the overthrow of European thrones by the sword.

These hard-used men were filled with the burning love of their country and their regiments. The founders of Sandhurst laid it down that the professional education of British officers ought to aim at producing, not corporals, but gentlemen. So long as it did so, they knew it would produce the kind of leader Englishmen would follow with a resolve of which Hugo knew nothing. It was pride, not servility:

> Pride in the continuing regiment – the personal individual loyalty which each private felt towards his corps – [which] gave to the British soldier a moral strength which the student . . . ought never to underestimate. It enabled him to stand firm and fight forward when men without it, however brave, would have failed. To let down the regiment, to be unworthy of the men of old who had marched under the same colours, to be untrue to the comrades who had shared the same loyalties, hardships and perils are things that the least-tutored, humblest soldier would not do. Through the dusty, tattered ranks the spirit of companionship ran like a golden thread.[7]

It was not just the soldiers, there was a national pride among the civilian poor who had a belief in the superiority of their country and its ways of life. For all its harshness and injustice, such simple folk thought there was no country like their own. These were the people who had reacted spontaneously with horror when they heard that the French king had been guillotined, the same people who had seen the curtains come down in the theatres in a recoil of shock at regicide, and whose minds, almost in an instant, had turned to war. There was something else which Hugo did not appreciate in his disparagement of the English: they may have followed a lord, but the subordination which Hugo despised was more a compliment than a taunt, the Englishman was wary of power, the islanders were careful to apply restraints to the exercise of it and would never tolerate tyranny They believed in the moral right of the individual to liberty, self-respect and the ownership of property. The Frenchman of the Revolution may have had his *égalité* – and been part of an extraordinary militarist empire which saw Vienna fall four times to their mercy. But Paris had fallen in 1814, it was about to fall again, and again in 1870, come within a whisker of it in 1914 and be laid low in 1940. The subservient islanders, meanwhile, experienced neither a tyrant nor invasion. The work of revolution in England would have to – and did – proceed in another more gradualist form.

As Napoleon left Paris on 11 June at the start of the Waterloo campaign, he had strongly fortified the city and also positions in advance of it, so far as the armies forming against him in the east were concerned. These redoubts were on the Seine, the Marne and the Saube, and among the passes of the Vosges hills, including Metz; Lyon was also guarded by a formidable force. As he prepared to do battle with the Prussians and the British, he could be in touch via a courier service to Lille or one of its telegraph trunking stations on the Paris line, and by these be in immediate contact direct with his outposts in Strasbourg, Metz and Lyon. However, he was not able to profit from this enormous strategic advantage; the cataclysm of Waterloo was so complete that it eliminated Napoleon as a military force, even as he held the strategic advantage in terms of the fast deployment or redeployment of his army, should a serious threat come from the east instead of from Wellington. As he left Paris, he exclaimed as he entered his carriage, 'I go to measure myself against Wellington.'[8] Taken in the aggregate, Napoleon was twice the man, but Wellington, while being a shadow of Napoleon's genius in the political sense, had fully the measure of Napoleon on the battlefield, and a greater respect for life and liberty.

Napoleon and Wellington were in the field with their armies in Belgium and there was no method of communicating available to either of them other than by the dispatch rider on horseback. Napoleon was alone with his army, now numbering over 70,000, all returning to him since his landing on the Côte d 'Azur on 1 March. As dawn broke on 18 June, neither Napoleon nor his men doubted their ability to destroy Wellington and reach Brussels by nightfall. Their triumph over the Prussians in a preliminary battle on 15 June, which had for the moment kept the two allies apart, had whetted their appetite for glory. They saw themselves on the verge of a new age, like that which had been delivered to them by their remarkable chain of victories in Italy in 1797. 'Nor was the urgent victory Napoleon needed the key only to political salvation. It would be a revenge for all the humiliations the English had heaped on him. Wellington was the one commander with a European reputation whom he had never beaten, and the British the one army.'[9] 'We will sleep tonight in Brussels', Napoleon told his officers, and but for the intervention of chance, or the Almighty as Hugo thought, they would have.

## Chance

The opening shots in the battle, the climax not just of a three-day campaign, but the whole Napoleonic era, were not fired until shortly before midday. During the previous night there had been a storm and torrential rain had drenched the battlefield; the very lateness of the hour, ordained to allow the ground to dry to permit the artillery some manoeuvrability, was to play its part in destiny. Blücher and his Prussian army had been badly mauled when, at dawn on 15 June, after one of his incredibly swift and secret manoeuvres, Napoleon had sprung across a river, concentrated his force and driven a wedge between Blücher and Wellington.[10] Napoleon argued that Blücher would retire to the east, and he detached Marshal Grouchy with 30,000 men to contain him; but Blücher had escaped annihilation and been able to withdraw in tolerable order into the night. Retaining contact with his defeated ally, Wellington fell back in good order, knowing that Blücher had promised that he would return to support Wellington's Anglo-German-

Dutch army when it, in its turn, was attacked by Napoleon. Late on the fateful day, in what Napoleon must have thought to be the devil's work, Blücher (having avoided being engaged by Grouchy) joined battle to save the day. Hugo, in his account of the battle paid particular attention to chance:

> What is wonderful in all battles on the scale of Waterloo is the part played in them by chance. The rain-sodden field, the sunken lane [in which large numbers of the French cavalry perished], the deafness of Grouchy [who failed to stop Blücher's intervention], the guide who misled Napoleon and the guide who led Blücher aright – chance was marvellously skilful in its ordering of that débâcle.

With some setbacks, the early phases of the battle went Napoleon's way, and were to be the cause of, first, the rumours, and then actual reports of defeat for Wellington that reached Brussels, and, as we will see, London as well.

Wellington's infantry were formed up in squares, resolutely his men would stand against a charge by Napoleon's cavalry, brandishing sabres and thundering towards them with cries of '*Vive l'Empéreur!*', the first rank threatening with the bayonet, while behind the well-drilled musketry took its toll. Where losses were great, the squares became smaller, discipline being the master of attrition. All this time Wellington rode about the battlefield, encouraging here, reordering there, and appraising all the time. Once, when chatting with the commanding officer of a square in which he had taken shelter he was heard to say, 'Oh, it will be all right; if the Prussians come up in time, we shall have a long peace.' But occasionally he looked at his watch. It was how long to nightfall, that he was calculating – he knew he could not survive that long – it was Blücher that he wanted. But, maintaining his own majestic certainty, he famously offered the remark, 'Hard pounding this, gentlemen, but we will see who can be pound the longest.' Throughout this time and during the bombardments which preceded each assault the British infantry patiently endured their fate. They seemed in their steady squares to be rooted to the ground. It was no battle of science, it was a stand-up fight between two pugilists, each milling away till one or the other was beaten.[11]

Chance now played her defining role. 'Each side was awaiting someone', wrote Hugo, 'and it was the technician who calculated rightly.' Napoleon awaited Grouchy whom he had summoned back to the battlefield, but he did not come; Wellington awaited Blücher who came, aided, it seems, by a peasant guide who knew the way. Seeing Wellington in his precarious state, Blücher ordered the attack with the notable words: 'We must give the English a breather.'

And all this happened – the Kings returned to their thrones, the master of Europe was caged, the *Ancien Régime* became the new régime, and all the darkness and light in the world change places – because on a summer afternoon a shepherd had said to a Prussian general in the wood, 'Go this way and not that way.'[12]

Everything Napoleon possessed had now to be staked on a final culminating bid for victory: chance had decided against him.

## Confusion

Three factors gave rise to unsubstantiated reports of Wellington's impending defeat during the day, rumours of which reached London. Before the battle began, Wellington could not know where Napoleon would strike: would it be a frontal assault (which, in fact, it turned out to be) or would the great general strike to the west? If Napoleon were to strike westwards, Wellington would be forced to expose Brussels, because it lay 12 miles (19km) behind Wellington's lines. For this reason Wellington wrote in the small hours of the morning of the 18th several letters warning the British ambassador at Brussels and others of this contingency. 'Pray keep the English quiet if you can', he told the former. Wellington also wrote a personal letter to one of his lady favourites, who was pregnant:

> Waterloo. Sunday morning,
> 3 o'clock. June 18, 1815
>
> My dear Lady Frances [Webster],
> As I am sending a messenger to Brussels, I write to you one line to tell you that I think you ought to take your preparations to remove from Brussels to Antwerp in case such a measure should be necessary. We fought a desperate battle on Friday, in which I was successful, though I had but very few troops. The Prussians were roughly handled, and retired in the night, which obliged me to do the same in this place yesterday. The course of the operations may oblige me to uncover Brussels for a moment, and may expose that town to the enemy; for which reason I recommend that you and your family should be prepared to move to Antwerp at a moment's notice.[13]

Thus was the ground laid for alarm to spread. Ney had led the main attack at about 1 o'clock. Wellington's lines being penetrated, one regiment of Hanoverian Hussars, led by its colonel, fled as far as Brussels, reporting that the French had gained the victory. During the afternoon, the city of Brussels was in a state of panic. Since 3 o'clock a stream of the wounded and fugitives had been pouring in; there had been so many in the rear of Wellington's lines that one of Blücher's men, who rode up to investigate and, seeing so many wounded and thinking it was a whole army, returned with a report that the British were defeated and in retreat. No one knew what was happening outside his own immediate vicinity, for, in the windless, oven-like, smoke-filled air, visibility was reduced to a few yards.[14] So great was the panic that it reached Louis XVIII, awaiting his destiny in Ghent. Hugo caught the moment: 'Then the Emperor straightened up in the saddle and for a moment sat pondering. Wellington had begun to withdraw: all that remained was to turn withdrawal into rout. He turned abruptly and ordered a dispatch to Paris with the news that the battle was won.'[15]

This premature news was relayed to Paris by the Lille–Paris telegraph line.[16] It was by this means, and its onward transmission by telegraph to Brest, that Napoleon's premature announcement came to the attention of Adm Lord Keith in Plymouth. When Napoleon had escaped from Elba, Keith was enjoying a well-earned retirement, he was already 69 years old and, as we have seen, he played a major part in the Navy's defence against invasion. He was brought out of retirement to take command of the Channel Fleet based in Plymouth. On 22 June he wrote to his daughter: 'There has been a great battle. I am anxious to hear the real event; I am not satisfied with the account. We seem to have been taken by surprise by Lord Wellington's ball.'[17]

The reference to the ball is to the event whereby news of the opening attacks in the Waterloo campaign arrived when Wellington was attending the Duchess of Richmond's ball in Brussels – an attendance which, far from being ill-judged, was designed to avoid civilian despondency and alarm. From Keith's letter we can adduce his scepticism about the veracity of the intelligence he had been given. Its source was almost certainly the premature announcement of victory by Napoleon, which Keith heard about from a dispatch by one of his captains, who had passed on the intelligence given to him by the captain of an American ship which had been boarded on the evening of 19 June and which had left Brest that morning. The report passed to Keith said that 'A boat was sent to him from the French frigate *Flore* in the outer roads this morning to communicate that a telegraphic message had arrived last evening [18 June] stating that Bonaparte had defeated Wellington.'[18]

Let us consider the logistics of how Napoleon's premature claim to have won the day at Waterloo could have arrived in Brest on the evening of the very day of the battle: is it credible? We are, of course, considering Napoleon's premature report, not the actual result. The battlefield was about 60 miles (96km) from the telegraph office in Lille – this would be about a six or seven hours' ride. The Brussels–Lille line had been closed in 1814 after Napoleon's abdication and we must assume that in 1815 the northern end of the line from Paris terminated at Lille, although it is possible that it stopped at the border with Belgium some 12 miles (19km), or more than an hour on horseback, nearer the battlefield. We do not know the time at which Napoleon sent his dispatch rider from the field, but if it was as late as

2pm, and remembering that the summer solstice was at hand, the rider could have got to the border or to Lille well before nightfall. The distance from Lille to Brest is over 500 miles (800km); could a telegraph message have reached Brest before nightfall on the 18th? – weather permitting, we have to conclude that it could. Evidently, the American captain was sceptical of the news, claming that the weather 'was thick', but this may have been his rationalization of his scepticism. It is incredible for a report to have been manufactured in Brest – one which, although it turned out to be premature, was correctly reporting what Napoleon sent in his dispatch. As we shall see, the news of the actual victory was to travel much slower in England. It was not just the American who was sceptical for Keith was wary of it too, but not because the telegraph in France was not working – it seems that it was – but probably because he simply did not trust the source; in this he was right for the wrong reasons, but the episode serves to illustrate the confusion which was caused by this and the other false reports reaching Brussels.

On the battlefield the reality was that, although not yet beaten, it was true that Wellington's position had decidedly worsened, for Ney had pierced his line.

> Wellington remained calm but he was white-lipped. The Austrian and French military attachés, who were with the English headquarters staff, believed that the day was lost. At five o'clock Wellington looked at his watch and was heard to murmur: 'Blücher – or darkness.' It was about this moment that a line of bayonets came into view in the distance, twinkling on the heights . . . This was the turning point.[19]

Then the last carnage began as Wellington shouted, 'Up Guards, and shoot straight!' The men of the Imperial Guard (who were with Napoleon at the end) felt the army giving way around them in the disorder of total rout:

> The shouts of '*Vive l'Empéreur!*' giving way to '*Sauve qui peu*', and amid disaster on every side they continued to advance forward, dying with every step they took. No man hesitated, no soldier of the line but was the equal of his general in courage, no man flinched from suicide.[20]

'His army was ruined at Waterloo,' wrote Lockhart, 'and a brief day of the second reign passed, without a twilight, into midnight.'[21] At last the confusion was ended: a dictatorship ended, and a whole system collapsed. Nothing if not fickle, the Paris crowds greeted the return of Louis XVIII on 8 July with dancing in the streets, as if to efface their enthusiasm of 20 March when they had been ecstatic at Napoleon's return.

## Sending the Message

It was after dark before Wellington was able to return to his inn in the village of Waterloo; exhausted, he slept for a few hours. He had not needed, as he had feared he might, to expose Brussels, to attack by a shift to the west. But he had exposed the city, not by manoeuvre nor by the false reports of defeat; he had exposed Brussels because of the narrowness of Napoleon's defeat – because Blücher, true to his promise, had turned up, but only just in time. After the anguished hours since the afternoon, Brussels slept that night knowing that it was redeemed; but what of the rest of the world? The Lille–Amsterdam line had been closed since the Peace of Paris in 1814 and we have seen that Brussels had no telegraphic liaison with Paris. As far as the telegraph was concerned, with the fall of Napoleon the previous year, Brussels had regressed back to the horse because the domestic telegraphs in both Belgium and Holland had been subject to destructive attacks by anti-French elements, both before and after the abdication.[22] The horse's day was not quite finally done. As Wellington gathered his thoughts in the inn, he found himself in the same position as Nelson after the Battle of the Nile and Collingwood after Trafalgar: great news had to be dispatched. It was the last great news, as it happened, to be delivered to London by the horse; the Waterloo dispatch was about to be prepared, once Wellington had recovered from his fatigue. But who was to play the role of Lt Lapenotière with his news of Trafalgar and Nelson; who was to be the new Lt Capel or Lt Duval with the news of the Nile and of India redeemed? Wellington rose in the early hours of 19 June to begin his dispatch to Lord Bathurst, Secretary of State for War and the Colonies but the rumours of defeat which were common currency in Brussels in the previous afternoon were to precede the news of what was a most profound and defining battlefield victory. It would take a whole war to extirpate Nazism; Bonapartism was eliminated in an afternoon.

## Major Percy

Wellington left the inn at Waterloo for Brussels early on the morning after the battle and finished his dispatch there. He was so moved by the losses of his friends that it shows in the dispatch; later it was described as if it were announcing a defeat instead of the greatest victory imaginable. Brussels too had to readjust its composure: the reports of defeat the previous afternoon, and spread who knows elsewhere, now had to be stood on their head. These rumours of defeat were to precede the dispatch home, where the same reversal had to be made – in London and by Keith in Plymouth. His official dispatch to the minister completed, Wellington entrusted it to his aide-de-camp, Maj Percy, who set off with it about midday on Monday, 19 June towards the coast about 70 miles (113km) away. Would he be the first with the news in London? In the post-chaise in which he travelled with the dispatch were also trophies which represented the climactic symbolism of the victory: two of the captured eagles of Napoleon's army. These, according to the Duke's instructions, Percy was to have 'the honour of laying at the feet of the Prince Regent'. (At this time George III (1738–1830) was suffering one of his bouts of madness; his son, later George IV (1762–1830), had become Prince Regent in 1810.) At Ghent, about halfway to the coast, Percy found that the news of the victory had preceded him, for Wellington had written a letter, sent before Percy's dispatch, to Louis XVIII, then in the town fretting over the outcome of the battle and whether he was to embark on a new, extended exile or another restoration.

At Ostend, the Navy took over: Maj Percy went aboard the 200-ton HMS *Peruvian*, which set off to cross the 70 miles (113km) of the southern North Sea to Dover. The journey should have taken only seven hours or so, but a dead calm stalled the ship, leaving the most vital news languishing in mid-Channel. Capt White, RN (1778–1828) of the *Peruvian* took control of the situation by leading a crew of six, one of whom was Percy himself, an oarsman at Eton College, to row themselves to England in a ship's gig.[23] Leaving their ship, evidently 'about noon', that is, about 24 hours after leaving Brussels, Percy's landfall was at Broadstairs on the Kent coast, itself a further 70 miles from London. The *Kentish Gazette* told its readers that it was:

> With exultation and pride do we this day communicate to our readers the details of one of the most glorious conflicts that ever adorned the British arms. At three in the afternoon of Tuesday [20 June – about 27 hours after leaving Brussels] the Hon Major Percy, aide-de-camp to our illustrious Hero, accompanied by Captain White . . . landed from a row boat near Broadstairs, with the dispatches . . . and . . . the Eagles . . . of two French regiments . . . with which they immediately proceeded . . . for the Metropolis.[24]

According to the newspaper, one of the eagles was 'much defaced with blood and dirt', the macabre details being given with a certain relish.

Unlike Lapenotière's landfall at Falmouth with the Trafalgar news, marked by a tablet, Percy's point of landfall has not been recorded; but there is one respect in which the circumstances accord with each other. Just as Vice-Adm Collingwood gave not a thought to using the telegraph at Portsmouth for Lapenotière's dispatch, so Wellington gave not a thought to the Deal telegraph, only 7 miles (11km) from Dover; why not? There are two possible reasons: the first would be the simple issue of interservice rivalry – why would Wellington want to gain most of a day in getting the news to London when its impact on the glory of his army would be dissipated and shared with the Admiralty, which, on this occasion, was not the close collaborator and campaign-winning resource which had been the case in the Peninsular War, won not much more than a year earlier? And the eagles, totems to the elimination of Bonapartism by his defeat in the field, why should they be separated from the news? All this gives a plausible case for Wellington's instructions to Percy to ride to London and give delivery in person. We must also examine whether, in fact, the Deal telegraph line had reopened after its closure, along with all the others, in 1814. If it were open, Capt White would certainly have known and would he not have gone to Deal to signal to the Admiralty that Percy was on his way, together with the news of the victory? In his excellent book, Wilson,[25] the worthy successor to, and collaborator with Mead,[26] discusses the myths of the news of Trafalgar and Waterloo arriving in London by telegraph – which which he correctly exposes – but in support of his rebuttal he states that, 'No telegraphs operated in this country in 1815. The shutters had ceased; the semaphores were not yet in service.' Wilson was wrong about this but right about the Waterloo news not arriving in London by telegraph. The papers of Lord Keith have in large measure been preserved.[27] The following extracts from them prove that the Plymouth telegraph, which, as we have seen, was a branch from the Portsmouth line, was open in June 1815 and in operation at the time that Napoleon was in captivity: 'an indistinct telegraph message was received'; 'in answer to the telegraph message'; 'upon the receipt of a telegraph message'; 'we understand by telegraph'; and 'we have sent you a telegraphic message today': these are just a few extracts from contemporary evidence.

As this final part of the story unfolds, I shall show that the news of Waterloo arrived in Portsmouth by the shutter telegraph, already reopened as the emergency legislation discussed in Chapter 10 was going through Parliament. Whether the Deal and the Yarmouth line, or, indeed, the coastal signal network, had been reopened after Napoleon's escape from Elba must remain moot. Unlike for Portsmouth and Plymouth, I have found no evidence with which to revise the previously received view. White would have known if the Deal telegraph were open. If it was, he could have communicated with London by separating from Percy and travelling the 12 miles (19km) to Deal by horse; in fact, he travelled with Percy to London; therefore, the total of the evidence available suggests little doubt that the Deal telegraph had not reopened.

In spite of Wilson's correct assertion that the news of Waterloo did not arrive in London by telegraph – there is not a shred of truth in it – the myth is repeated on the Internet with the gross error of its being confused by an interrupted telegraphic message: 'Wellington defeated . . .', which, it is wrongly averred, gave rise to the reports of the calamity at Waterloo – we have already seen that false reports of Wellington's defeat were around at the time, there is no need to make up a new one. The story is not just apocryphal but downright wrong. It was first put about, Wilson[28] tells us, in the *Encyclopaedia Britannica* of 1824, when it was said that a report being sent up from Plymouth of Wellington's victory at Salamanca in 1812 was stopped by fog at a critical point in the message allowing the truncation to give an utterly misleading inversion: the whole message should have said 'Wellington defeated the French at [Salamanca]'. Even at the time or in the years which followed, the myth grew that the truncated message 'Wellington defeated . . .' was the cause of a stock exchange sell-off. The very idea that the Admiralty would put half a message into the public domain – one that could only spread the alarm and despondency on which the myth-makers rely – is as absurd as it is unsupported by evidence. It was always a fantasy, now propagated afresh, and embellished with the nonsense that it was this truncated message that was the reason for the selling on the London stock exchange before Percy arrived. We have already seen that, thanks to the initial beating that Blücher suffered on 15 June, followed by the reports of defeat in general circulation in Brussels on the afternoon of the 18th, there was plenty of material to support the circulation of rumours of defeat in London on Tuesday or Wednesday, 20 or 21 June; there is no need to create a new reason for these reports.

Looking for Lord Bathurst at his office and home in Downing Street, the Secretary of State for War and addressee of Wellington's dispatch, Percy was told that he and other government dignitaries were being entertained at a dinner at 44 Grosvenor Square; the speculation and fretting among those dinner guests as they considered the rumours of defeat and awaited official word from Wellington can be imagined. Hotfoot, Percy continued his journey and delivered the dispatch which brought forth the most extraordinary, joyous celebrations of what was, without doubt, the most important news in the lifetime of any who heard it: Wellington had defeated Napoleon in the field, Bonapatism was in its death-throes. The first and only duel between Wellington and Napoleon had been fought, but, unlike the rumour that had preceded it, the result was good. A fourteen-year old girl, who was sleeping in the house when Percy interrupted the dinner party, recalled her memories of the event in old age:

> An officer in a scarlet tunic with gold on it and brandishing the dispatch came tearing into her father's house, followed by two other men, all asking for Lord Bathurst and crying out 'Victory . . . Victory . . . Bonaparte has been beaten . . .'. She saw Major Percy's face and noticed how tired and dishevelled he looked and watched him rush through the open door from the hall into the dining-room, and a moment later heard renewed bursts of cheering from the men

> inside. Then, her father, Lord Bathurst, came out, and standing outside the front door facing Grosvenor Square he announced the news to the great crowd.[29]

Until the 1990s there was a public house behind the south front of Grosvenor Square called 'The Waterloo Dispatch', in celebration of Percy's arrival and Bathurst's announcement on or near the spot. Sadly it is no more; such a destruction, we might note, would not happen in France without some memorial to mark the spot.

Maj Percy had one last duty to perform: the captured eagles still had to be presented to the Prince Regent who was attending a ball in St James's Square together with his brother, the Duke of York and Lord Castlereagh, the Foreign Secretary, not long returned from Vienna. The story is told that:

> The Prince Regent had opened the ball and the couples were taking their places for the first . . . [dance] when there was suddenly an unexpected interruption. A sound of distant cheering, which soon grew louder and louder, was heard above the music. The dancers broke away from their partners, dashed to the windows which were flung wide open as it was a sultry evening, and the orchestra faltered and finally stopped. A most extraordinary sight met the eyes of . . .[the] guests. . . . a great crowd of people, waving and shouting, filled the square below.[30]

Maj Percy had arrived, 'such a dusty figure', observed the surprised hostess; much to her consternation, she having taken so much trouble to impress her guests with the important people who had graced her ball, the proceedings broke up in a pandemonium as the eagles were presented to the Prince Regent by the wearied, blood-stained, dishevelled spectacle who had completed his task, begun about 60 hours earlier, by gloriously upstaging the hostess. What took place in government offices that night is not recorded, but the following day the news was on its way on laurel bedecked mail coaches to every city in the land.

On 23 June the news of Wellington's victory reached Norwich, suggesting that it was taken there by mail coach and not via the Yarmouth telegraph, which like the Deal line, had probably not reopened. The Portsmouth telegraph, and its branch to Plymouth, most certainly was working for, on 26 June *The Hampshire Chronicle* include the following piece:

> The Message – 'BONAPARTE DEFEATED' – received here [Portsmouth] by a telegraphic communication, on Thursday [22 June] noon, produced the most heartfelt joy and enthusiasm: and every arrival since, tends to increase our exultation, as they all show

> more the brilliancy and importance of the victory gained. Ships of war were dispatched to the French coast to fire a royal salute, with the colours of England, Holland, and Prussia flying, and afterwards to hoist the white flag over the tri-coloured. From this having been practiced in the close of the late war, it will prove an antidote, amongst the good subjects of France to Bonaparte's freedom of the press.

The Portsmouth telegraph had obviously by then been reopened and was working in time to carry the news of Waterloo.

# 13
# Napoleon: Capture

*'St Helena!', exclaimed Napoleon. 'Sir, it is surely preferable to being confined in a smaller place in England, or being sent to France, or perhaps Russia.'*
'Russie! Dieu garde!', was his reply.[1]

*The last, but not the least of Napoleon's victories was won at St Helena. There he created the Napoleonic legend, and there he lived long enough to see his own career in perspective, and to reinterpret it in tune with the forces of liberalism and nationality which were to shape the Europe of the nineteenth century.*[2]

*There is no last word, there is no end. The argument goes on.*[3]

## After the Battle

It was easy to be critical of the lenient policy that had allowed Napoleon's escape from Elba; according to a definitive history of the period, there is no room for doubt about where the blame lies for what led up to Waterloo, and the suffering in the battle: 'The tens of thousands of casualties, French, Prussian, Hanoverian, Dutch and British were a direct consequence of the Tsar's blundering generosity in granting Elba to Napoleon.'[4]

This is a reference to the great mistake of 1814 in not forcing an unconditional surrender; such a policy would undoubtedly have brought many casualties in 1814 instead of at Waterloo, but their scale could hardly have matched that of the great killing match in Belgium. To say 'once bitten, twice shy' would be too trite: there was not a single voice in power after Waterloo to protect Napoleon, save for a few who either had already or would soon desert or betray him. He was not to be allowed a second escape; there was to be no new Elba, it was to be captivity this time. But he still had to be captured; after his defeat at Waterloo Napoleon became a fugitive. When political control of a country changes hands by violence, the measure of who is the master is usually by who is in control of communications – today it would be television and radio – in Paris in 1815 it was the telegraph. We have already seen that Napoleon's claim to have won the battle was relayed to Paris on 18 June via the Lille telegraph and that this false report reached Brest and ultimately Lord Keith in Plymouth. When Napoleon had joined his army and taken it north on what became known as the Waterloo Campaign, he left Paris in the hands of his collaborator, a man whom he had raised to prominence, the duplicitous Fouché; it was of Fouché and Talleyrand, who had encouraged the Egyptian expedition, that Napoleon was to remark later that he would have remained Emperor if he had had them put to death.

Talleyrand had been a bishop, but as a political leader and diplomat he served in the top levels of most of the regimes that governed France from 1789 and into the post-Napoleonic era. By taking diplomatic appointments abroad, he had escaped the Terror, but he had been back in Paris to help to prepare the ground for the *coup d'etat* that saw Napoleon become First Consul and rise to ultimate political power. Talleyrand served him well, but their views diverged after 1805, by which time Talleyrand regarded Napoleon's ambitions as dangerously excessive.

Fouché was an incorrigible schemer who ultimately paid the price of exile, not because he betrayed Napoleon, but because, having been elected in 1792 to the National Convention, he had voted to execute Louis XVI; this event was proscribed after the Bourbon restoration of 1815. An enthusiastic revolutionary, in 1793 he had ruthlessly suppressed the counter-revolutionaries in Lyon. He had schemed for the overthrow of Robespierre in 1794 and, after foreign diplomatic appointments, he was recalled to Paris to become Minister of Police and was a supporter of Napoleon in the 1799 coup. His elaborate police system was well organized and highly efficient, especially at internal spying, but, being involved in political manoeuvring against Napoleon, he was dismissed in 1802 only to be reinstated in 1804, after he had uncovered a British-financed plot to assassinate Napoleon. In conformity with his character, he was ousted again in 1810, after intriguing with England. When Napoleon returned in 1815, the opportunistic Fouché was reappointed Minister of Police, but secretly corresponded with the allies to secure his future and he became president of the provisional government established after Waterloo and continued for a time to serve Louis XVIII. The law proscribing those responsible for the death of Louis XVI forced him into exile in 1816, where he died in obscurity. But his work was done in 1815, when Napoleon's grip on the levers of power was prised off by Fouché; by his hand, not Wellington's, Napoleon was doomed to exile and captivity.

Well might Napoleon have rued leaving Fouché in charge. We must examine how this duplicitous man used the telegraph. He it was, through his control of the government machine, including the police (Britain was ruled at this time without a police force) and with the telegraph his tool, the arch manipulator.

Paris is nearly 200 miles (320km) from Waterloo but, thanks to the telegraph conveying from Lille Napoleon's false report of victory, Fouché organized a 100-gun salute to be fired in honour of the Emperor's success on the following day. Paris, fickle as ever, was jubilant and proclaimed that the glory of France was secured, and dejection filled the hearts of the Royalists. But on the morning of the 21st it was learned that Napoleon had arrived the night before, alone, at the Elysée Palace. The secret could no longer be kept: a decisive battle had been fought, lost and, as a force, the French army had ceased to exist. It was time for control over the telegraph and for the other levers of government to change again;[5] Fouché was up to the job.

As we have seen, the false report of Napoleon's claimed victory went down the line to Brest: the news of the reality of the French defeat was carried to Paris by the Lille telegraph on 20 June 1815; while, on 23 June, Napoleon's abdication was sent down all the lines and on 4 July the news of the capitulation of the French army before Paris was given by telegraph.[6] At some stage or other, control over the telegraph lines, without actually leaving Fouché's hands, moved from being in the hands of a supporter of Napoleon – that is to say, a supporter for as long as he was still at the head of his army – to remaining in the same hands, but those of a treacherous man, now openly his enemy. Was it as a friend of Napoleon that a telegraph message was sent to Brest suddenly ordering the French frigate *Hortense,* reportedly the fastest vessel in the French navy, to make ready for sea? This message, the source of which is the same American captain who told of the false claim of Napoleon's victory over Wellington, was reported on 19 June.[7] Because this was before the general news flash of the French defeat, it suggests that it was a precautionary order in case of trouble for Napoleon. Fouché's self-interest lay, he thought, in helping Napoleon to make himself scarce, so that the former could take control in Paris. The American captain reported that the *Hortense* was:

> . . . bending sails in the inner roads [of Brest] last evening [18 June] and was to be in the outer roads today [19 June]. The people say that she is to take off Bonaparte in the event of defeat and the further success of the Royalists in the south . . . inhabitants of Brest are generally averse to Bonaparte and long for peace and the Bourbons, and in fact any government that will give them peace.[8]

Napoleon made no attempt to regain his throne by military means (as would, of course, have been his natural instinct to do), in spite of the fact that he still had considerable resources available to him, more, in fact, than he had had after his appalling losses, from which he had rallied, on the retreat from Moscow and his defeat at Leipzig. Napoleon still had call on 400,000 men and, but for Fouché's treachery and that of others, he would probably have continued the fight.[9] With his enemy Fouché now in control in Paris and with the civilian population again showing support for the Bourbons, with the Coalition armies totalling 600,000 approaching from the east and Wellington following Blücher to Paris, and with the French telegraph network now in the hands of his enemies, with the tables turned, and Napoleon being able to communicate only at the speed of the horse, it is not altogether realistic to think of him being able to organize a defeat of the Coalition. To create a civil war and go down fighting would have been his possible exit if he had chosen this route, but he did not. With his tide ebbing, the political whirlpools and currents were too much to overcome. Acknowledging his dénouement, and in a statement which showed more greatness than hubris and which allows him to tower in history above the Nazi tyrant, he said, 'I have not come back from Elba to have Paris run with blood'; on 23 June he abdicated.

According to Hamilton-Williams,[10] in the final analysis Napoleon's defeat

> Had been caused by men that he himself had placed in positions of power and, although mistrusting them, had failed to remove, particularly Talleyrand in 1814 and Fouché in 1815. Napoleon had believed that his own ability, his genius, would suffice to keep these untrustworthy men under control. In this he had deceived himself. In 1814, before leaving Paris for the front, he could have imprisoned Talleyrand . . . as both a precaution and a lesson to others. Likewise in 1815 . . . he should on leaving Paris have ordered . . . [the imprisonment] of Fouché . . .

As we have seen, Victor Hugo saw it differently: had Napoleon won at Waterloo (and with the Coalition on his track, survived the certain rerun somewhere else), it would have been counter to the flowing tide of the nineteenth century: 'it was time for the great man to fall'.[11] It was also time for him to be captured, and, as he saw it, succumb to the treachery of his enemies.

## Blockade

As soon as it had been known that Napoleon had escaped from Elba, the whole government/military organization in London had been thrown into alert; to say panic may be overstating the case, but not by a lot. Nobody had dreamed of the new scenario, and there were no contingency plans in place; it was an uncomfortable time for all concerned in government. The Admiralty, as we have seen, were thought by some to have been responsible for the escape. Although this charge would not stand up, the Admiralty had certainly been wrong-footed and were not to be caught out again; they remobilized the Navy's blockade of the French ports. Additionally, in support of this they took steps to reopen the Plymouth and Portsmouth shutter telegraph lines; a culture of preparedness and a loathing of being misled were to have a continuing influence on the Admiralty. Even as the shutter telegraphs were being closed down again after Napoleon was incarcerated below the Equator, Popham was talking to them about semaphore, and, in due course, a brand new telegraph line to Portsmouth based on semaphore technology was opened in 1822.

But in April 1815 Lord Keith was ordered out of retirement to organize the blockade; taking up command of the Channel Fleet, he hoisted his flag on board HMS *Ville de Paris** on 29 May. His instructions were to resume the blockade and assist the Royalists in La Vendée region of France near La Rochelle. In the period leading up to the Waterloo Campaign nothing much happened at sea, although a tireless vigilance on the cruising stations was maintained. We have already seen that Keith, although he was sceptical of its veracity, was alerted to the false report on 22 June of Wellington's defeat. He heard the official report of the French defeat via London on 24 June: the news arrived in a dispatch brought from London by the mail coach. It is intriguing how the Keith Papers demonstrate the way in which the telegraph was reserved for operational commands of the Navy; unlike in France, diplomatic traffic went by the mail coach – the mail at this time took two days (only) to reach Plymouth – a dispatch sent with a Monday date would routinely arrive in Plymouth on the Wednesday. In contrast, the news of Marshal Ney's, capture was telegraphed to the King in Paris on 18 August 1815.[12]

On 28 June, Keith heard from Lord Melville, First Lord of the Admiralty, that there was a possibility of Napoleon's attempting to escape from an Atlantic coast port; this arose from reports in London of a request by Fouché on behalf of Napoleon for a passport to the USA, one which showed Fouché's interest in having Napoleon out of the way. Napoleon left Malmaison, near Paris, on 29 June for Rochefort, arriving on 3 July, still in the hope that a passport would have been brought from London. With the military option looking bleak, he now had the choice of running the

---

* This ship's name sounds as if it were a French prize converted to the Navy's use: it was not, but it was named after one that had been a generation earlier: the 110-gun French flagship was at the time the greatest prize that had been won by the Navy; she was taken by Lord Rodney in 1782 at the Battle of the Saintes during the American Revolutionary War. The new 110-gun ship of the same name which replaced her combined superior sailing performance as well as fire power and was one of the Navy's most powerful battleships. Before Lord Keith flew his flag from her in Plymouth in 1815, she had done sterling service earlier in the war in the Western Approaches as the flagship of Adm Sir William Cornwallis.

gauntlet of Keith's blockade or surrender. Keith was informed by Melville that:

> Reports have reached HM Government from various quarters that in the event of adverse fortune it was the intention of Bonaparte to escape to America. If there is any truth in these statements he will in all probability make the attempt now, unless he should be forcibly detained in Paris. If he should embark in a small vessel from one of the numerous ports along the coast of France it may be scarcely possible to prevent his escape; but if he should wait till a frigate or sloop of war can be fitted out for him, you may perhaps receive information of such preparation and may thereby be enabled to watch and intercept her. At any rate it is desirable that you should take every precaution in your power with a view to his seizure and detention should he endeavour to quit France by sea.[13]

And two days later, on 30 June:

> I wrote last night . . . in answer to the telegraph message that all arms for the succour of the Royalists should be punctual . . . We have fresh reports every hour of Bonaparte's intention to escape – he pretends for England, we think America. It is of great consequence to intercept him and we reckon your vigilance.[14]

Keith was already on notice, without the reminder, that his blockade was now the front line; but he was well up to the job. On 3 July he received Melville's dispatch, dated 1 July:

> I am commanded by my Lords Commissioners of the Admiralty to acquaint your Lordship that a proposition reached HM Government last night [30 June] from the present rulers of France [this was Fouché's work] demanding a passport and safe conduct for Bonaparte and his family to proceed to America. To this proposition HM Government have returned a negative answer; and it now seems more probable than ever that Bonaparte will endeavour to effect his escape, either to England, or what is much more likely to America.
>
> Your Lordship will therefore repeat to all your cruisers the orders already given with further directions to them to make the strictest search of any vessel they may fall in with; and if they should be so fortunate as to intercept Bonaparte, the captain of HM ship should transfer him and his family to HM ship and there keeping him in careful custody should return to the nearest port of England with all possible expedition. He should not permit any communication

> whatsoever with the shore, and he will be held responsible for keeping the whole transaction a profound secret until their Lordships' further orders shall be received.[15]

On 3 July Keith replied to Melville:

> . . . in consequence of your letter of the 1st inst. relative to the expected departure of Bonaparte for America, I have sent out for the purpose of intercepting him, with orders in strict conformity to their Lordships' directions, the *Swiftsure* to the north of Cape Finisterre, the *Vengeur* in the trade of the Channel thirty leagues to the westward of Ushant [about 90 miles (145km); that is, in the Atlantic] and the *Glasgow* off Brest, with directions to . . . [the captain to distribute the orders among the cruising fleets] . . .[16]

This more or less routine reply was sent, it should be noted, by mail coach and not telegraph. Meanwhile, out at sea, Keith's second in command, Rear-Adm (later Adm) the Hon Sir Henry Hotham, dispatched back to Keith:

> . . . Since I heard of Bonaparte's abdication I have been most anxious in adopting every measure I could devise to intercept him . . . I consider every part of the coast under my control . . . well guarded, and a tolerably good outside line of ships too; but two more frigates could well be bestowed . . . one to join the *Bellerophon* and another for the Loire, where I have only two brigs. . . .
>
> As I am quite alone, if your lordship can send me any vessel for communication I should be thankful; of those . . . your Lordship was good enough to send me, the *Helicon*, *Telegraph* and *Nimble* are absent on voyages to England . . .[17]

The reference to the *Telegraph* is to a 12-gun schooner, which had achieved minor fame in October 1813 as Wellington invaded the south of France. A French ship, the 16-gun *Filibustier* found herself liable to capture in the mouth of the Bayonne River and the *Telegraph* attacked her, and, seeing that other English ships were approaching, the *Filibustier* set herself on fire and ultimately blew up. The gallant little *Telegraph* was observed by Napoleon[18] after the Navy had taken him, but her luck ran out when she was lost in a shipwreck in the West Indies in 1817.[19]

On 8 July Napoleon went aboard the *Saale*, having embarked from the beach at Fouras, some 15 miles (24km) south of Rochefort. So far as Keith was concerned, however, the reports of Napoleon's whereabouts were conflicting: on 30 June he told his wife, 'I am seeking Bonny on the sea'; on

1 July, 'It is said that Bonny is in London. I do not believe it', and finally, on 2 July, 'I am sending out all I have to look for Bonny if he takes to the sea'.[20] The British blockade was increased by fourteen men-of-war, which had sailed from Portsmouth on 1 July.[21] Keith's total force consisted of over thirty ships, all with orders to search vessels of every type: no ship nor battery dare molest them, it was as massive a use and demonstration of overwhelming sea power as can be imagined, a further dividend from Trafalgar. The several possible points of departure for Napoleon were covered by warships operating in coastal waters and, in addition, a double line of cruisers further out to sea stretched from Ushant, to cover the Western Approaches in addition to cover along the whole Channel coast to Finisterre.

On board the *Saale* plans were discussed about which course to pursue should the passport not be granted. Should the frigates try to fight their way through? Should the emperor return to the mainland and put himself at the head of the remnants of his army? Should he make use of a vessel put at his disposal by the American consul at Bordeaux?[22] All these possibilities were considered, and the evidence seems plain in suggesting that trying to reach the USA was the favoured option; but there was the awesome blockading power of the Royal Navy to consider. According to Lockhart,[23] none of his group nor the captains of vessels that may have attempted to run the blockade accepted that it was possible to escape the constricting force that was being applied. 'Wherever wood can swim,' intoned Napoleon, 'here I am sure to find this flag of England.' This was an echo of his words seventeen years earlier, on hearing of the catastrophe at the Battle of the Nile, when a solitary sigh issued from Napoleon's breath. 'To France,' he said then, 'the fates have decreed the empire of the land – to England that of the sea.' In this, of course, he was only right about England, and until Jutland, a whole century later, this remained the unalloyed truth.

But on the high seas off Rochefort in1815, the power of the Royal Navy was never more graphically displayed to Napoleon. Negotiations were started with Capt Maitland, the master of HMS *Bellerophon*; both ship and master were destined for key roles in the next few weeks. The *Bellerophon,* known affectionately by her crews as the '*Billy Ruffian*', had already achieved fame and been a thorn in Napoleon's side: she had been a participant in Nelson's victories at the Nile and Trafalgar. At the Nile, after engaging the French 120-gun flagship, *L'Orient,* she was badly damaged herself, with over 200 casualties; at Trafalgar, her captain (Cooke) was to die. From the shore, one of Napoleon's Marshals (Count Bertrand) sent a message, dated 9 July, to Maitland:

> Monsieur L'Admiral, The Emperor Napoleon, having abdicated from power and chosen the USA for a refuge, has embarked in the two frigates, which are in the roads for the purpose of reaching his

> destination. He is a waiting the passport from the British Government . . . which compels me to send you the present flag of truce to ask if you have any knowledge of the said passport, or if you think it may be the intention of the British Government to impede our passage to the USA. I should be extremely grateful if you would give me any news you may have . . .[24]

Maitland's reply was both proper and uncompromising:

> . . . I have the honour to acquaint you [that] I cannot say what the intentions of my Government may be: but the two countries at present being in a state of war, I cannot allow any ships of war to put to sea from the port of Rochefort. As to the proposal . . . of allowing the Emperor to proceed in a merchant vessel, it is out of my power, without the sanction of my commanding officer (Sir Henry Hotham . . .) to allow any vessel, under whatever flag she may be, to pass with a personage of such consequence. . . .[25]

The whole business of Napoleon's surrender, arguments over his status and his objection to being sent to St. Helena is a drama of its own; of his part in it Maitland wrote an account,[26] which Sir Walter Scott called 'as fine, manly and explicit account as ever was given of so interesting a transaction'. Reflecting Maitland's perception of what was going on in the minds of the fugitives, he dispatched immediately to Hotham, 'The two people who brought the letter seem very anxious to convince me that [Napoleon could still rejoin his armies] . . . and make some stand . . .'

Of Maitland it was later said that he was too easy-going on Napoleon while on board, but he knew his duty so far as capturing him was concerned and he was not out-foxed. Napoleon went on board the *Bellerophon* on 14 July, intending to put himself at the mercy of the Prince Regent.

## How the News of Napoleon's Being Taken Arrived

There could not be any hotter news of the whereabouts of Napoleon or that he had been taken: would London be the first to know about Maitland's prize, via France? Or would the news travel faster across the sea? On 23 July the mail coach came into Plymouth, decorated with laurel in celebration of the fact that Napoleon had been taken; the news, therefore, was in the public domain in London on 21 July. On that day Melville sent a dispatch to Keith in Plymouth: 'If we are to believe the official article from the Maritime Prefect at Rochefort in the French newspapers received today, . . . Bonaparte surrendered on the 14th or 15th to the *Bellerophon* [and is] . . . on board that ship.'

Melville repeated his instruction that Napoleon should be detained on board and that 'No person, whether in HM service or not, who does not belong to the ship, should be suffered to go on board, either for the purpose of visiting the officers, or on any pretence whatever, without permission from the Admiralty.'[27]

Rochefort never had a link to the French telegraph network, before or after this period. Nantes, some 100 miles (160km) north of Rochefort had a link created by a branch from the Paris–Brest line at Avranches, but this did not open until much later.[28] The news which Melville was passing on to Keith, in the form of Paris press reports, must have travelled from Rochefort overland via Paris, for it had taken six or seven days for it to cover the total distance of over 500 miles (800km).

Because the Keith correspondence has largely survived and because references are made in it to the telegraph, we can deduce that a message was sometimes sent by both methods; but not in the case of the news of Napoleon's capture. Keith had plainly not received advance notice of London's intelligence by telegraph, because, while the news of the capture (received via French newspapers) was on its way on 22 July, being rushed through Hampshire, Dorset and Somerset, Keith, in a bizarre duplication, was busy penning a dispatch to Melville telling *him* the same momentous news, just in from one of his ships:

> Captain Sartorius of HM ship *Slaney* has this moment landed with the enclosed dispatch from Captain Maitland of the *Bellerophon* by which it appears that Bonaparte proposed on the 14th inst. to embark on board the *Bellerophon* and throw himself on the generosity of the Prince Regent.
>
> There is a General Gourgaud* on board the Slaney who is charged with a letter to the Prince Regent, of which a copy is enclosed, and as I understand from the captain of the Slaney that he refuses to deliver that letter to any other person than H.R.H. I have directed that he is to remain on board the *Slaney* and ordered her to Torbay there to await their Lordship's commands.
>
> . . . I have ordered Captain Sartorius [himself] to convey this despatch as he was present with Captain Maitland through the whole transaction.[29]

It is deeply perplexing to observe that this momentous news was not dispatched in either direction by telegraph, for there could have been be no

---

*Gen Gougraud's conversations with Napoleon at St. Helena were published in Latimer, E. Wormley, *Talks of Napoleon at St. Helena* (1903).

more pressing traffic on the line. It was, after all, to meet the human need for faster intelligence and the giving of orders that the telegraph had been invented over twenty years earlier; it is utterly inconceivable that such news would not have been telegraphed in France (remember Marshal Ney). Perhaps it was sent by telegraph but because no record of traffic has been retained and because we are left only with the hard-copy archive, it appears that the message was sent only by coach. This must be considered as the more likely, perhaps due to fog: if Keith had telegraphed ahead to say that Sartorius was coming surely he would have made mention of it in his dispatch. It is not that the telegraph was not in Keith's mind, for his dispatch continues:

> I shall send directions to Torbay to-morrow morning to meet Captain Maitland, enforcing the orders contained in your letter . . . and if my presence should be considered useful there I shall hold myself in readiness to set off upon receipt of a telegraph message to meet any instructions their Lordships may address to me there.[30]

It remains a mystery why the telegraph was not used to convey the news in either direction of the capture. So, we have to conclude that as Capt Sartorius travelled up the London Road, anxious for the journey like Lt Lapenotière and Maj Percy before him and with Keith's dispatch and a copy of Napoleon's letter to the Prince Regent, he believed that it was he who was carrying great news which would be received with acclamation in London. But only if it was, in fact, news; he must have had the extraordinary and deflating experience of seeing the laurel-bedecked mail coach – the one whose arrival in Plymouth with the news we have just been considering – going the other way with the same news. It is not recorded whether, in fact, the two coaches stopped for a conversation; it is more likely that Sartorius pressed on for London, even if he had noticed the mail coach in time to hail it.

The reference in Keith's dispatch to Torbay and the telegraph exposes an interesting aside: the Plymouth branch of the shutter telegraph passed only a dozen miles or so (about 20km) inland from Torbay and a facility existed for telegraphic traffic for Torbay, either from Plymouth or London, to be carried on horseback from the telegraph station to the officer commanding.

That completes the story of how Lord Keith, the Admiralty and the Government received the news: what about the public? According to the *Royal Cornwall Gazette*, published in Truro on Saturday, 28 July 1815:

> The first intelligence of the surrender of . . . [Napoleon] reached this country through the medium of the *Moniteur* [the official French newspaper, and not always reliable]. An article in that paper from the Maritime Prefect of Rochefort, dated 15 [July], announced

> that . . . [Napoleon] had embarked on board the *Epervier* brig, . . . [under] a flag of truce; that he proceeded for the English cruising station, and soon joined the English ship *Bellerophon*, [under] Capt. Maitland [on 14 July], which immediately hoisted the white flag at the mizzen and received . . . [Napoleon] and his attendants on board. An Aid-de-camp of Prince Schwartzenburgh brought an official account of this event to the Austrian Ambassador in London, on Friday . . . [21 July] . . . and the arrival of the *Bellerophon* first at Torbay and afterwards at Plymouth, substantiates the case beyond any doubt. . . . [Napoleon] is NOW A PRISONER ON BOARD A BRITISH MAN OF WAR, IN PLYMOUTH SOUND.

From this report it seemed that Napoleon gave himself up by seeking out the British blockade ship; to use the expression 'seeking out' sounds like the acceptable spin as the cover for the thwarted passport plan, for, if it had been issued, Napoleon would have been sailing into the sunset, waving to the *Bellerophon* as he went. The *Royal Cornwall Gazette* continued:

> The *Bellerophon*, with the white flag at the mizzen, the yellow (or quarantine flag) at the fore, and the British pendant at the main mast, must be, under present circumstances, a most interesting object; and it is not to be wondered at that the curiosity of Englishmen should have adopted every expedient in order to procure a sight of the man who once 'made the nations tremble' . . .

Thus, Lord Keith had the once-great man and his entourage on one of his ships and it fell to him to handle this remarkable event some 200 miles (320km) from London. The shutter telegraph was functioning, but, as we have seen, this appeared to be used mostly by the Admiralty for operational matters concerning the fleet, practically all the historic exchanges between ministers in London and Keith were conducted by mail: the mail traffic up and down what we now call the A39 and the A30 over the following two weeks was considerable. But news was coming in from the sea as well: in a dispatch from the captain of HMS *Chatham* off Brest and dated 20 July:

> It is with extreme satisfaction that I have the honour of acquainting your Lordship that a flag of truce is just arrived with an officer charged by the Commandant at Brest and the French Admiral with letters addressed to the Commander of the British Squadron, informing me that Brest and its dependencies have submitted to their lawful sovereign, . . . I shall . . . hoist the Royal Flag of France and fire a Royal Salute.[31]

The long wars with France were drawing to their close.

## Napoleon, the Tourist Attraction

On 24 July the *Bellerophon* anchored in Torbay, about 40 miles (64km) from Plymouth round Start Point; on the same day Keith wrote to his wife: 'Bonny is in Torbay with 5 generals and 60 persons in all; but I am obliged to prohibit all intercourse with the ship, as all Plymouth would have been off to gape at him.'[32]

On the same day, Capt Sartorius arrived with Keith's dispatches to Melville, who wrote back to Keith:

> I am much obliged to you remembering me in directing Capt Sartorius to come to Wimbledon; he arrived there between three and four this morning and we have since had a Cabinet on the business . . . you will be able to judge whether if there is any influx of small boats getting round the ship from curiosity, it may not be necessary to have guard boats to keep everything at a distance . . . [we thought of leaving Napoleon at Torbay but] . . . I thought it on the whole better and more secure to trust to Plymouth . . .[33]

It seems that the movement of the *Bellerophon* was not directed from London by telegraph, because she was not ordered round to Plymouth until 26 July, presumably after Melville's instructions of the 24th arrived by mail: Napoleon was not to be allowed ashore. So, while the government decided what to do with the fallen tyrant, he was detained on board for several days. As the *Royal Cornwall Gazette* reported, he quickly became a tourist attraction:

> . . . thousands upon thousands of visitors flocked to the place, and swarmed in boats of all kinds upon the Sound, surrounding the ship and doing their utmost to obtain a glance at the man who had been a terror to Europe, but who now was a prisoner of war. The Emperor frequently came on deck, and placing himself in the gangway gratified the curiosity of the crowd.[34]

The scene was captured at the time by a young Plymouth artist, who later acquired renown as Sir Charles Eastlake, President of the Royal Academy for many years. Eastlake made a special study of the prisoner on the deck of the *Bellerophon*, making several sketches from a boat,[35] jostling among the tourists; no one was allowed on board, the captain and the crew were to be Napoleon's only intimates. The resulting picture, painted in a studio later, was said to be 'the best and latest portrait ever painted of him'[36] and was put on public display in Plymouth in December 1815, for the high admission price of 1 shilling (5p). The important painting is now held at the National Maritime Museum, Greenwich.

Some sixty or more years later, a French artist Jules Giradet, about whom little is known, other than that he was born in 1856, painted the scene around the *Bellerophon* on Plymouth Sound. It is doubtful whether he had any material to hand for him to bring to mind the scene other than the contemporary newspaper reports, and, quite possibly, the description of the scene in Jewitt's *A History of Plymouth* of 1873. The painting is undated, but it was bought by Plymouth Art Gallery in 1909 where it now hangs.

The scene was also captured in some decorative windows of the Guildhall in Plymouth; in four different lights aspects of the war and Napoleon's stay on the *Bellerophon* were depicted; one of them showed Lord Keith being introduced to him; but Wellington and Nelson also featured in the celebration of victory, reflecting their decisive triumphs against his ambitions. They were an important part of Plymouth's civic heritage, which, in an event drenched in irony, were destroyed in 1941 by the bombs of an enemy whose tyrannical leader combined having no better success than Napoleon, with none, lamentably, of his redeeming features.

## Napoleon to be Sent to St Helena

On the morning of 30 July Lord Keith received a telegraphic message to the effect that a representative of the government, Sir Henry Bunbury, was on his way from London. He duly arrived later that day, with dispatches containing the determination of what was to be done with Napoleon. On the following day Keith and Bunbury visited Napoleon on *Bellerophon* to inform him of his fate, which Melville explained to Keith:

> It would be inconsistent with our duty to this country and to His Majesty's allies if we were to leave to General [the government refused to acknowledge him as emperor] Bonaparte the means or opportunity of again disturbing the peace of Europe and renewing all the calamities of war. It is therefore unavoidable that he should be restrained in his personal liberty to whatever extent may be necessary to secure our first and paramount object. The island of St Helena has been selected for his future residence . . .[37]

If he could not get to America, Napoleon wished to be kept captive in England, the country which had the honour to have been the greatest and most enduring obstacle to his ambition. His letter to the Prince Regent had been delayed in delivery long enough for it to have had no effect; the government were not going to compromise on Napoleon's fate. Keith's instructions, which travelled to Plymouth in the mail, were clear: Napoleon was not to be allowed to set foot in England, but was to be transferred from the *Bellerophon* (bringing to an end her magnificent role in the Napoleonic Wars) to HMS *Northumberland* (another ship that had served under Nelson in the Mediterranean), to be taken to St. Helena. On 3 August instructions were received by telegraph for the *Bellerophon* to set sail to make rendezvous with the *Northumberland*: the telegraphed message was 'indistinct', perhaps due to the weather, but the instructions were confirmed in a dispatch which arrived in the mail on the following day. Melville's dispatch, dated 3 August, illustrates well the use of the telegraph for directing and receiving intelligence of ship movements ('I shall not write . . . till I hear by telegraph that . . . [the ship] has sailed'), while using the mail for government business:

> We have sent you a telegraphic message today for Bonaparte to take a cruise till everything is ready for him, and we have sent a messenger with a similar order; he ought to arrive at Plymouth to-morrow afternoon. [We have heard by telegraph that]. . . the *Northumberland* has sailed from Portsmouth . . .[38]

St Helena was no Elba: it was a staging post controlled by the East India Company for vessels bound for the Cape and India, located in the tropics in the South Atlantic, some 1,200 miles (1,930km) west of Africa and 15° below the Equator. Having escaped once from exile, it was not to be allowed to happen again, not only was Napoleon to be on a remote island far from Europe, he was to be guarded night and day.

## Napoleon's Legacy

I have already noted Geyl's great book, *Napoleon: for and against*, the objectivity, with every point of view represented, and the calmness with which he reviews the by then nearly 150 years of writing about Napoleon (especially so when one considers that he wrote it in occupied Holland) will ensure its place as an enduring reference work. As Geyl says of Napoleon, 'There is no last word, there is no end', and still 'The argument goes on'. As an illustration of Geyl's objectivity this must suffice:

> I doubt whether the French nation is more intelligent, more reasonable, and more peaceful than another. I should certainly not call it more bellicose or more fickle, but it has had its unintelligent unreasonable periods, when it was a worry to its neighbours. It was . . . a most willing tool in the hands of Napoleon, and after his death the credulous dupe of the legend.

There is no shortage of illustrative material by which the French celebrate their glory: the monument at Boulogne is, in this respect, sublime; a celebration of the love of Napoleon by his soldiers; of the politicization of the glory of his name and not at all, as we British might suppose, a further example of the French capacity for honouring failure. That we faced out the threat of invasion, represented by the camp of Boulogne, is off the point of the 164ft (50m) column, with the figure of Napoleon upon it, with his gaze permanently fixed on what he could never have – England. On 21 September 1804, when activity at the camp was at a high pitch, with constant training for the troops in embarking and disembarking, the Commander-in-Chief, Marshal Soult, issued the following order:

> The troops of the Camp of Boulogne wishing to give a proof of their admiration and devotion to the monarch who rules over the destinies of France, have resolved to erect a monument, capable of resisting the ravages of time, in order to perpetuate the memory of his greatness and glory; and to testify to their love and fidelity to the First Emperor of the French, before all the world and all generations. To raise a memorial, for all time, of our hero's creation of an Order [the Legion d'Honneur] to reward honour and bravery.
>
> And lastly, to consecrate the spot where the Emperor Napoleon came to share the work and hardships of his soldiers, to train them for new conflicts, and to prepare the way for the success of his vast enterprise.[39]

The foundation stone of the monument was laid on the next anniversary of the *coup d'etat* (6 November) that had brought Napoleon to power, and it was to be funded from subscriptions by the men of the army. The French navy under Adm Bruix joined themselves to these sentiments and the people of Boulogne, themselves wishing to be associated with the project, provided 11 acres (45,000sq.m) of land on the cliffs just north of Boulogne for its site. Unhappily, but in the nature of such affairs, by 1814 the column (expected to be completed in four years) had grown to only 62ft (19m). As might be expected, after the Restoration no funds were forthcoming to complete the work, and in a defiant gesture the bronze earmarked for the bas-reliefs, itself taken from the battlefield of Austerlitz, was confiscated and used for the royalist project of making a statue of Henry IV (to be placed on the Pont-Neuf in Paris).[40] To the rescue of this sorry tale came the politicization of the memory of Napoleon.

Louis Philippe had been crowned 'King of the French' in 1830 and, in a populist gesture to Napoleon, reflecting the Thiers influence, he had the monument completed and sanitized by a focus on the Legion d'Honneur.

The inscription on the column, in the box below, translates as follows:

> ON THIS SHORE ON 16 AUGUST 1804
> IN THE PRESENCE OF LA GRANDE ARMÉE
> NAPOLEON PRESENTED DECORATIONS OF
> THE LEGION D'HONNEUR
> TO SOLDIERS AND CIVILIANS WHO HAD DESERVED
> WELL OF THEIR COUNTRY
>
> THE CORPS COMMANDED BY MARSHALL SOULT
> AND THE FLEET UNDER THE ORDERS OF ADMIRAL BRUIX
> WISHED TO PERPETUATE THE MEMORY OF THE
> DAY BY A MONUMENT
>
> LOUIS PHILIPPE I, KING OF THE FRENCH
> COMPLETES THIS COLUMN
> CONSECRATED
> BY NAPOLEON'S GRANDE ARMÉE
> 1840

Plainly, the completion of the column started by Napoleon's soldiers and finished by Louis-Philippe was a politically inspired piece of symbolism, a monument to Napoleon's greatness. But there was one final twist to the story concerning the statue of Napoleon just as it was being hoisted into position: was it a royalist with a sense of irony or an Englishman with an impish delight who had vandalized it? For horror of horrors, on the night before the hoist someone carved on Napoleon's left eyeball one solitary word: a word to cheer the heart of every Englishman – 'Waterloo'.[41]

But there is one thing the English cannot assert, that the column outside Boulogne is a blatant copy of Nelson's Column in Trafalgar Square. As we have seen, although the column was not completed until 1840, it was designed in 1804; Nelson's column is much later, the design of Trafalgar Square being dated 1828. If either were a copy of the other, the finger of plagiarism points not to Boulogne but to London.

Yet there is more to Napoleon's legacy than a column on the Boulogne littoral. He left behind solid and permanent edifices of civil government and a network of telegraphs across France – across Europe until he was defeated, and across the Channel too. Moreover, I have already speculated on what might have been if Napoleon's mind had focused on Sir Francis Ronalds's electrical experiments, completed in the year after Waterloo. Britain may have vanquished the man but certainly not the legend for there, next to his tomb in Les Invalides, is a statue of the Emperor bearing the emblems of the

Empire, a hero still, in spite of his failure. But above all, Napoleon reminds us that we are islanders, at our best when the outlook is bleak. Napoleon the failed invader gave us our belief in ourselves; he begat our own legendary heroes, Nelson and Wellington; he also bequeathed us a well-drilled plan for invasion defence which was still in the files at the War Office,[42] ready to be applied when the next tyrant, egged on by the successors to Foch, threatened us in 1940. But we must focus back on telegraphy, for, thanks to Napoleon, we had our shutter telegraphs again and, later, our semaphores were built because of the shock waves of his '100 days'.

Even in death, Napoleon caused the telegraphs to stir, not in England, because there was no telegraph, the shutter telegraphs were closed again after Waterloo and the Portsmouth semaphore line did not open until 1822, but in France, on 5 July 1821, a message was sent from Calais on the telegraph to Paris reporting his death.[43] We have seen the extent of Napoleon's influence on the Admiralty's attitude towards telegraphy during his lifetime – a good defence against invasion depended on surefooted commands to the ships of the Navy – catching a tide was made possible by the telegraph. But the escape from Elba left scar tissue on the Admiralty's psyche; even if they could not reasonably be blamed for his escape, and certainly not for his being given his Mediterranean kingdom in the first place, they had been badly wrong-footed. So, even after his death, Napoleon continued to have an influence on the Admiralty and the attitude to telegraphy. In France, the telegraph never faltered on his passing, the French centralizing tendency found in it an essential instrument of government, but in England it was different. The evidence of Napoleon's influence on telegraphy in England is this: if the Peace of 1814 had endured, if Napoleon had remained in Elba, some new stimulus, some catalyst, would have been needed to induce the Admiralty to reinvest in a telegraph line, but there was none after Napoleon. The Congress of Vienna gave a peace which predated the railways by only fifteen years; the shortening of journey times which followed could not possibly make a new case for visual telegraphy, either in peace or war. This is true even without the influence of the electric telegraph that followed the railways. No, we can be certain that, if Napoleon had not escaped from Elba, not only would England's use of the visual telegraphs have stopped in 1814, it would, almost certainly, never have been resurrected, except perhaps for shipping use.

In this scenario, of a permanent peace in 1814, what would Sir Francis Ronalds have done in 1816 with his electrical telegraph? The Admiralty were trying to save money and, with no new war in contemplation, they would not have been interested, as they had indeed already shown. Perhaps Ronalds would have offered it to the nascent newspaper industry, one that could make money out of fast news transmission. But there is no speculation about Napoleon's legacy of the semaphore line to Portsmouth.

He never lived to know of its existence, but it was his legacy to England, because the Admiralty had been caught napping, and it was not to happen again. Popham's semaphore was in the ascendancy and, with the chastening experience of being caught off-guard fresh in mind, the Admiralty started experimenting with what proved to be a superior visual system to the shutter, and without this we certainly would not have had the Admiralty to Portsmouth semaphore telegraph line, so much of the fabric of which, unlike the shutter telegraphs, remains today. It was to Napoleon that a nod might have been given – which should have been given – when the command was uttered between 1822 and 1847, 'Send it by semaphore'.

## The Telegraph on St Helena

Napoleon harboured a deep resentment of his being consigned to St Helena and lost no opportunity for vituperative complaint against his confinement and for disagreeable personal attacks on the governor, Sir Hudson Lowe. All these complaints reached Europe and were believed by those disposed to be sympathetic to the captive. The official policy, unbending as it was, had been cast in the light of the Elba experience and was not unconscionably harsh. A visitor to St Helena observed:

> There never, perhaps, was a prisoner, so much requiring to be watched and guarded, to whom so much liberty and range for exercise was allowed. With an officer he may go over any part of the island: wholly unobserved, his limits extend four miles – partially observed, eight – and overlooked twelve [about 6, 13 and 19km]. At night the sentinels certainly close round Longwood itself.[44]

Longwood was a barn of a country house, dedicated to Napoleon and his group, albeit some of whom spilled over into outlying annexes; it is difficult to imagine, in all the circumstances of Napoleon's story, a more liberal regime.

There is a final twist in the story of the old telegraphs during the wars with France: it involves one of the key figures in English telegraph history – Rear-Adm Sir Home Riggs Popham, and his influence on the telegraph on St Helena, since, when Napoleon arrived there in 1815, the island was no stranger to the telegraph. In 1802 Col Robert Patten, of the East India Company, became governor of the island, then administered by the company. Patten had been posted from India where, at that time, there was no telegraph. In January 1803, Popham had called at the island and stayed for two or three weeks waiting for a convoy which he was to escort to England. In May of the same year the governor reported on his new telegraph system. The system owed nothing to the existing shutter telegraph at home with which the governor, fresh from India, would not have been familiar in any case, but it did have features in common with Popham's flag telegraph system, which, as we have seen, was later introduced to and adopted by the Navy, and used at Trafalgar. This combination – the recognizable Popham imprint and the timing of his visit – at the least suggests that Popham had a seminal influence on the telegraphic system installed on St Helena. Popham left there in mid February 1803;[45] in May the governor reported that his new telegraph system

> Is found completely to answer the intended purpose by conveying information in a simple, easy, clear and distinct manner . . .
>
> I was led to prefer the sort of Telegraph I have adopted composed of a frame of wood and balls, because our stations are generally upon the heights having the sky behind which renders such objects distinctly visible . . . With only four balls [arranged in different configurations], 100 different signals can be distinctly made. . . the system adopted is a species of communication in cypher . . .

The reference to cipher is important. Although the Chappe telegraph system used a code, as did the Navy thanks to Popham, the English land telegraphs never did. Here is the Popham imprint: the St Helena telegraph did not need to spell out a message letter by letter, but, by means of a vocabulary book, prearranged combinations of balls could give the desired message.

Popham had done his pioneering work on a telegraphic vocabulary in 1800 while in the same ship, the *Romney*, on which he was still serving when she called in at St Helena in 1803. Wilson[46] gives no credit to Popham for the telegraphic vocabulary used there; he observes that Popham visited the island in 1806 (which he did) and suggests that 'he merely made a few improvements' to the telegraph. This analysis completely overlooks Popham's 1803 visit, of which Wilson may have been unaware, and the fact that the St Helena telegraphic system has a considerable amount in common with Popham's naval telegraphic code, which he had already invented before the 1803 visit. Moreover, in demonstration of Popham's contemporary fluency with codes, in 1803 Popham produced, at the request of the East India Company, a version of his code suited to their own ships (known as 'Indiamen'). Their special need can be illustrated by code no.160 which meant 'Are the natives friendly?', while no.161 meant, 'Are they numerous?'[47] Because Popham had been thinking about telegraphy for nearly twenty years before his work for the Company and his visit to the island in the same year, it is with reasonably certain that Popham influenced Patten rather than vice versa.

Whatever Popham's influence on the St Helena telegraphic system might have been, it was put to good use after the *Northumberland* arrived with Napoleon on 15 October 1815:

> The rusty pulleys of the aerial telegraph installed by the previous governor were cleaned; and an office was set up. . . [at Longwood] making it possible to communicate immediately to the authorities the information that:
>
> *All is well with respect to General Bonaparte and family*
> *General Bonaparte is unwell*
> *General Bonaparte is out, properly attended, beyond the cordon of sentries*
> *General Bonaparte is out but within the cordon of sentries.*[48]

All this was routine and consistent with the report cited above, and these signals were probably telegraphed daily. In ascending levels of anxiety, the codebook had further signals to offer: *General Bonaparte has been out longer than usual, and is supposed to have passed the sentries not properly attended.* There would, of course have been a monumental flap if the following signal had ever been hoisted: *General Bonaparte is missing.*

These coded signals demonstrate two things: in relation to his supervision, even if his movement was free, how closely Napoleon was monitored (much to his unceasing objection); and, in relation to telegraphic practice, how prearranged signals could be sent, if a vocabulary had been set up, without the need to spell out the whole message letter by letter.

In 1820, soldiers of the XXth Regiment of Foot took on the responsibility for the guard over Napoleon. This regiment, originating from Devon, had started recruiting in Preston, Lancashire in the bleak days of the Revolutionary war in 1798–99; this marked the first association with the county for a regiment which was later to be renamed the Lancashire Fusiliers. There was an irony in the XXth of Foot guarding Napoleon: the Regiment had served in the Peninsula and, among other battle honours, it was proud of Vittoria and Toulouse (a battle which Wellington won early in 1814, after he had crossed the Pyrenees and following Vittoria). Even before that, they had fought against the army that Napoleon had abandoned in Egypt. Twelve grenadiers of the XXth bore his coffin to the grave.[49] As if to prove the point about the benefits of an alphabetic system of telegraphy and the limitations of one based on a vocabulary, on 5 May 1821, the Lancashire lad who was on signal duty that day must have been dismayed, when he looked up the vocabulary book, to find just like Pasco at Trafalgar, what he needed was not there; there was no signal in the book for: *General Bonaparte is dead.*

# Notes

### Ch.1 When Speed Was Measured by the Horse and the Sailing Ship

1 *Cymbeline*, III, ii.
2 *The Macmillan Family Encyclopaedia* (1980).
3 *The Handbook of Communication by Telegraph* (1842).
4 Webster, G., *The Roman Imperial Army* (1969).
5 Collingwood, R.G. and J.N.L. Myres, *Roman Britain and the English Settlements* (1937).
6 Cornwall Library Service.
7 *Naval Miscellany*, vol.2 (1928).
8 Holzmann, G.J. and B. Pehrson, *The Early History of Data Networks* (1995).
9 Bryant, Sir Arthur *The Age of Elegance 1812–1822* (1950).
10 King. H.C., *The History of Telescopes* (1955).
11 Porter, R. (ed.), *The Cambridge History of Science*, vol.4, *Eighteenth-Century Science* (2003).
12 Crawley, C.W. (ed.), *The New Cambridge Modern History*, vol.9, *War and Peace in an Age of Upheaval 1793–1830* (1969).
13 Allen, N., *Through the Letter-box* (1988).
14 International Telecommunications Union, *From Semaphore to Satellites* (1965).
15 Appleyard, Rollo, quoted in *Pioneers of Electrical Communication* (1930).
16 Ibid.
17 Bryant, *The Age of Elegance* (1950).
18 Crawley, *The New Cambridge Modern History*, vol.10 (1969).
19 Ibid.
20 Ibid.

### Ch.2 The Ordnance Survey

1 Quoted in W.A. Seymour (ed.), *A History of the Ordnance Survey* (1980), a book of considerable scholarship from which has been gleaned much of the history of mapping in the period covered here.
2 Crawley, C.W. (ed.), *The New Cambridge Modern History*, vol.9, *War and Peace in an Age of Upheaval 1793–1830* (1969).
3 Ibid.
4 Harley, J.B., 'The Society of Arts and the surveys of English counties 1759–1809', *Royal Society* of Arts, vol.112, pp.43–46, 119–24, 269–75, 538–43.
5 British Library, Map Library, K.Top.VI. 97.
6 Seymour, W.A. (ed.), *Origins of the Ordnance Survey* (1980).
7 Ibid.
8 Close, Sir Charles, *The Early Years of the Ordnance Survey* (1926).
9 Ibid.
10 PRO, WO 30/115. Quoted in Seymour, *A History of the Ordnance Survey* (1980).
11 Brown, L.A., *The Story of Maps* (Boston, 1949), p.257.
12 Close, *Early Years of the Ordnance Survey* (1926).
13 King, H.C., *The History of Telescopes* (1955).
14 In a matter beyond the scope of this book, it was the first ever instrument which could

make allowance for 'spherical excess': the effect on a triangle of its sides being on a curved surface, for instance, the earth.
15 King, *History of Telescopes* (1955).
16 O'Donoghue, Y., *William Roy 1726–1790, Pioneer of the Ordnance Survey* (1977).
17 Mudge, W. and I. Dalby, *An Account of the Operations Carried on for Accomplishing a Trigonometrical Survey of England and Wales 1784–1796* (1799).
18 O'Donoghue, Ylonde, *William Roy,* 1726–1790, *Pioneeer of the Ordnance Survey* (1977).
19 Skelton, R.A., *Geographical Journal,* vol.128 (1962).
20 Close, *Early Years of the Ordnance Survey,* (1926).
21 Lockhart, J., *The History of Napoleon Buonaparte* (1906)/

### Ch.3 The First Telegraphs and the French Revolution

1 *Toilus and Cressida,* III, iii.
2 Quoted in Desmond Clarke, *The Ingenious Mr Edgeworth* (1965).
3 Rhys, E. (ed.), *The Hampstead Annual* (1897).
4 From the memoirs of Richard Lovell Edgeworth, quoted in Clarke, *The Ingenious Mr Edgeworth* (1965).
5 Clarke, Desmond, *The Ingenious Mr Edgeworth* (1955).
6 Quoted in G. Wilson, *John Gamble and the First British Military Telegraph* (unpublished; available in the library of the Royal Corps of Signals, Blandford).
7 From the memoirs of Richard Lovell Edgeworth, quoted in Clarke, Desmond, *The Ingenious Mr Edgeworth* (1965).
8 Tollemache, B. (ed.), *Richard Lovell Edgeworth, a Selection from His Memoirs* (1896).
9 Young, A., *Travels in France and Italy* (1792–94).
10 Mercier, L.-S., *Tableau of Paris* (Amsterdam, 12 vols, 1782–88).
11 Geyl, P., *Napoleon: for and against* (1949).
12 Young, *Travels.*
13 Doyle, W., *The Oxford History of the French Revolution* (2002).
14 Ibid.
15 Holzmann, G.J. and Bjørn Pehrson, *The Early History of Data Networks* (1995).
16 Ibid.
17 Chappe, I. and Chappe, A., *Histoire de la Télégraphie* (1824), quoted in Holzman and Pehrson, *The Early History of Data Networks* (1995).
18 Holzman and Pehrson, *The Early History of Data Networks* (1995).
19 Quoted in Holzman and Pehrson, *The Early History of Data Networks* (1995).
20 Carlyle, T., *The French Revolution* (2002 edn).
21 Quoted in Holzman and Pehrson, *The Early History of Data Networks* (1995).
22 Ibid.
23 Lakanal, J.,*Rapport sur le télégraphe du citoyen Chappe, fait au nom du Comité d'instruction publique & de la Commission nommé par décret du 27 avril dernier* (1793).
24 Tuck, O., 'The Old Telegraph', *The Fighting Forces* (Sept. 1924).
25 Wilson, G., *The Old Telegraphs* (1976).
26 From a lecture given by Capt F.J. Bolton, 12th Regiment and quoted in *Royal United Services Institute,* vol.7 (1864).
27 Quoted in Holzman and Pehrson, *The Early History of Data Networks* (1995).

## Ch.4 The Development of the Chappe Telegraph

1 Crawley, C.W. (ed.), *The New Cambridge Modern History*, vol.9, *War and Peace in an Age of Upheaval* (1969).
2 Holzman, G.J. and B. Pehrson, *The Early History of Data Networks* (1995).
3 Porter, R. (ed.), *The Cambridge History of Science*, vol.4, *Eighteenth-Century Science* (2003).
4 Chappe, I. and A., *Histoire de la Télégraphie* (1824), quoted in Holzman and Pehrson, *The Early History of Data Networks* (1995).
5 Crawley, *The New Cambridge Modern History*, vol.9 (1969).
6 Holzman, G.J. and Pehrson, B., *The Early History of Data Networks* (1995).
7 Ibid.
8 Bryant, A., *The Years of Endurance 1793–1802* (1942).
9 Crawley, *The New Cambridge Modern History*, vol.9 (1969).
10 Quoted in G. Wilson, *John Gamble and the First British Military Telegraph* (unpublished; available in the library of the Royal Corps of Signals, Blandford).
11 Koenig, D., *Scientific Monthly*, vol.59 (Dec. 1944).
12 Holzman and Pehrson, *The Early History of Data Networks* (1995).
13 Edelcrantz, A.N., *Treatise on Telegraphs* (in Swedish, 1796), quoted in Holzman and Pehrson, *The Early History of Data Networks* (1995).
14 Tuck, O., 'The Old Telegraph', *The Fighting Forces* (Sept. 1924).
15 Holzmann and Pehrson, *The Early History of Data Networks* (1995).
16 From a lecture given by Capt. F.J. Bolton, 12th Regiment and quoted in *J. Royal United Services Institute*, vol.7 (1864).
17 Tuck, 'The Old Telegraph', *The Fighting Forces* (Sept. 1924).
18 Wilson, G., *The Old Telegraphs* (1976).
19 Translated from a quotation in Rollo Appleyard, *Pioneers of Electrical Communication* (1930).
20 Holzman and Pehrson, *The Early History of Data Networks* (1995).
21 Wilson, *The Old Telegraphs* (1976).
22 Holzman and Pehrson, *The Early History of Data Networks* (1995).
23 Koenig, *Scientific Monthly*, vol.59 (Dec. 1944).
24 Holzman and Pehrson, *The Early History of Data Networks* (1995).

## Ch.5 The Telegraph is Developed in England

1 *Henry VI*, Pt III: V, vi.
2 Gamble, Revd J., *An Essay on the Different Modes of Communication by Signals; containing an history of the progressive improvements in this art, from the first account of beacons to the most approved methods of telegraphic correspondence* (1797; earlier edition published in 1795).
3 Ibid.
4 Wilson, G., *The Old Telegraphs* (1976).
5 Ibid.
6 Gamble, Revd J., *An Essay on the Different Moden of Communication by Signals* (1797).
7 Wilson, *The Old Telegraphs* (1976).
8 British Library Map Library, Maps M.T.6. b.2. (14).
9 Lindley, J. and W. Crossley, *Memoir of a Map of the County of Surrey – from a Survey made in the years 1789 to 1790.*
10 PRO WO 30/55.
11 PRO WO 78, Maps and plans.
12 The map is available in Camden Public Library, Theobalds Road, London WC1.
13 *Norfolk Archaeology*, vol.35 (1973); Munday, Revd J.T., *The Yarmouth and London Telegraph.*

## Ch.6 Telegraphy as it Developed at Sea

1 Kent, Capt B., *Signal! A History of Signalling in the Royal Navy* (1993).
2 Ibid.
3 Ibid.
4 Ibid.
5 Ibid.
6 Ibid.
7 Tunstall, B., *Naval Warfare in the Age of Sail: the Evolution of Fighting Tactics* (1990).
8 Popham, H., *A Damned Cunning Fellow* (1991).
9 *Mariner's Mirror*, vol.271, no.4 (Oct. 1941).
10 *Naval Chronicle*, vol.27 (1912).
11 Popham, *Damned Cunning Fellow* (1991).
12 Navy Records Society, *The Barham Papers*, vol.2 (1890).
13 Popham, *Damned Cunning Fellow* (1991).
14 Ibid.
15 Ibid.
16 Ibid.
17 Crawley, C.W. (ed.), *The New Cambridge Modern History*, vol.9, *War and Peace in an Age of Upheaval* (1969).
18 Mahan, Capt A.T., *Influence of Sea Power in the War of the French Revolution* (1893).
19 Holmes, T.W., *The Semaphore* (1983).
20 Baylis, Lt Col. T.H., *The True Account of Nelson's Famous Signal* (1905).
21 Popham, *A Damned Cunning Fellow* (1991).
22 Harris, Sir N. (ed.), *The Dispatches and Letters of Vice-Admiral Lord Viscount Nelson* (1844).
23 Kent, Barrie, *A History of Signalling in the Royal Navy* (1993).
24 Popham, Sir H., *Telegraphic Signals or Marine Vocabulary* (1812).

## Ch.7 The Revolution at War

1 Maffeo, S.E., *Most Secret and Confidential: Intelligence in the Age of Nelson* (2000).
2 Lockhart, J.G., *The History of Napoleon Bonaparte* (1829).
3 PRO, WO 30/58.
4 Ibid.
5 Ibid.
6 PRO, WO 30/56.
7 Ibid.
8 PRO, WO 1/407.
9 PRO, MR 1200, *Military Sketch of the Country round London pointing out the Positions to cover the Capital* (Sept. 1801).
10 PRO, WO 30/66, pp.86–87.
11 Ibid., p.83.
12 Gamble, Revd J. *An Essay on the Different Modes of Communication by Signals; containing an history of the progressive improvements in this art, from the first account of beacons to the most approved methods of telegraphic correspondence* (1797; earlier edition published in 1795).
13 PRO, WO 40/10.
14 Tuck, O., *The Old Telegraph, The Fighting Forces* (Sept. 1924).
15 Neale, J.P. and E.W. Brayley, *The History and Antiquities of the Church of St. Peter, Westminster* (1823).
16 Tuck, *The Old Telegraph, The Fighting Forces* (Sept. 1924).

17 Wilson, G., *John Gamble and the First British Military Telegraph* (unpublished; available in the library of the Royal Corps of Signals, Blandford).
18 Lockhart, J.G., *The History of Napoleon Bonaparte* (1829).
19 Based on Elizabeth Wormley Latimer, quoted in *Talks of Napoleon at St Helena* (1903).
20 Geyl, Pieter, *Napoleon: for and against* (1949).
21 Holzman, G.J. and B. Pehrson, *The Early History of Data Networks* (1995).
22 Édouard Driault, quoted in Geyl, *Napoleon: for and against.*
23 Mme de Staël, quoted in Geyl, *Napoleon: for and against.*
24 Édouard Driault, quoted in Geyl, *Napoleon: for and against.*
25 Lockhart, *The History of Napoleon Bonaparte* (1829).
26 Ibid.
27 Ibid.

**Ch.8 'He Brings Great News'**

1 *Macbeth*: I, v.
2 *Proverbs* 25, 25.
3 In a letter to Earl Spencer, First Lord of the Admiralty, from 'The mouth of the Nile', 9 August 1798.
4 From a poem is signed simply 'R', *Royal Cornwall Gazette*, 23 Nov. 1805.
5 From a poem by Chas. F. Forshan; ibid., 26 Oct. 1905.
6 Hibbert, C., *Nelson: a Personal History* (1994).
7 Dane, C., *He Brings Great News* (1944). Although this is a fictional account of how the Trafalgar news arrived in London, it was researched meticulously.
8 Allen, D. and A. Cross, 'Lieutenant Lapenotière's ride from Falmouth to London, 4–6 November 1805', *The Nelson Dispatch* (*Journal of the Nelson Society*), vol.7, part 12.
9 *Royal Cornwall Gazette*, 9 Nov. 1805.
10 Whitfield, H.F., *Plymouth and Devonport: in Times of War and Peace* (1900).
11 Poale, P.A.S., *The History of the Town and Borough of Penzance* (1974).
12 Villiers, A., *The Battle of Trafalgar* (1965).
13 Dane, *He Brings Great News: a story* (1944).
14 Lavery, B., *Nelson and the Nile* (1998).
15 PRO Adm 1/5347, quoted in Lavery, *Nelson and the Nile* (1998).
16 Lavery, *Nelson and the Nile* (1998).
17 Ibid.
18 Ibid.
19 Harris, Sir N. (ed.), *The Dispatches and Letters of Vice-Admiral Lord Viscount Nelson* (1844).
20 Knight, C., *Autobiography* (2 vols, 1861).
21 Ibid.
22 Lavery, *Nelson and the Nile* (1998).
23 Ibid.
24 Ibid.
25 Corbett, J.S. (ed.), *The Private Papers of George, second Earl Spencer* (1794–1801) (1913).
26 Lockhart, J.G., *The History of Napoleon Bonaparte* (1829).
27 Harris, Sir Nicholson (ed.), *Dispatches and Letters of Vice-Admiral Lord Viscount Nelson* (1844).
28 Gachot, H., *Le Télégraph Optique* (1967).

**Ch.9 'There are Bitter Weeds in England'**

1 Bryant, Sir Arthur, *The Years of Endurance 1793–1802* (1942).
2 Ibid.
3 Geyl, P., *Napoleon: for and against* (1949).
4 Wilson, G., *The Old Telegraphs* (1976).
5 Gachot, H., *Le Télégraph Optique* (1967).
6 Bryant, Sir Arthur, *Years of Victory 1802–1812* (1944).
7 Maffeo, S.E., *Most Secret and Confidential: Intelligence in the Age of Nelson* (2000).
8 Bryant, *Years of Victory* (1942).
9 Geyl, P., *Napoleon: for and against* (1949).
10 Lepercq, J. and L., *Il y a 200 ans . . . Le Camp de Boulogne* (2003).
11 Grueber, H.A., '*The Descente en Angleterre*', Medal of Napoleon I in *Numistmatic Chron.*, 4th Ser., VII (1907), pp.434–39.
12 Bryant, *Years of Victory* (1942).
13 Ibid.
14 'Biographical Memoirs of The Right Honourable Lord Keith', *Naval Chronicle*, vol.10 (1803).
15 Fone, J.F., 'Signalling from Norwich to the Coast in the Napoleonic Period', *Norfolk Archeology*, vol.52, part 3 (1996), pp.356–61.
16 Hudleston, Capt R., 'The Coast Signal Stations and the Semaphore Telegraph', *Mariner's Mirror*, vol , no.7 (July 1911).
17 Ibid.
18 *Mariner's Mirror*, vol , no.9 (Sept. 1911).
19 Goodwin J., 'Naval and Military Co-operation and Control over Invasion Warnings', *Fortress*, no.15 (Nov. 1992).
20 PRO, WO 133/12.
21 Wilson, *The Old Telegraphs* (1976).
22 Wilson, J., *A Soldier's Wife: Wellington's Marriage* (1987).
23 Gurwood, Lt Col, *The Dispatches of Field Marshal the Duke of Wellington, During his Various campaigns from 1799 to 1818*, vol.6, p.224 (1838).
24 From the Keith Papers, quoted in: *Mariner's Mirror*, vol.1, no.9 (Sept.1911).
25 Ibid.
26 Bryant, *Years of Victory* (1942).
27 Ibid.
28 Goodwin, 'Naval and Military Co-operation'.
29 Ibid.
30 Ibid.
31 *Norfolk Archaeology*, vol.35 (1973).
32 Laphorne, W.H., 'Flying the White Ensign at St. Peter's', *Bygone Kent*, vol.11, no.10.
33 Hudleston, 'The Coast Signal Stations', *Mariners' Mirror* (vol.1, no.7, July 1911).
34 Bryant, *Years of Victory* (1942).
35 Harris, Sir N. (ed.), *The Dispatches and Letters of Vice-Admiral Lord Viscount Nelson* (1844).
36 Bryant, *Years of Victory 1802–1812* (1942).
37 Lepercq, *Il y a 200 ans . . . Le Camp de Boulogne* (2003).
38 Nicolay, N., *Napoleon at the Boulogne Camp* (1907).
39 Ibid.
40 Ibid.
41 Bryant, *Years of Victory 1802–1812* (1942).
42 Crawley, C.W. (ed.), *The New Cambridge Modern History*, vol.9, *War and Peace in an Age of Upheaval* (1969).

43 Gibbs, M.G., *The Military Career of Napoleon the Great* (1904).
44 Lepercq., *Il y a 200 ans . . . Le Camp de Boulogne* (2003).

### Ch.10 From Boulogne to Elba, via Moscow and Leipzig

1 Bryant, A., *The Great Duke or the Invincible General* (1971).
2 Chandler, D., *The Campaigns of Napoleon* (1967).
3 Wilson, G., *The Old Telegraphs* (1976).
4 Gachot, H., *Le Télégraph Optique,* (1967).
5 *Hampshire Telegraph* and *Sussex Chronicle,* 11 Nov. 1805.
6 Lewis, M., *A Social History of the Navy, 1813–1815* (1960), quoted in Crawley, C.W. (ed.), *The New Cambridge Modern History,* vol.9, *War and Peace in an Age of Upheaval* (1969).
7 Gibbs, M.B., *The Military Career of Napoleon the Great* (1904).
8 Villiers, A., *The Battle of Trafalgar* (1965).
9 *Hampshire Telegraph* and *Sussex Chronicle,* 11 Nov. 1805.
10 Wilson, G., *The Old Telegraphs* (1976).
11 Chandler, *Campaigns of Napoleon* (1981).
12 Ibid.
13 Ibid.
14 Adolfe Thiers, quoted in: Geyl, P., *Napoleon: for and against* (1949).
15 Gabriel Hanotaux, quoted in: Geyl, P., *Napoleon: for and against* (1949).
16 Wilson, *The Old Telegraphs* (1976).
17 Ibid.
18 Geyl, P., *Napoleon: for and against* (1949).
19 Ibid.
20 Ibid.
21 Thiers, quoted in Geyl, P., *Napoleon: for and against.*
22 Édouard Driault, quoted in Geyl, P., *Napoleon: for and against.*
23 Ibid.
24 Ibid.
25 Ibid.
26 Quoted by courtesy of Scotia Philately Ltd.
27 Geyl, *Napoleon: for and against.*
28 Bryant, *Years of Victory 1802–1812* (1944).
29 Ibid.
30 Ibid.
31 From the General Station Regulations of 1809, quoted in: Holzman, G.J. and B. Pehrson, *The Early History of Data Networks* (1995).
32 Fisher, H.A.L., *Bonapartism,* quoted in Bryant, *Years of Victory* (1942).
33 Bryant, *Years of Victory* (1942).
34 Geyl, P. *Napoleon: for and against.* (1944)
35 Bryant, *Years of Victory 1802–1812* (1942).
36 Ibid.
37 *Naval Chronicle,* vol.16 (1806).
38 Cochrane, Capt Lord Thomas, *The Autobiography of a Seaman,* 2 vols (2nd edn, 1860–61).
39 Morriss, R., in Le Fevre, P. and R. Harding, (Ed.), *Precursors of Nelson* (2000).
40 Navy Records Society, *The Barham Papers,* vol.3 (1910).
41 Bryant, *Years of Victory* (1942).
42 Bryant, *The Age of Elegance 1812–1822* (1950).
43 Bryant, *Years of Victory* (1942).

44 Henderson, J., *The Frigates* (1970).
45 Urban, M., *The Man who Broke Napoleon's Codes: the Story of George Scovell* (2001).
46 Bryant, *Years of Victory* (1942).
47 Holzman and Pehrson, *The Early History of Data Networks* (1995).
48 Bryant, *Years of Victory* (1942).
49 Bryant, *The Age of Elegance* (1950).
50 Lockhart, J.G., *The History of Napoleon Bonaparte* (1829).
51 Quoted from an original letter by courtesy of Scotia Philately Ltd.
52 Wilson, *The Old Telegraphs* (1976).
53 Lockhart, *The History of Napoleon Bonaparte* (1829).
54 Quoted from an original letter by courtesy of Scotia Philately Ltd.
55 Lockhart, *The History of Napoleon Bonaparte* (1829).
56 Wilson, *The Old Telegraphs* (1976).
57 Bryant, *The Age of Elegance 1812–1822* (1942).
58 Lockhart, *The History of Napoleon Bonaparte* (1829).
59 Wilson, *The Old Telegraphs* (1976).
60 Adolfe Thiers, quoted in Geyl, P. *Napoleon: for and against* (1944).
61 Lockhart, *The History of Napoleon Bonaparte* (1829).
62 Geyl, *Napoleon: for and against* (1944).
63 Bryant, *The Age of Elegance 1812–1822* (1942).
64 Albert Sorel, writing over 70 years after the events, quoted in Geyl, P., *Napoleon: for and against* (1949).
65 Koenig, D., *Scientific Monthly*, vol.59 (Dec. 1944).

## Ch.11 Napoleon: Escape

1 Dumas, A., *The Count of Monte Cristo.* Although this famous story is fiction, it gives a good insight into the politics of the period and of the role of the telegraph in France; it was written in 1844-5, when the telegraph was still in routine use.
2 Ibid.
3 Ibid.
4 Wilson, G., *The Old Telegraphs* (1976).
5 Ibid.
6 Lockhart, J.G., *The History of Napoleon Bonaparte* (1829).
7 Hansard, 12 Apr. 1815.
8 Ibid.
9 Ibid.
10 Ibid.
11 Holmes, T.W., *The Semaphore* (1983).

## Ch.12 Napoleon: Defeat

1 Bryant, Sir Arthur., *The Great Duke* (1971).
2 *Henry VI*, Part I, IV, v.
3 Hugo, V., *Les Misérables* (trans. Norman Denny, 1976).
4 Ibid.
5 Crawley, C.W. (ed.), *The New Cambridge Modern History*, vol.9, *War and Peace in an Age of Upheaval* (1969).
6 Hugo, *Les Misérables* (trans. Norman Denny), (1976).
7 Bryant, Sir Arthur, *The Age of Elegance 1812–1822* (1950).
8 Lockhart, J.G., *The History of Napoleon Bonaparte* (1829).

9 Bryant, *The Age of Elegance* (1950).
10 Ibid.
11 Bryant, *The Great Duke* (1971).
12 Hugo, *Les Misérables* (trans. Norman Denny), (1976).
13 Bryant *The Great Duke* (1971).
14 Ibid.
15 Hugo, *Les Misérables* (trans. Norman Denny) (1976).
16 Wilson, G., *The Old Telegraphs* (1976).
17 Perrin, W.G. and C. Lloyd (eds), *The Keith Papers* (Navy Records Society, 1927, 1950, 1955).
18 Ibid.
19 Hugo, *Les Miserables* (trans. Norman Denny) (1976).
20 Ibid.
21 Lockhart, *The History of Napoleon Bonaparte.* (1829).
22 Wilson, *The Old Telegraphs* (1976).
23 Colby, R., *The Wellington Dispatch: The Story of the Duke of Wellington's Official Despatch on the Battle of Waterloo and Its Journey to London* (HMSO, 1965).
24 *Kentish Gazette*, 23 June 1815.
25 Wilson, *The Old Telegraphs* (1976).
26 See references to Cdr H.P. Mead, RN and his articles in the Preface.
27 Perrin, and Lloyd (eds), *The Keith Papers* (Navy Records Society, 1927, 1950, 1955).
28 Wilson, G., *The Old Telegraphs* (1976).
29 Colby, *The Wellington Dispatch* (1965).
30 Ibid.

### Ch.13 Napoleon: Capture

1 Perrin, W.G. and C. Lloyd (eds), *The Keith Papers* (Navy Records Society, 1927, 1950, 1955).
2 Crawley, C.W. (ed.), *The New Cambridge Modern History*, vol.9, *War and Peace in an Age of Upheaval* (1969).
3 Geyl, P., *Napoleon: for and against* (1949).
4 Crawley, *The New Cambridge Modern History*, vol.9.
5 Lockhart, J.G., *The History of Napoleon Bonaparte* (1829).
6 Wilson, G., *The Old Telegraphs* (1976).
7 Perrin and Lloyd, *The Keith Papers.*
8 Ibid.
9 Hamilton-Williams, D., *Waterloo: New Perspectives, the Great Battle Reappraised* (1993).
10 Ibid.
11 Hugo, V., *Les Misérables* (trans. Norman Denny, 1976).
12 Wilson, *The Old Telegraphs* (1976).
13 Perrin and Lloyd, *The Keith Papers.*
14 Ibid.
15 Ibid.
16 Ibid.
17 Ibid.
18 Latimer, E. Wormley, *Talks of Napoleon at St. Helena* (1903).
19 Clowes, W. Laird, *The Royal Navy: a History* (7 vols, 1897–1903).
20 Perrin and Lloyd, *The Keith Papers.*
21 Gates, W.G., *Naval History of Portsmouth* (1901).
22 Perrin and Lloyd, *The Keith Papers.*

23 Lockhart, *The History of Napoleon Bonaparte* (1829).
24 Perrin and Lloyd, *The Keith Papers.*
25 Ibid.
26 Maitland, F.W., *The Surrender of Napoleon* (1826).
27 Perrin and Lloyd, *The Keith Papers.*
28 Wilson, G., *The Old Telegraphs* (1976).
29 Perrin and Lloyd, *The Keith Papers.*
30 Ibid.
31 Ibid.
32 Ibid.
33 Ibid.
34 Jowett, L., *A History of Plymouth* (1873).
35 Bracken, C.W., *A History of Plymouth* (1931).
36 Jowett, *A History of Plymouth* (1873).
37 Perrin and Lloyd, *The Keith Papers.*
38 Ibid.
39 Nicolay, F., *Napoleon at the Boulogne Camp* (1907).
40 Ibid.
41 Ibid.
42 PRO, WO 30/58.
43 Wilson, *The Old Telegraphs* (1976).
44 Lockhart, *The History of Napoleon Bonaparte* (1829).
45 Popham, Hugh, *A Damned Cunning Fellow* (1991).
46 Wilson, *The Old Telegraphs* (1976).
47 Popham, *A Damned Cunning Fellow* (1991).
48 Martineau, G., *Napoleon's St. Helena* (1968).
49 Surtees, Maj Gen G., *A Short History of XX The Lancashire Fusiliers* (1955).

# Appendix
# Routes of the Shutter Telegraph Stations from the Admiralty

None of the shutter telegraph buildings has survived; although their locations can usually be established, the exact spots are not always known. The information below is from several sources; distances in brackets (given in format: miles/kilometres) are from the corresponding station nearer to London.

**Deal**

Opened 1796, closed 1814; total distance: 70/113; longest carry: 11.2/18.

1. Admiralty
2. 36 West Square, Southwark (1¼/2); existing house, later converted to semaphore
3. Nunhead (3/5); Telegraph Hill Gardens, New Cross
4. Shooters Hill (4½/7); on the south shoulder of the hill
5. Swanscombe (10½/17); just south of the A2
6. Gad's Hill (6¾/11); Telegraph Road
7. Callum Hill (10/16); near Lower Halstow
8. Beacon Hill, Faversham (8/13); Beacon Hill, 2/3.2 W of Faversham: (branch to Sheerness)
9. Shottenden (5/8); Shottenden Hill
10. Barham Downs (11.2/18); about ½/0.8 NNW of Womenswold
11. Betteshanger (5.6/9); Telegraph Farm
12. Deal (4.3/7); Navy Yard.

*Branch to Sheerness*

1. Tonge (4/6.4 from Beacon Hill junction); Telegraph Hill
2. Barrow Hill (5/8); E of Queenborough-in-Sheppey
3. Sheerness (2.3/3.7); Sheerness Dockyard.

**Portsmouth**

Opened 1796, closed 1814; reopened 1815, closed 1816?; total length: 65/105; longest carry: Beacon Hill–Portsdown Hill: 11½/18.5.

1. Admiralty
2. Chelsea (1.7/2.7); East Wing of Royal Hospital
3. Putney Heath (4/6.4); near Telegraph Inn, Telegraph Road
4. Cabbage Hill (8/13); Telegraph Hill, S of Chessington Zoo
5. Netley Heath (8.4/13.5); Hackhurst Downs, near Gomshall
6. Hascombe (8.4/13.5); Telegraph Hill, ½/0.8 SE of church
7. Blackdown (7.8/12.6); 1½/2.4 E by N from Fernhurst Church
8. Beacon Hill (10/16); 1½/2.4 ESE from South Harting

9. Portsdown Hill (11.5/18.5); site of Gamble's 1795 experimental telegraph, near Bedhapmton
10. Portsmouth (5/8); Southsea Common.

**Plymouth Branch**

Opened 1806, closed 1814; reopened 1815, closed 1816?; total length: 152/245; longest carry: Rockbere–Haldon Hill: 10/16:

1. Chalton Down (5.8/9.3); 1/1.6 W of Chalton Village
2. Wickham (7.7/12.4); 1¼/2 E by N from church
3. Town Hill (9/14.5); 2/3.2 ESE from South Stoneham church
4. Toot Hill (5.7/9.2); 2½/4 SE of Romsey
5. Bramshaw (9.5/15.3); 2¼/3.6 W of village
6. Pistle Hill (9.2/14.8); 2¾/4.4 SE of Cranbourne church
7. Chalbury (4.8/7.7); close to church (N of Wimborne Minster)
8. Blandford Race Course (8.6/13.8); site of Royal Corps of Signals depot
9. Belchalwell (5.2/8.4); 4/6.4 S of Sturminster Newton
10. Nettlecombe Tout (5.2/8.4); 2/3.2 S of Mappowder
11. High Stoy (5.8/9.3); Telegraph Hill, 1/1.6 NNW of Minterne Magna
12. Toller Down (7.8/12.6); 2½/4 W of Rampisham
13. Lambert's Castle (9.7/15.6); 4½/7.2 E of Axeminster
14. St. Cyrus (4.7/7.6); St. Cyrus Hill, 1/1.6 NNW of Honiton
15. Rockbeare (7/11.3); 6½/10.5 E of Exeter
16. Haldon Hill (10/16)
17. Knighton (9.2/15); 2/3.2 ESE of Bovey Tracey
18. Marley (9/14.5); Telegraph Hill, 4/6.4 ENE of Ashburton
19. Ivybridge (8/13)
20. Saltram (5.4/8.7); 1/1.6 W of Plympton Earle
21. Mount Wise, Plymouth (4,8 miles).

**Yarmouth**

Opened 1807, closed 1814; total length: 136.5/220; longest carry: Royston–Gog Magog Hills and Newmarket, both 11.7/18.8, the longest carry of any shutter telegraph station:

1. Admiralty
2. Royal Hospital Chelsea (1.8/2.9); on top of the West Wing
3. Hampstead (5.4/8.7); Telegraph Hill
4. Woodcock Hill (6.5/10.5); about ½/0.8 SSE of Borehamwood station
5. St. Albans (8/13); on top of fifteenth-century clock-tower
6. Dunstable (11.3/18.2); on high ground 2/3.2 S of town
7. Lilley Hoo (9/14.5); Telegraph Hill, 4½/7.2 W of Hitchin
8. Baldock (9.4/15); probably on Hickman's Hill, 2/3.2 S of town
9. Royston (8.1/13); high ground 1/1.6 S of town
10. Gog Magog Hills (11.7/18.8); about ¾.8 S of town
11. King's Chair, Newmarket (11.7/18.8); 1½/2.4 SE of town
12. Icklingham (9.8/15.8); Telegraph Plantation
13. Barnham (6.7/10.8); uncertain location.
14. East Harling (8.8/14.2); Telegraph Hill, 1/1.6 E of town
15. Carleton Rode (7.3/11.8); Telegraph Farm, 2/3.2 NW of village
16. Wreningham (5.4/8.7); on high ground near church
17. Mousehold (8.2/13.2); Telegraph Lane, from Thorpe Road
18. Strupmshaw 6.6/10.6); hill S of church
19. Yarmouth (10.8/17.4); on South Gate.

# Chronology

**1763**
25 Dec — Claude Chappe born.

**1776**
4 July — The American Revolution begins, leading to war with France.

**1783**
Oct — End of the American Revolutionary War sees the end of hostilities with France. Cassini proposes the connection by triangulation of Paris with Greenwich.

**1784** — Work on the connection of Paris to Greenwich by triangulation started.

**1787**
31 July — Ramsden's 3ft theodolite placed on Hounslow Heath.
17 Oct — Cross-Channel trigonometrical connection made: both sides of the Channel can now be fixed on maps.

**1789**
14 July — Storming of the Bastille begins the French Revolution. The 'Great Fear' was marked by widespread insurrection, burning and looting throughout France.
6 Oct — Following the March of the Women on Versailles, Louis XVI and his Queen are removed, virtually as prisoners, to the Palace of the Tuileries in Paris.

**1790**
14 July — On the first anniversary of the Revolution and to mark national unity celebrations are held on the Champs de Mars in Paris: from May to October, the royal family were able to live in the Palace of St. Cloud, just outside Paris.

**1791** — Work on the triangulation of Britain led to the founding of the Ordnance Survey Office within the Board of Ordnance.
2 Mar — Claude Chappe successfully demonstrated his telegraph to officials in Brûlon.
1 Oct — Ignace Chappe became a member of the Legislative Assembly and lobbied for telegraph trials.

**1792** — Early telegraph experiments at L'Etoile in Paris broken up by riotous mobs.
24 Mar — Claude Chappe's revised telegraph system presented to the new Legislative Assembly.
20 Apr — Legislative Assembly declared war on Austria.
29 July — The 500 Marseillaise, responding to the call for volunteers to defend France, arrived in Paris singing the *Marseillaise.*
10 Aug — Following new outbreaks of civil disorder, there was an armed invasion of the Tuileries: the Swiss Guards were massacred and the King arrested; Napoleon was a witness to these events.
13 Aug — King Louis removed to the Temple.

| | |
|---|---|
| 2–6 Sep | Parisian mobs thrill to the public executions of prisoners by guillotine. Telegraph experiments at Belleville, Paris, attacked by mobs thinking that Claude Chappe was attempting to communicate with the King imprisoned in the Temple. |
| 22 Sep | First French Republic established. |
| **1793** | |
| 21 Jan | Louis XVI executed by guillotine, followed by the Reign of Terror of 1793–94, led by Robespierre; the Terror became identified with ruthless centralized revolutionary government. |
| 1 Feb | France declared war on England and Holland. |
| 12 July | A demonstration of the Chappe brothers' telegraph system a complete success. |
| 4 Aug | Telegraph line from Paris to Lille ordered. |
| 3 Nov | Marie Antoinette, wife of Louis XVI, executed. |
| **1794** | |
| 1 June | In the 'Glorious First of June' eight French warships destroyed by the Royal Navy. |
| 16 July | Paris–Lille telegraph line declared open. |
| 27 July | Robespierre overthrown and guillotined next day. |
| 15 Aug | Chappe's telegraph brought news to Paris of the victory at Le Quesnoy; start of the age of communication from a distance. Duke of York (Commander-in Chief of the British Army) shown a model of Chappe's system and an alphabet of the system was found on a French prisoner-of-war; the Duke ordered his chaplain the Revd John Gamble, a mathematician, to investigate. |
| **1795** | |
| Apr | The report by Gamble on the French telegraph system is given to the Admiralty who authorize trials. |
| 6 Aug | Gamble conducted a trial for the Admiralty of his five-shutter telegraph in Portsmouth. |
| 25 Sep | After trials of Gamble's shutter system, the Admiralty authorized work using Murray's six-shutter system on lines connecting London to Deal and Portsmouth. |
| 5 Oct | Napoleon subdued a royalist rising in Paris. |
| **1796** | |
| 27 Jan | Shutter telegraph line to Deal finished, to be followed later in the year by the line to Portsmouth. |
| Nov | French plan to invade north-east England abandoned. |
| 15 Dec | French invasion fleet sailed from Brest for Ireland, hoping to make common cause against England, but, underestimating the difficulties and risks, failed. |
| **1797** | |
| Jan | French invasion fleet, stormbound and demoralized, abandoned plans to invade Ireland without putting any troops ashore. The French lost ten ships to storm, collision or capture. |
| 14 Feb | At Battle of Cape St Vincent, Adm Jervis (supported by Cdr Nelson) inflicted massive damage on Spanish fleet as it left Straits of Gibraltar, eliminating Spain as major maritime power. |
| 16 Feb | In ignorance of the Spanish naval defeat, French invasion force left Brest. Unfavourable winds prevent landing aimed at capturing Bristol; instead the French landed near Fishguard in Pembrokeshire; the invasion failed, but effect was to ignite a spontaneous patriotic reaction of national unity. |
| 11 Oct | At Battle of Camperdown off their own coast, Dutch navy suffered heavy defeat at the hands of the Royal Navy; the invasion threat was, for the present, broken. |
| 17 Oct | Reputation of a previously little known French commander Napoleon Bonaparte |

| | |
|---|---|
| | enhanced when, after a stunning campaign in Italy, he took charge of negotiating the terms of the Franco/German Treaty of Campo Formio. |
| 26 Oct | Napoleon appointed commander-in-chief of the Army of England. |
| Nov | French authorized telegraph lines to Strasburg and Brest. |
| 5 Dec | Napoleon arrived in Paris and made supreme commander. |

**1798**

| | |
|---|---|
| 15 Jan | Displaying fallibility in understanding the vulnerability of England to revolt in Ireland and discounting the reality of a new uprising, Napoleon rejected the arguments of Irish nationalists for a new invasion of Ireland as a means to defeat England. |
| 10 Feb | Napoleon toured the invasion ports. Although his interventions accelerated the French naval building programme, he realized that it would be many years before the French could build sufficient warships to achieve command of the sea and that without it an invasion of England would be risky. |
| 27 Mar | Unknowing that Napoleon was reappraising an early invasion, the British government introduced a parliamentary bill to facilitate the development of volunteer units already springing up locally, soon numbering over 150,000 men. |
| 19 May | The French fleet sailed from Toulon bound for Egypt. |
| 1 July | Napoleon reached Alexandria, having taken Malta on the way. |
| 1 Aug | Nelson inflicts catastrophe on the French at the Battle of the Nile. |
| 7 Aug | Paris–Brest telegraph line opened. |
| 22 Aug | French invasion force successfully disembarked on the west coast of Ireland, but failure awaited. |
| 16 Sep | With no way of knowing of the defeat in Ireland, reinforcements sailed from Brest. |
| 12 Oct | Royal Navy intercepted French fleet bound for Ireland, capturing six warships. |

**1799**

| | |
|---|---|
| 4 June | George III took birthday salute of volunteer forces in Hyde Park; examples of it repeated all over the country, reflecting the continuing invasion alarm. |
| 24 Aug | On hearing of French defeats at the hands of coalition forces, Napoleon left Egypt for France. |
| 9 Oct | Napoleon arrived back in France. |
| 6 Nov | After a *coup d'état,* Napoleon appointed First Consul by which he concentrated power into his own hands and through which order and regularity were restored; the first French Revolution came to an end; Napoleon sent a propaganda message down the telegraph system. |

**1800**

| | |
|---|---|
| | Napoleon introduced unifying cultural, civic and legal reforms, doing much to establish his ultimate status; success at home was matched by military victories on the Continent. |
| | The new century saw telegraph trunk lines in operation from Paris to Lille, Strasburg and Brest. |
| | Rear-Adm Popham developed his telegraphic code using flags, ultimately in universal use in the Navy; its use at Trafalgar allowed tactical control of the battle to be seized by Nelson. |

**1801**

| | |
|---|---|
| 1 Jan | The United Kingdom of Great Britain and Ireland came into being. |
| 2 Apr | Nelson defeated the Danish fleet at the Battle of Copenhagen where, famously, he puts the telescope to his blind eye and ignored the order to disengage. |
| 1 Oct | Preliminary terms agreed with France for ending war. |

**1802**

| | |
|---|---|
| 27 Mar | Although the Royal Navy was undefeated and growing in strength, neither side could achieve decisive victory on land; Britain and France (along with Spain and Holland) were tiring of their war and signed the Treaty of Amiens (ending the period known as the 'French Revolutionary Wars', running since 1792; but few believed that Napoleon would be satisfied). |

**1803**

| | |
|---|---|
| | French efforts to build their navy continued, leading to renewed fears of invasion in England. Napoleon ordered the extension of the telegraph, connecting Paris to Boulogne. |
| 8 Mar | Alarmed by developments, George III alerts Parliament to the danger from France; mobilization of the militia. |
| 17 May | England declared war on France. |
| 6 July | Nelson, in HMS *Victory* and in command of the Mediterranean fleet, joined the fleet blockading Toulon. |

| | |
|---|---|
| **1804** | A spurt of activity produced more coastal telegraph stations for defence against French invasion. In France the Depillion coastal semaphore provided a strategic communications advantage over the Royal Navy. |
| 18 May | Napoleon declared Emperor, later to be crowned by the Pope. The whole effort of the French directed to an invasion of England by the short sea route. |
| 20 July | Napoleon visited the headquarters of the Grande Armée in Boulogne. |
| 2 Dec | Napoleon's coronation. |

**1805**

| | |
|---|---|
| 23 Jan | Claude Chappe committed suicide. |
| Apr | Villeneuve's fleet escaped through the Straits of Gibraltar. |
| 3 Aug | Napoleon joined Grande Armée at Boulogne for the chance to cross the Channel, with over 2,000 boats in the Channel ports, which could lift over 150,000 men. |
| 23 Aug | Napoleon gave up attempt to outwit the Royal Navy by a dash across the Channel: in a volte-face he ordered the Grande Armée to break camp and march to the Danube. |
| 2 Sep | Capt Blackwood, of the frigate *Euryalus*, brought news to Nelson, resting at Merton, that Villeneuve's fleet was in Cadiz. |
| 15 Sep | Nelson sailed from Portsmouth in *Victory*, as commander of the combined British fleets. |
| 21Oct | Battle of Trafalgar: Spanish and French fleets virtually destroyed; Nelson died a hero. The Royal Navy's command of the seas was supreme. |
| | Admiralty authorized extension of the Portsmouth shutter telegraph line to Plymouth. |
| 6 Nov | News of Trafalgar arrived at the Admiralty, overland from Falmouth, without using the shutter telegraph to Portsmouth. |
| 2 Dec | Napoleon defeated Russians and Austrians at Austerlitz. |

**1806**

| | |
|---|---|
| 9 Jan | Nelson buried in St. Paul's Cathedral after state funeral. |
| Nov | Berlin Decree: Napoleon, needing a new way to make England bend to his will, imposed a boycott of English trade by European states. |

**1807**

| | |
|---|---|
| | Admiralty authorised new shutter telegraph line to Great Yarmouth. |

| | |
|---|---|
| Nov | England responded to Berlin Decree by requiring all neutral shipping to be licensed by an English port.<br>Lyon connected to Paris by telegraph. |
| **1808** | |
| | Peninsular War broke out after Portugal refused to cease trading with Britain. Wellington assembled a magnificent British army supplied by an unchallenged Navy. |
| 25 June | Yarmouth shutter telegraph line commissioned. |
| **1809** | Telegraph line to Lyon extended across the Alps to Milan. |
| **1810** | Weakened British economy, aggravated by bad harvests in 1808 and 1809, sees wave of bankruptcies. |
| Oct | As Venice is connected to Paris via Milan, work started on telegraph extension to Amsterdam. |
| **1811** | Nadir of British economic fortunes. |
| **1812** | |
| June | Napoleon invaded Russia with an army of 600,000. |
| Oct | After Battle of Borodino, Napoleon advanced to Moscow from which its citizens fled and the city was fired. With no winter quarters, retreat from Moscow began; barely 20,000 of the French army survived. |
| **1813** | After the chaotic winter, a final coalition emerged which ultimately defeated Napoleon. |
| Feb | Russia recruited Prussia as first member of the coalition. |
| June | Britain joined coalition. |
| Aug | Austria joined coalition forming the quadruple alliance. |
| 16–18 Oct | Napoleon defeated at Battle of Leipzig, French army of nearly 200,000 routed and suffered two-thirds casualties. |
| 10 Nov | Wellington completed his victories in Iberia; the French retreated over the Pyrenees, pursued by Wellington. |
| **1814** | |
| 17 Feb | Napoleon, forsaking his last chance to save his throne, rejected the allies' terms. |
| 9 Mar | The allies, continuing in congress, consolidated coalition by the Treaty of Chaumont, settling the basis for continuing the struggle, and a mutual defence plan against future French aggression. As the congress disbanded, Tsar Alexander, risking leaving Napoleon to his rear, undertook direct march on Paris. |
| 12 Mar | Wellington, advancing north, reached Bordeaux, where the population, disdaining Napoleon, called for restoration of the Bourbon monarchy. |
| 28 Mar | Coalition leaders settled their war aim: expulsion of Napoleon from France. |
| 30 Mar | Russian troops occupied the high ground of Montmartre; fall of Paris. |
| 31 Mar | Tsar made triumphal entry into Paris. |
| 6 Apr | Future Louis XVIII summoned from exile. During the month Napoleon abdicated and left Paris for Elba.<br>French telegraphs stopped at the French border. |
| 30 May | Treaty of Paris brought war against Napoleon to temporary end; representatives of the European powers to be sent to Vienna within two months for a peace congress. |

| | |
|---|---|
| June | Most of the principal statesmen and sovereigns first adjourned to London as guests of the government to celebrate peace in Europe. |
| July | Admiralty decided to close down all four shutter telegraph lines. |
| Sep | Congress of Vienna convened. |
| Nov | Orders given by the Admiralty to break up all coastal telegraph stations from Norfolk to Devon. |
| Dec | At the year's end, proceedings at Vienna took place in an atmosphere of anger, bitterness and frustration as the former allies contemplated a new war among themselves. |
| **1815** | |
| 1 Mar | Napoleon escaped from Elba and landed on the Riviera. |
| 6–7 Mar | During the night news of his escape arrived in Vienna. |
| | Work started on reopening Portsmouth and Plymouth telegraph routes. |
| 13 Mar | The eight signatories of the first Treaty of Paris, all in Vienna for the Congress, declared Napoleon an outlaw and made plans to hold Europe with three separate armies, one led by Wellington. The coalition was reformed with unprecedented speed. |
| Late Mar | Napoleon, back in Paris, assembled new government; Louis XVIII fled to Ghent. |
| 9 June | Act of the Congress of Vienna signed in the Schönbrunn Palace. |
| 16 June | Bill to allow state acquisition of land for telegraph stations introduced in Parliament. |
| 18 June | Napoleon suffered crushing defeat at Waterloo; Wellington's victory, aided just in time by Blücher, saw him become one of the most famous men in European history. |
| 22 June | News of Waterloo arrived in Portsmouth by telegraph. |
| 7 July | Allies staged second triumphal entry into Paris, followed next day by Louis XVIII's return. Napoleon, being unable to escape from Rochefort, surrendered to the Royal Navy; taken to Plymouth and then into exile on St. Helena. |
| Aug | Telegraph line to Plymouth carried operational naval orders while Napoleon held prisoner on HMS *Bellerophon.* |
| 20 Nov | Second Treaty of Paris signed; end of the Napoleonic war; France and Britain never subsequently at war with each other. |
| **1821** | |
| 5 May | Napoleon dies on St Helena; when the news reached Calais it was telegraphed to Paris. |
| **1822** | Semaphore line connecting the Admiralty with Portsmouth opened. |
| **1840** | |
| 15 Dec | Napoleon, reinstated as hero of the French, disinterred from St Helena, given funeral in Paris and entombed in Les Invalides. |
| **1847** | Railway link between Waterloo Station and Gosport completed, enabling the electric telegraph connection to be made via a submarine cable under Portsmouth harbour. |
| 31 Dec | Admiralty shuts down semaphore lines; last operational link to the Napoleonic wars removed. |

# Bibliography

Allen, Natalie, *Through the Letter-box* (1988)
Allen, Thomas, *History of the Counties of Surrey and Sussex* (1829)
Appleyard, Rollo, *Pioneers of Electrical Communication* (1930)
Arnold, James R., *Crisis on the Danube, Napoleon's Austrian Campaign of 1809* (1990)
Bablot, Michel *et al.*, *Le Patrimoine des Télécommunications Françaises* (2002)
Barratt, Thomas J., *The Annals of Hampstead* (1972)
Bayliss, Lt Col T.H., *The True Account of Nelson's Famous Signal* (1905)
Birkhead, Alice, *The Story of the French Revolution* (1917)
Bracken, C.W., *A History of Plymouth* (1931)
Brayley, E.W., *A Topographical History of Surrey*, vols 1–5 (1841–48)
Bridge, Maureen and John Pegg (eds), *Call to Arms* (2001)
Broome, Capt Jack, RN, *Make Another Signal* (1955)
Bryant, Sir Arthur, *The Age of Elegance 1812–1822* (1950)
*The Years of Endurance* (1942)
*The Great Duke or the Invincible General* (1971)
*Years of Victory 1802–1812* (1942)
Burton, Anthony, *The Canal Builders* (1981)
Capez, José and Florent Lepercq, *Il y a 200 ans . . . Le Camp de Boulogne* (2003)
Carlyle, Thomas, *The French Revolution* (2002)
Chandler, D., *The Campaigns of Napoleon* (1967)
Clarke, Desmond, *The Ingenious Mr Edgeworth* (1965)
Close, Sir Charles, *The Early Days of the Ordnance Survey* (1926)
Clowes, Sir W.L., *The Royal Navy: a History* (1897–1903)
Colby, Reginald, *The Waterloo Despatch: The Story of the Duke of Wellington's Official Dispatch on the Battle of Waterloo and Its Journey to London* (1965)
Collingwood, R.G. and J.N.L. Myres, *The Oxford History of England: Roman Britain and the English Settlements* (1937)
Conolly, J., *Philanthropic Vocabulary and Code of Signals* (1821)
Colby, R., *The Waterloo Dispatch* (1965)
Corbett, Julian S. (ed.), *The Private Papers of George, second Earl Spencer, First Lord of the Admiralty, 1794–1801* (1913)
Crawley, C.W. (ed.), *The New Cambridge Modern History*, vol.9, *War and Peace in an Age of Upheaval* (1969)
Dane, Clemence, *He Brings Great News: a Story* (1944)
Doyle, William, *The Oxford History of the French Revolution* (2002)
Gachot, Henri, *Le Télégraph Optique* (1967)
Gamble, Revd J., *An Essay on the Different Modes of Communication by Signals* (1797)
Gates, William G., *The Naval History of Portsmouth* (1901)
Geyl, Pieter, *Napoleon: For and Against* (1949)
Gray, Victor and Aspey, Mélanie (eds), *The Life and Times of N.M. Rothschild, 1777–1836* (1998)

Gurwood, Lt Col, *The Dispatches of Field Marshal the Duke of Wellington, During His Various Campaigns from 1799 to 1818* (1838)
Hamilton-Williams, David, *Waterloo: New Perspectives, the Great Battle Reappraised* (1993)
*Handbook of Communication by Telegraph* (1842)
Harris, Sir Nicholas (ed.), *The Dispatches and Letters of Vice-Admiral Lord Viscount Nelson* (1844)
Henderson, James, *The Frigates* (1970)
Hibbert, Christopher, *Nelson: A Personal History* (1994)
Holmes T.W., *The Semaphore* (1983)
Inwood, Stephen, *A History of London* (1998)
Holzmann, Gerard J. and Björn Pehrson, *The Early History of Data Networks* (1995)
International Telecommunications Union, *From Sempahore to Satellites* (1965)
Jowett, L., *A History of Plymouth* (1873)
Kent, Barrie, *A History of Signalling in the Royal Navy* (1993)
King, Henry C., *The History of the Telescope* (1955)
Knight, Miss Cornelia; Lady Companion to the Princess of Wales, *Autobiography* (1861)
Knight, Roger (eds. Peter Le Fevre and Richard Harding), *Precursors of Nelson* (2000)
Latimer, Elizabeth Wormeley, *Talks of Napoleon at St. Helena* (1903)
Laughton, Sir John Knox (ed.), *Letters and Papers of Charles, Lord Barham, 1758–1813* (Naval Records Society, 3 vols, 1907–11)
Lavery, Brian, *Nelson and the Nile* (1998)
Lecky, Halton Stirling, *The King's Ships* (1913–14)
Lepercq, J. and Lepercq, L. *Il y a 200 ans . . . Le Camp de Boulogne* (2003)
Lockhart, John Gibson, *The History of Napoleon Bonaparte* (1829)
Longmate, Norman, *Island Fortress: The Defence of Great Britain1603–1945* (1991)
Maffeo, Steven E., *Most Secret and Confidential: Intelligence in the Age of Nelson* (2000)
Maitland, F.W., *The Surrender of Napoleon* (1826)
Marriott Leo, *What's Left of Nelson* (1995)
Manning, O. and W. Bray, *The History and Antiquities of the County of Surrey* (3 vols, 1804, 1809, 1814)
Neale, J.P. and E.W. Brayley, *The History and Antiquities of the at the Church of St. Peter, Westminster* (1823)
Nicolay, Fernand, *Napoleon at the Boulogne Camp* (1907)
O'Donoghue, Ylonde, *William Roy, 1726–1790, Pioneer of the Ordnance Survey* (1977)
Ogilvy, James S., *A Pilgrimage in Surrey* (1914)
Nalder, Maj Gen R.F.H., *The Royal Corps of Signals: A History of its Antecedents and Development (circa 1800–1955)* (1958)
Parker, Eric, *Highways and Byways in Surrey* (1908)
Pasley, Lt Col C.W., *Description of the Universal Telegraph* (1822)
Perrin, W.G. and Christopher Lloyd (eds), *The Keith Papers* (Navy Records Society, 1927, 1950, 1955)
Pickering, John, *A Lecture on Telegraphic Language* (1833)
Pool, P.A.S., *The History of the Borough of Penzance* (1974)
Popham, Adm Sir Home, *Telegraphic Signals or Marine Vocabulary* (1812)
Popham, Hugh, *A Damned Cunning Fellow* (1991)
Porter, Roy (ed.), *The Cambridge History of Science*, vol.4, *Eighteenth-century Science* (2003)
Rhys, Ernest (ed.), *The Hampstead Annual* (1897)
Rolt L.T.C., *Navigable Waterways* (1969)
Ronalds, Francis, *Descriptions of an Electric Telegraph* (1823)
Rothschild, Lord, *The Shadow of a Great Man* (1982)
Sidebottom, J.K., *The Overland Mail* (1948)

Swanton, E.W. and P. Woods, *Bygone Haslemere* (1914)
Seymour, W.A. (ed.), *The Origins of the Ordnance Survey* (1980)
Sharp, Henry A., *A Historical Catalogue of Surrey Maps* (1929)
Southgate, G.W., *England 1793–1914* (1951)
Surtees, Maj Gen G., *A Short History of XX The Lancashire Fusiliers* (1955)
Thomson, Alice, *The Singing Line* (1999)
Tollemache, Beatrix L., *Richard Lovell Edgeworth, a Selection from his Memoirs* (1896)
Tunstall, Brian, *Naval Warfare in the Age of Sail: the Evolution of Fighting Tactics* (1990)
Villiers, Alan, *The Battle of Trafalgar* (1965)
Wilson, Geoffrey, *The Old Telegraphs* (1976)
Warner, Oliver, *Nelson* (1975)
Watson, J. Steven, *The Oxford History of England: The Reign of George III 1760–1815* (1960)
Whitfield, H.F., *Plymouth and Devonport: in Times of War and Peace* (1900)
Wilson, Joan, *A Soldier's Wife: Wellington's Marriage* (1987)

# Index

# Index

# Index

# Index

# Index